The Fall Girl

"In Clark's latest, a clash of personalities brings new tumult to the Santa Clara DA's office and exposes corruption in the California criminal justice system. Clark has a savvy hand with the dramas of prosecutorial life and a knack for drawing sharp, interesting characters."

—CrimeReads

"Clark's legal experience again translates into superior fiction."

—*Publishers Weekly*

"*The Fall Girl* shows Marcia Clark at her absolute best. The book is her leanest to date yet packs as big and brash a punch as any of her previous works."

—Criminal Element

Final Judgment

"The plot twists are both plausible and shocking in this intelligent page-turner. Fans of whodunits featuring ethical dilemmas will be pleased."

—*Publishers Weekly* (starred review)

"With its fast-moving plot and winning characters, this fourth entry in the Brinkman series will keep readers turning pages and rooting for Sam."

—*Booklist*

"The book marks a welcome return for Marcia Clark, who is in fine form. Beyond the requisite questions of whodunit and why, she explores the gray areas of morality, where notions of right and wrong lie firmly in the eye of the beholder. A fiery finale to the Samantha Brinkman saga."

—Criminal Element

"The final book in the Samantha Brinkman series is a thrill ride with twists and turns."

—Red Carpet Crash

"A gripping read. Recommended."

—Long and Short Reviews

"We may not always agree with her motives, but one thing's for sure: if you are arrested for a crime, you want Samantha Brinkman on your side."

—Woman around Town

Snap Judgment

"Samantha Brinkman, Clark's flawed but sympathetic Los Angeles defense attorney protagonist, must deal with more than one explosive case in her highly suspenseful third outing . . . Clark keeps up the frenetic pace but never allows the plot's tricky developments to overwhelm her characterizations."

—*Publishers Weekly* (starred review)

"A twisting plot informed by Clark's legal know-how will keep readers turning pages."

—*Booklist*

"Fans of Clark's legal thriller series featuring defense attorney Samantha Brinkman will be pleased to learn that this third installment (after *Moral Defense*) continues to deliver fast-paced plotting and savvy style laced with a healthy dose of humor. Clark, once again, nimbly handles the warp and weft of her interwoven characters and storylines, knitting them into a satisfying conclusion that will leave readers eagerly anticipating another Brinkman episode."

—*Library Journal*

"Marcia Clark has a proven talent for storytelling that transcends novels . . . and *Snap Judgment*, like her other books, masterfully illustrates that prowess. Propulsive plotting, visceral action, dexterous dialogue, and a palpable sense of time and place all conspire to make for an undeniably exhilarating read. And just when you think you've got it all figured out, she flips the script. If you haven't yet become a convert for team Clark, you owe it to yourselves to do so. This is one pleasure that won't leave you feeling the least bit guilty."

—Criminal Element

"*Snap Judgment* sees the return of a terrific character in Samantha Brinkman. Marcia Clark renders the world of high-stakes law and flexible morals in perfect three-dimensional clarity."

—Authorlink

"Marcia Clark certainly knows the ins and outs of the litigation business, and fans will be thrilled with this new mystery."

—*Suspense Magazine*

Moral Defense
An Amazon Best Book of the Month: Mystery, Thriller, & Suspense Category

"*Moral Defense* by former Los Angeles prosecutor Marcia Clark has it all: a hard-charging lawyer heroine, tough-as-nails cops, realistic yet somehow lovable 'bad guys,' as well as fly-by-the-seat-of-your-pants pacing and page-turning twists."

—Associated Press

"In Clark's outstanding sequel to *Blood Defense* . . . [she] deepens her already fascinating lead, while adeptly juggling several subplots."

—*Publishers Weekly* (starred review)

"This second in the Brinkman series (after *Blood Defense*, 2016) is a nonstop ride marked by legal and moral gray areas, with a cliff-hanger epilogue. Another Clark legal thriller that's hard to put down."

—*Booklist*

"A murdered family leaves only one survivor in this second roller-coaster case for Los Angeles attorney Samantha Brinkman . . . [The case] builds to a rare intensity."

—*Kirkus Reviews*

"Clark's formidable experience lends itself to this exhilarating novel."

—RT Book Reviews

"Riveting and suspenseful."

—*Crimespree Magazine*

"It's a complex, tightly woven plot, and as is the case with all of Clark's novels, the page-turning journey—through sensitive and controversial issues—to the surprise ending is not without considerable twists and turns."

—The Big Thrill

"You'll be thrilled with [Marcia Clark's] second Samantha Brinkman mystery, *Moral Defense*, in which your assumptions as to whodunit will be wrong. This book has a complicated moral compass and an ending you don't see coming."

—*Elle*

Blood Defense

"Former LA prosecutor Clark kicks off a promising new series with this top-notch whodunit . . . Clark sprinkles jaw-dropping surprises throughout and impressively pulls off a shocker that lesser writers can only envy."

—*Publishers Weekly* (starred review)

"On the heels of FX's blockbuster television series, *American Crime Story: The People v. O. J. Simpson* . . . Simpson prosecutor-turned-author Clark . . . launches a new legal thriller series. Unlike in her well-received Rachel Knight books, which featured an LA prosecutor, Clark's latest calls on her earlier career as a criminal defense attorney to fashion protagonist Samantha Brinkman. Verdict: Clark's deft handling of her characters through a multilevel maze of conflicts delivers an exhilarating read."

—*Library Journal*

"Clark, who served as a prosecutor for the trial of O. J. Simpson, clearly knows this world well. She has the most fun when she's showing readers the world of celebrity trials, from the media circus, the courthouse crowds, the crazies, and the police to the inner workings of the trial itself. You'll push yourself to finish the final pages just to keep pace with the defense team's discoveries."

—Associated Press

"Once again, Marcia Clark has reinvented herself—and the results are stellar. Her knowledge of the criminal justice system is unrivaled, as is her understanding of how the media influences public opinion of high-profile trials—and the actions of those involved. But the real magic of Clark's writing is her dynamic, richly textured characters and the visceral, often gritty settings they frequent."

—*Hartford Examiner*

TRIAL
BY
AMBUSH

MURDER, INJUSTICE, *and*
the TRUTH ABOUT *the* CASE
of BARBARA GRAHAM

TRIAL

BY

AMBUSH

MARCIA CLARK

THOMAS & MERCER

Published by Thomas & Mercer, Seattle

www.apub.com

Amazon, the Amazon logo, and Thomas & Mercer are trademarks of Amazon.com,
Inc., or its affiliates.

ISBN-13: 9781662515965 (hardcover)
ISBN-13: 9781662515958 (paperback)
ISBN-13: 9781662515941 (digital)

Cover design by Richard Ljoenes Design LLC
Cover image: © Herald Examiner Collection / Los Angeles Public Library

Printed in the United States of America
First edition

TRIAL
BY
AMBUSH

FOREWORD

I have a vivid memory of the moment I knew—once and for all—that I was going to write about Barbara Graham. It was when I saw the photo. Wearing a prison-issue dress, seated next to her lawyer, Barbara Graham, just thirty years old and the only woman in the room, is looking up at the sea of reporters—all men, their cameras and lights pointing down at her. A few of them are on bended knee, leaning toward her like nervous lovers about to propose. A palpable intensity radiating from the scene makes it feel as though Barbara could be consumed on the spot by the sheer energy pouring down at her. She stares over her shoulder at them, her expression fearful, bewildered. She looks vulnerable, small, and very alone. The antithesis of all the news coverage I'd read that painted her as a vicious and cold-blooded, albeit beautiful, murderer.

© *Herald Examiner Collection / Los Angeles Public Library*

My reaction was visceral. I could feel my body recoil at the thought of being at the center of that kind of attention. I had no conscious thought that I might—on some level—identify with her. Not then, anyway.

But until I saw that photo, I hadn't been sold on the idea of writing about Barbara Graham. The realization that I had to write about her case didn't come as a thunderclap. It was a gradual thing. Like a sentence written word by word over time, its meaning unclear until I finally saw how it had to end. The idea of writing a book about a real criminal case—as opposed to crime fiction—didn't make much sense to me at first. As a practicing criminal lawyer, I've spent most of my adult life immersed in true crime. First as a defense attorney in private practice, then as a prosecutor in Los Angeles County, and now for the past sixteen-plus years as an appellate lawyer. I had true crime coming out of my ears. I lived it. So whenever someone suggested that I write a true crime book, I'd think, "What for? I've got enough of my own cases to worry about."

And yet, a few years ago, as I wrapped up the appeal on what felt like my millionth murder case, the idea started to take root. In rare quiet moments, I could feel myself warming to the possibility, thinking, "That might actually be cool." But the thought didn't initially spur me into action. I had this idea that when the time was right, the universe would make it happen. A story would appear that'd strike me like a bolt of lightning, and I'd know this was the *one*. At that point, since the universe had already been so helpful, I was sure it'd see that I'd need a break from my own caseload—not to mention other projects. I'd write a note to self to thank the universe when it was time to put together the acknowledgments for the book, and off I'd go, ready to embark on the journey.

Shockingly, none of the above occurred.

A couple of years passed with no such great epiphanies. I'd thought I was doing my part by keeping an open mind, ready to receive the lightning bolt when it came, but apparently the universe was busy elsewhere. It finally dawned on me that if I really wanted to do this, I'd have to go on the hunt and find the case myself.

I knew I'd have to choose carefully, that it had to be a case I was passionate about. I'd been warned about how much work was involved in writing nonfiction. Months—maybe years—of research that'd require a lot of patience (unfortunately not a personal strength) and tenacity (I'm okay on that front—some say borderline obsessive, but what do those quitters know?). That kind of total immersion, living with the case day in and day out over the course of months and maybe years, meant that I'd have to be deeply invested in the case.

But I wasn't exactly a stranger to that kind of dedication. I'd had to invest long hours for weeks, and sometimes months, at a time on my appellate cases. So I had some idea of what that meant. And now, having accepted the harsh reality that I'd have to do some digging, I'd thought finding the right case would be a snap. I'd been collecting articles and newspaper clippings of crime stories for years, thinking I might turn them into a true crime limited series, or use them as inspiration for a novel. I'd been stuffing them into manila folders that I kept in a drawer of my filing cabinet. Now, those folders had multiplied to the point they took up four drawers. So I was sure my only problem would be deciding which one to choose. But as I plowed through one story after another, I realized they weren't really all that intriguing. Bizarre, creepy, even gruesome, but if I was going to devote at least a year of my life to a true crime story, it had to be about more than just the scary monster lurking in the shadows.

This, I was now forced to concede, was going to be a tall order. A case like that wouldn't be so easy to find. I surfed the internet, dug into published—but unheralded—cases, even browsed cheesy true crime magazines, and . . . nothing.

I was starting to think I'd set myself up for failure when, purely by accident, in a footnote at the bottom of a page about another case, I found a mention of Barbara Graham. I'd like to say it was a eureka moment. It wasn't.

In fact, the very first things I read about the case almost made me reject it out of hand. First of all, it was an old case—the murder and the trial took place in 1953—which meant research was going to be a problem. I definitely wouldn't get to do any in-person interviews. Everyone involved would be dead and gone. Even worse, it was big news at the time. The '50s version of "the Trial of the Century." It inspired an Oscar-winning film, *I Want to Live!*, starring Susan Hayward as Barbara Graham. I was sure that meant the story had already been plumbed from all angles. Especially the trial.

And that's what interested me most: what had happened in that courtroom. Because no matter what witnesses say to the cops or reporters, the closest you'll get to the truth of a case is the trial itself, which shows what they said under oath, what the lawyers did, and how the judge ruled. But with all the attention the case got, there were bound to be books, papers, and articles of all kinds about everything connected to the case—the trial in particular. What more would there be to say?

Still, I decided to do a little surfing just to make sure there was nothing left to add. I checked out newspaper archives for articles written during the trial. They offered some information about who was testifying and the gist of what they said, but the writing was so feverishly arch, and the details so frequently conflicting, it left me unsure of what to believe. In short, the coverage was little better than a gossip column.

And surprisingly, there hadn't been all that much written about the case in the years following the trial. I found a couple of podcasts that devoted a single episode to the case and some short magazine articles, a few of which called Barbara's guilt into question, but none went into enough depth to make a compelling case for innocence. For the most part, the stories just took a superficial swipe at the incongruity of a beautiful young woman who—in collaboration with two hardened thugs—committed the brutal murder of an elderly woman. I did run across one article in an online magazine that went after the unduly negative press coverage of Barbara. Which was interesting. But it, too, offered only the barest outline of the case and the evidence. None of the articles was recent—that online magazine piece came the closest to something current, and it'd been published over ten years ago. And while all the articles and podcasts mentioned that there'd been a trial, none of them discussed what had actually gone on in that courtroom.

Two books had been published about the case. One, *Proof of Guilt*, by Kathleen Cairns, was excellent, but it didn't discuss the trial either. The other, *The Case of Barbara Graham*, by Bill Walker, was a short paperback published in 1961 that summarized the highlights of the trial, but the selective nature of what was emphasized and—importantly—what was left out gave me pause about its reliability. And as I delved into the research and actual writing of this book, I discovered that in fact, its account of the trial was biased and inaccurate in some very crucial respects.

So there hadn't been any reliable, in-depth examination of the trial. That was good. Very good. The trial was what I'd been drawn to from the moment I'd found the case. And it now seemed I had a virtually open field.

But I was also intrigued by the article about how poorly Barbara had been treated by the press. I admit that issue had some personal resonance for me. During the O. J. Simpson trial, I barely recognized myself in the person reporters described as the lead prosecutor in the case. It was a helpless feeling to read the exaggerated accounts and flat-out misrepresentations of me, but there was no way to stop them. So I stopped myself and quit reading.

But when I checked out some of the news stories about Barbara, I saw how much worse it could get. The descriptions of her were snide, relentlessly critical, and obsessed with her looks. Every story seemed to start and end with some comment about her hair, her makeup, her clothes, and most of all, her cavalier attitude. They'd reduced her to a stereotype, the femme fatale of noir novels, beautiful but with a block of ice for a heart.

Yet the widely acclaimed 1958 film had been accused of painting an overly sympathetic picture of her, showing her to be a devoted mother who'd been falsely accused and framed by unscrupulous cops. So what changed? How did Barbara Graham go from the villainess nicknamed by the press as "Bloody Babs" to misbegotten victim?

That intrigued me too.

And I also found some interesting personal connections to the case. Just odd little coincidences. Like the fact that I'd lived within a mile or two of the crime scene—a quiet suburban neighborhood in Burbank; the fact that the lead prosecutor, J. Miller Leavy, had been an icon in the Los Angeles District Attorney's Office, where I'd been a prosecutor for fourteen years; and that I'd spent a decade working in the courthouse across the street from the courtroom where Barbara's trial was held.

Then I saw that photo. Barbara, surrounded by a roomful of reporters, all men, hovering over her, and the expression of fear on her face as she looked at them over her shoulder. That did it. My decision was made. I was going to write about the trial. I needed to know the truth about the case, and the only way to do that was by finding out what had happened in court. Especially when it came to Barbara, who—per the media accounts—didn't seem to belong on either Murderers' Row or the saintly pedestal the film had set up for her. The contrast alone between the scorn and derision heaped on Barbara during the trial and the heart-wrenchingly sympathetic treatment she got in the film showed there was a truth that still hadn't been told about this case.

What she'd actually done, what evidence had been presented to prove that, and why the prosecution had taken the rare step—even back then—of seeking the death penalty for a woman could only be discovered by finding out what went on in that trial.

That meant if I was going to write this book, there was only one source reliable enough to do it right: the reporter's transcripts that recorded the actual testimony of witnesses, the rulings by the judge, and the arguments of counsel. The problem was I didn't think they still existed. Based on what I knew from handling criminal appeals, court reporters only have to keep their trial notes for ten years. The trial took place in 1953, over seventy years ago.

My only hope lay in the fact that this was a death penalty case. That must mean the court reporters had to keep their trial notes longer. But . . . seventy years? That was a lot to hope for.

I found a website for the court reporters. It had a form for requests, and there was a phone number at the bottom. I called the number, got a recording, and left a message saying I just needed to find out whether the transcripts for the case had been destroyed. I waited a few days, but I knew court reporters are busy people. They're an amazing bunch of humans, and our system of justice would collapse without them. But they don't have a lot of time to chat. So I went ahead and filed the written request. Two weeks went by with no response. I was antsy. I'd been getting more and more invested in the case. The longer I had to wait, the more painful it was going to be if I had to abandon ship. I decided to call the number listed for one of the offices. And lucked out. An actual court reporter answered the phone. I explained my dilemma. She assured me the transcripts had to exist. "It's a death case, right?" she said. "Right," I said, "so how long do you have to keep them?" She replied, her tone matter of fact, "Death cases? Forever."

Hallelujah! But keep them where? That she didn't know. But she suggested court archives in downtown Los Angeles. I looked up the address and saw that it was just half a block away from where I'd worked when I was a prosecutor, assigned to Central Trials on Temple Street. Oddly, I'd never been there before.

The archives building was a fascinating place. Tucked underground behind the courthouse on Temple Street, it was a subterranean cavern packed from floor to mile-high ceiling with files. I recognized the color-coded heavy-bond manila folders I used to see in courtrooms and the clerk's office. I filled out the file request form, dropped it into the box, and crossed my fingers.

When the clerk called me up to the window, I thought, "He has to have the transcripts. *Has* to." He frowned at the slip of paper. "I don't know. I don't think we keep them that long. But let me go check."

He trotted over to a table where four older men seemed to be taking a break. One of them rubbed his chin and shrugged; the others shook their heads. My heart sank.

I'd hit a dead end. Already. "No dice, huh?" I asked.

He pushed his glasses up and tapped some keys on his computer. "Actually, there's a chance we might have the file on microfiche. Do you want to wait while I look?"

Of course I did. He told me to come back in half an hour. I went outside and walked around, trying to distract myself from the possibility of failure. A lot had changed since I'd left the district attorney's office in 1995. I looked up and tried to spot the window of my old office on the eighteenth floor. A wave of nostalgia washed over me as I remembered how many times I'd looked out on the city from that window after a long day in court. I still cherished those days—the ones before the Simpson trial.

I noticed the space behind the building had been turned into a park. It used to be a parking lot—a coveted spot that required a special pass because it was close to the office. The park was a much prettier idea, but I wondered where the prosecutors and public defenders had to park now. Hopefully, not in the old Chinatown lot, half a mile away, where I'd had to park for years before I'd earned that special pass. I'd had a habit of working long hours—I loved the quiet time after everyone had left for the day—and the trek from Temple Street to Hill Street in the dark was dangerous. Dangerous enough to make me buy my first handgun.

I saw that someone was shooting a film or TV show across the street at city hall—a location favored for its imposing facade and dramatic entrance. The film crew and actors were milling around the set, but the people who'd stopped to gawk at them were more interesting: one was dressed in silver sequins from head to toe, and the woman with him was dressed in thigh-high platform boots and pink hot pants . . . remember those? She did. And she rocked them.

I checked my phone and saw that the clerk had texted me to say he was ready. I hurried back, and the guards waved me through.

I moved up to the clerk's window and held my breath as I asked, "So what do you think?"

"It seems we do have it on microfiche, but it's about a thousand pages. It'll take a while to print out. Do you want the whole thing?"

"Yes, please." But I had a feeling this wasn't going to be what I wanted. From what I'd read, the trial had taken weeks. The reporter's transcripts had to total a lot more than a thousand pages. "Can you tell if the reporter's transcripts are included?"

"Not yet. But if you only want—"

"No, no. I'll take whatever you have. That's fine."

He told me to come back the following day, and it'd be ready and waiting for me.

And it was. I took the stack of pages to my car. Too anxious to wait until I got home, I quickly flipped through the pages. With a sinking feeling, I saw that this wasn't the reporter's transcript. It was the clerk's transcript. The clerk's transcript only has written documents, like motions and subpoenas and the minute orders—the daily recording of events by the court clerk. The minute orders say things like, "Court reconvenes, all parties and the jury present." Or "Court recess declared until 1:30 p.m." So the clerk's transcript doesn't have the actual witness testimony. It still might have some important information—and as it turned out, it really did—but it didn't have the most important part of what I needed.

Desperate, I reached out to Kathleen Cairns, the author of *Proof of Guilt* (which I highly recommend), which discussed Barbara's life and her case but focused on the death penalty, not the trial. I asked if she had any idea how I could get my hands on those reporter's transcripts. She was a gem: helpful, smart, and kind. She boosted my flagging spirits. She was sure the state archives would have those transcripts.

I immediately reached out to the archives, but the answer was maddeningly slow in coming. It took months of emails back and forth to make sure they had any records of the trial, and even once they confirmed they did, they couldn't tell exactly what they had. So the archives might hold what I needed . . . or not.

The day the three boxes got delivered, I stared down at them. Had I scored the holy grail? Or just a bunch of official documents of no particular interest? The size and weight of the boxes looked about right, like some of the bigger appeals I've handled.

It took me a few minutes to cut the tape and look inside. And then I saw . . . "Volume One—Reporter's Transcript." I had them! The trial transcripts. All four-thousand-plus pages of them.

I cleared off my desk, pulled the rubber band off the thick stack of pages, and dived in.

Now, I could tell the whole story, the story no one had yet told.

THE STORY OF
BARBARA GRAHAM

CHAPTER ONE

The evening of March 8, 1953, was cool, even brisk, in the quiet Southern California suburb of Burbank. On the tree-lined Parkside Avenue, a light breeze gently wafted through the leaves. Mabel Monahan, a widow who lived alone in a charming ranch-style house on that street, was blissfully unaware of what the next twenty-four hours would hold. She was getting ready to go to her regular Sunday-night poker game with her close friend Merle Leslie. Although Mabel was sixty-four years old and walked with a slight limp—an old injury suffered in a car accident—she knew how to party.

Mabel and Merle had met during their vaudeville days back in the '30s. Merle and her husband managed a vaudeville troupe, and Mabel was, among other things, a roller-skating star. She'd performed in carnivals and sideshows and at times went by the name Madam Martinez to bill herself as a palm reader. It was on the vaudeville circuit that she'd met her late husband, George Monahan, a spectacular ice-skater who was a featured performer at state fairs, outdoor events, and—of course—carnivals. They started out as a roller-skating team performing across the country and wound up as husband and wife. It was an unconventional but exciting and even glamorous life.

But by 1953, Mabel had traded in her wild nomadic days for the cozy house on the corner of Parkside Avenue and Orchard Drive. Back then, it was about as quiet as any small suburban town in You-Name-It, USA. Wide streets; kids playing in front yards; swing sets and fruit trees in backyards; and a little mom-and-pop grocery store tucked in among the houses where mothers could send their nine-year-olds to pick up a carton of milk. I know the area well, having lived just a few miles away in the neighboring town of Glendale in the eighties, and it was still a peaceful little haven then, ideal for young families.

Even so, Mabel Monahan kept her windows closed and her doors locked with a chain and always used the peephole when someone came knocking. She wasn't a paranoid safety freak. She was just security conscious. Having lived in hotels for most of her life, where someone—usually a man—was posted at the front desk, standing between her living space and the outside world, Mabel wasn't accustomed to the solitary, unprotected feeling of a house—with all those windows, not to mention front and back yards.

Mabel had never planned or hoped to own a home. The house on Parkside Avenue fell into her lap. At the time, it seemed to be one of the luckiest of lucky breaks.

It was a gift from her daughter, Iris, who got the house in the divorce settlement from her ex-husband, the brilliantly successful casino owner and real estate investor Tutor Scherer. He and Iris met when she auditioned to perform as a singer and dancer in the floor show of the Ship Café, his restaurant bar and lounge that was a popular haunt during Prohibition. Iris, following in her parents' footsteps, had a bent for the performing arts, and Tutor hired her on the spot. Tutor, a bootlegger as well as a restaurant owner, was one handsome, smooth-talking operator, and Iris fell hard for him. After a few years, they married.

But Iris's dreams of connubial bliss failed to take into account the realities of being married to a sharp-eyed dealmaker like Tutor, who always had his sights trained on the next big score. Seeing the end of Prohibition on the horizon, Tutor wisely moved out of booze and into gambling—at first in Los Angeles (where he quickly learned he'd have to compete with big-time gangster Mickey Cohen), then in the safer—and more open—pastures of Las Vegas. There, he invested in casinos, founded the Pioneer Club, and diversified into other real estate holdings. All this wheeling and dealing meant Tutor wasn't home much. Still, Iris might've managed to live with his absences were it not for the fact that they so often included extracurricular activities. Entrepreneurial obsession was one thing, but adultery was quite another. After thirteen rocky years, Iris divorced him, then remarried and moved to New York.

Tutor gave her a generous divorce settlement of over $100,000 in cash, expensive jewelry, and . . . the Burbank house on Parkside Avenue. But Iris, now living in New York, didn't need the home or want the reminder of her life with Tutor. So Mabel, for the first time in her life, became a homeowner. And somehow that expensive jewelry also found its way into her hands. She was known to carry it around in her purse to show off to her friends and fellow poker players. Whether Tutor knew Mabel wound up with the jewelry he'd bestowed on Iris is an open question. But I have a feeling he wouldn't have minded. Although Iris was out of his life, Tutor remained close with Mabel and visited her often when he was in town.

On the night of March 8, 1953, as Mabel got ready to go out to her poker game, she packed that jewelry and about $500 in cash—the equivalent of over $5,000 today—in her oversize black purse.

Lyda Newton, a mutual friend of Mabel's and Merle's, picked them up at about 8:00 p.m. and drove them to Albert Marino's house in Sherman Oaks, a nearby suburban city in the San Fernando Valley, where the poker party was getting underway. They played and partied until 1:00 a.m., then went to the Silver Broiler for "lunch." Lyda dropped them back at Mabel's house at 3:00 a.m., and they talked until 4:30 a.m., then hit the hay. The next day, March 9, Mabel made them breakfast, and that afternoon, Merle's husband came to pick her up. They chatted until the couple left at 2:00 p.m. Merle later called to check in on Mabel at 6:00 p.m., and they talked on the phone briefly. It was the last time Merle would ever speak to her longtime friend.

Mabel had settled in to read a book, a mystery titled *The Purple Pony Murders*, when someone rang the doorbell. It was 8:30 p.m. She wasn't expecting anyone. She went to the door and peered through the peephole. A petite young woman in a long coat was looking up at her. Mabel asked who she was and what she wanted. The woman answered, clearly distressed, "My car broke down and it won't start. It's stuck out in the middle of the street. There doesn't seem to be a phone booth nearby, and I don't know anyone in this neighborhood. Could you please let me use your phone so I can call for help?"

And then, Mabel, the vaudevillian trouper who was nobody's fool, made her fatal mistake. She opened the door. She stepped back, expecting to lead the woman to the phone. But she managed only a short bark of surprise . . . before the door slammed shut.

Two days later, on March 11, 1953, at 11:30 a.m., gardener Mitchell Truesdale showed up for work at Mabel's home. He noticed the floodlights were still on. That was weird. When he went to ring the doorbell to get the key for the backyard gate, he saw that the front door was ajar. Even weirder. Mabel always kept her doors, windows—every point of access—locked. He pushed the door a little farther open and called out, "Mrs. Monahan? It's me, Mitchell." But he got no answer.

He moved inside and looked down the short hallway that opened onto the living room. That's when he saw that the living room and carpets were "tore upside down," and there was blood, lots of it. He closed the door and called his friend, Burbank police detective Carl Lane.

When Lane arrived, they briefly searched the house together. There was blood on the wall just inside the doorway, on the walls in the hallway, on the living room rugs and furniture, and on the wall of the hallway on the left that led to a linen closet and the den . . . and beyond that, the house had been ransacked. Or as Lane would later testify, everything in the house had been "radically disarranged."

Lane backed out of the living room and turned down the hallway that led to the den. And there he found Mabel. She was lying on the floor, face down, her body half in and half out of the linen closet, her hands tied behind her back. There was blood on her head, a pillowcase underneath it, a bloodstained cloth wrapped around her neck, and a cloth strip with a knot in the center lying on the floor near her head.

Lane stared in shock. This just didn't happen, not in this peaceful little neighborhood—and certainly not to an elderly widow. He called the station and waited for the lead investigator to arrive.

That turned out to be Lieutenant Robert Coveney—who would later become Captain Coveney of the Burbank Police Department. Lean, clean shaven, with the short haircut typical of cops—and just about every other man on the street in the '50s—he had a determined set to his jaw and the skeptical air of a good detective. He'd be the driving force behind every move throughout the investigation and trial—for better, and for much, much worse.

Coveney and his team did a full search and found even more blood: on the leather-covered piano and on the nearby walls in the living room, on the partition between the living room and dining room, on the carpet in the entry hall and hall closet, and on the rug that was in front of the closet. Coveney also found another strip of cloth with a knot in the center—like the one near Mabel's head—in the front room behind the sofa.

It was a scene of screaming violence and chaos, the house ripped apart from top to bottom. Whoever did this was expecting to score a big hit and was hell bent on finding it. But when the police searched Mabel's closet, they came to a screeching halt: hanging on a hook was her big black purse, and in it was almost $500 in cash, along with fistfuls of jewelry—good jewelry, like diamond rings, earrings and brooches, and platinum bracelets. The stash was worth thousands. Even crazier, that closet had been thoroughly ransacked and the other purses in it had been turned inside out and thrown to the floor.

Now the cops were facing two questions: Not just *who* did it, but why?

CHAPTER TWO

Mabel Monahan had never been famous in life, but her bizarre, lurid death made her an overnight celebrity. Just one day after her body was discovered, news of her murder exploded across the country. From California to New Hampshire and many states in between, Mabel Monahan suddenly became a household name: "Mabel Monahan, Once Actress, Killed"; "Mabel Monahan Found Slain in Her Residence"; "Wealthy Widow Beaten to Death in California"; "Former Actress Found Dead in Closet"; "Former Actress Found Murdered—Mabel Monahan's Body Discovered in Burbank Home." And in the *Valley Times*, the hometown newspaper for the Burbank area, it was splashed across the front page in large, bold type, above the fold, complete with a recent photo of Mabel, looking over her shoulder, hair coiffed, in a flowered dress, and a photo of the typical '50s ranch-style house that was now an infamous crime scene: "Find Burbank Widow Bludgeoned to Death."

With eyes around the nation now focused on the case, the pressure to slap handcuffs on someone was high. The Burbank Police Department door knocked the entire neighborhood, canvassed every repairman and tradesperson working in the area, and put out feelers to every unofficial source—i.e., informant—on the street. But . . . nothing. They hit one dead end after another. Apart from a few reports describing the whining of Mabel's black Labrador (funny how often dogs seem to be the first to sound the alarm), no one had seen or heard anything out of the ordinary. Forensic evidence was a bust too. Surprisingly, given the way the house had been turned inside out, there were no fingerprints. On the other hand, science and technology back then weren't what they are today. There was no "touch DNA" or closed-circuit street cameras or Ring cameras. It was 1953. Transistor radios were just about to come out, a pound of round steak was fifty-three cents, and the two most popular television shows were *I Love Lucy* and *Dragnet*.

So the police were left with no eyewitnesses and no physical evidence. Desperate for answers, they turned to Mabel's connection to her ex-son-in-law, Tutor Scherer. Tutor's early foray into the world of gambling and bootlegging could've left him with some dangerous enemies—like the notorious gangster Mickey Cohen, who was known to control the underworld gambling operations in Los Angeles. It seemed a likely explanation—and so far the only one—for targeting the elderly widow. The press ate up the sensational hook and jumped in with both feet, announcing that gambling interests might lie at the bottom of the slaying: "Slaying Linked to Clark Gaming";[1] "Gambling Link Is Sought in Widow Strangulation."

The one good thing about the gambling angle was that it was easy to check out. As confirmed by all of Mabel's friends, she and Tutor Scherer were close. If he knew of any enemies who might've hated him enough to kill her, Tutor would surely say so. Lieutenant Coveney made a beeline for the deluxe resort in Palm Springs, a popular desert retreat in Southern California, where Tutor was vacationing. But Tutor, though shocked and saddened by the news of Mabel's death, shut down that angle with a definitive shake of the head.

"I'm sorry as hell Mabel got knocked off," he said. "We always got along swell, even after the divorce. I just don't know why anyone would kill her. It must have been the work of a prowler or burglar."

But maybe the robbers thought Tutor had used the house to hide some casino profits? Again, Tutor nixed the idea: "I never had a safe of

---

1   This was a reference to Clark County in Nevada.

any kind in that house. I think a guy who keeps large sums of cash or jewelry where he lives is just begging to be knocked over."

Likewise, Scherer waved off the press hype that there was some link between the murder and Las Vegas gambling, saying, "There just isn't any connection. Iris got no interest in that town from the divorce settlement—only the cash, some jewels, and the Burbank house, which I knew the old gal liked so much."

But actually, Tutor *was* involved—though he surely didn't know it, and neither did the cops. At least, not then.

The first real break came a week after the murder, when the Burbank police got a tip from a longtime CI—confidential informant—known as Indian George. He admitted he and four criming buddies had plotted to burglarize the Monahan house two years earlier. They'd even cased the house, but nothing more ever came of it. And helpful George not only gave up the names of his confederates, but he also gave up the reason why Monahan was targeted. According to the criminal rumor mill, Iris had done well in the divorce settlement and scored a bundle of cash plus lots of expensive jewelry, and it was all stashed in a safe in the Parkside Avenue house.

The police ran the names he'd given them. All four had rap sheets. Three were reportedly associates of Mickey Cohen. But the focus landed on the two "box men"; i.e., safecrackers: William Upshaw and Baxter Shorter. When the cops hauled them into the station, they both vehemently denied ever having cased the Monahan house or knowing anything about the murder. But after hours of intense grilling during a twenty-four-hour stint in custody, Upshaw caved. Shorter—who was a close friend—had told Upshaw he knew who'd done the murder, but he hadn't named names.

Upshaw offered Coveney a deal: let him and Shorter out, and he'd get Shorter to tell him who'd committed the murder. The police were in a tough spot. Legally speaking, they could only hold Shorter and Upshaw for forty-eight hours without filing charges, and twenty-four of them were already gone. Unless the cops managed to come up with enough evidence to file charges on them by the following day—a very unlikely prospect—they'd have to cut them loose anyway. Coveney, in no position to turn him down, agreed. But he played tough, giving Upshaw just two days to produce a name, or else . . .

Or else . . . what? The cops couldn't file charges for casing the house back in 1951. It's not a crime to look at a house. And besides, the uncorroborated word of an ex-con accomplice was legally worthless. Coveney might've been threatening to keep an eye on them in case they made a slipup in the future, but at that point, he had zero leverage.

So Upshaw and Shorter were free . . . for the moment. But they were nervous. They didn't realize Coveney's threat was as empty as his evidence locker. Upshaw, under pressure to meet Coveney's deadline, was making Shorter sweat. He pushed Shorter to get a lawyer—he just happened to have one in mind—and make a deal with the DA. It worked. Shorter ran for legal cover, and when the lawyer heard what he had to say, he immediately reached out to the district attorney, Ernie Roll. The lawyer came on strong, demanding full immunity for his client. Shorter would make the entire case for them.

It was a big ask, but Roll knew this might be their only chance to finally crack the case, and he couldn't afford to give Shorter a chance to change his mind. He drafted a stenographer and convened a meeting with Shorter and his lawyer that same day, bringing along a coterie of advisers: Adolph Alexander, one of the deputy district attorneys who'd later handle the trial; Burbank police chief Rex Andrews; and Lieutenant Robert Coveney. Selling the cops on a deal for an accomplice can be a tough proposition. Understandably, they don't want to see a criminal walk. Especially one who was involved in a murder. But this time, the chief was on board. It'd been more than two weeks since that gardener had found the body, and they still had no suspects and no clue. DA Roll was on board too . . . in theory. But he insisted on hearing what Shorter had to say before making any promises. He didn't want to "buy a pig in a poke."

Shorter was your typical career criminal. He'd served time in prison for burglary and had a record of arrests for forgery and larceny dating back to 1927. A solidly built, dark-haired man with a five o'clock shadow and a mischievous grin, he'd recently been busted for drunk driving and was awaiting trial.

And it turned out, he was up to his neck in the whole ugly scheme, from the day the burglary plot was hatched to the night it all ended in disaster. A third party, whom he'd promised not to name, had recommended him for the Monahan job.[2] Shorter said he'd met with two men at their motel on March 7, 1953, who introduced themselves only as Jack and John. They described a plan to burglarize the Monahan house. The man named John said he knew Tutor Scherer personally, that he'd ridden from Las Vegas to Los Angeles with him, and that Scherer was carrying a shoebox filled with money. Shorter had heard the story before about Tutor Scherer supposedly bringing boxes of cash from Las Vegas, and he admitted that he had indeed cased the location with Indian George and the others back in 1951. He'd been thinking about that big score ever since. Now was his chance to make it happen.

They decided to go have a look at the Monahan house. Shorter, the only one who knew where it was, gave the directions to Parkside Avenue. Jack said he already had two other men and a woman to do the job and that Shorter could just sit in the car and act as a lookout. Shorter's take—just 10 percent—wasn't much. But it wasn't bad considering his only real "work" would be to make sure they went to the right house.

The heist was set for the evening of March 9. They met up in the parking lot across from the Smoke House Restaurant, an old-school dinner house with red leather booths, dark wood, and low lighting.

---

2   It was later revealed that this third party was none other than William Upshaw. In return for the favor of getting him a lawyer, Upshaw had made Shorter promise not to admit he'd been involved when Shorter gave his statement to the cops.

That restaurant, located across the street from the Warner Bros. Studios in Burbank, is still in business, and it's a landmark.

The Smoke House Restaurant was just a few minutes away from the Monahan house. As the group of four men and a woman huddled together in a car that was supposedly stolen, the man named Jack laid out the plan: "We'll send the girl in first," referring to the woman, whom Shorter thought was named Mary. He couldn't remember what she looked like.

Jack said they had only two guns and asked Shorter if he had one. He didn't. He said he'd thrown his gun away a while ago. But Shorter saw "Mary" put a small .38 special revolver into her purse. They drove to the scene of the crime in two cars: Shorter drove with a man named Emmett, and Jack followed in a separate car, accompanied by John and "Mary." Everyone wore gloves. They parked, and the woman went to the front door. The plan was for her to get the older woman to open the door by saying her car broke down and she needed to use a phone. Once inside, she was supposed to pull out the gun and force the older woman to lie down on the couch. Then John was to go in and tie her up with sheets and pillowcases.

The gambit worked: Mabel Monahan opened the door. Shorter said he heard Mabel give "just a short scream one time. In fact, I wasn't sure about it." The door then slammed shut. (The man named John entered the house right after "Mary" and before the door closed, but Baxter Shorter didn't seem to have noticed that.) Meanwhile, Shorter, Emmett, and Jack stayed in their cars and waited. After some time passed, Emmett got nervous. The older woman (Mabel) should've been secured by then, and John should've already come out to get them. Emmett and Shorter went to Jack's car to confer. Jack told Emmett, "Take my gun and go in and see what's wrong. They've been in there too long for one woman."[3] Emmett took the gun and went into the house. Shorter stayed in the car with Jack.

---

3   The passages in quotes are taken directly from the transcript of Shorter's statement.

Some time passed, and then Emmett came out and said, "She is finally tied up. Come in and help us look." Jack told Shorter to stay in the car and keep a lookout for "things." He then went into the house. A few minutes later, Jack beckoned him inside, saying, "There's nothing here." Shorter entered the house, and when he turned left down a hallway, he saw Mabel Monahan lying on the floor. Even though at this point it'd been days since the murder, Shorter's horror at the sight of her was still apparent.

Shorter said,

> She is beaten horribly. There is blood all over the rug and everything. As I enter the door, the woman is moaning. The woman with us bends down to John. He is holding the old lady's head down on the rug, on the carpeting. The woman says, "Go on and knock her out." So Emmett takes a nickel-plated gun out and starts slugging her in the temple. I said, "My God, in Heaven's name what are you doing?" I grabbed him by the shoulder and turned him over on his fanny and everybody looked at me. I said, "This was totally unnecessary. This isn't the way that it was supposed to have been at all. This is no good." I went out of the room and when I came back in, the other man was still holding her down and she was still making noises, moaning, not very loud. I said, "Jesus Christ, this is no good. This woman's in bad shape. She is hardly breathing. Now take that gag off her. You didn't have to do that." So John looked up at Jack and said, "Shall I do what he said? What's the difference? She's not going to give us any more trouble." So he took the gag out of her mouth and from what I read in the paper there was something tied around her throat. I didn't notice that. At that time I was awful sick, deathly sick, after seeing that poor woman. So they said, "We wanted you to see that the information you gave

us was wrong." "Well," I said, "John, you came down with Scherer and he brought the shoe box full of money with him, isn't that right?" He said, "Yes, you're right, I did, but not here." So they said, "We want to show you there is no safe here at all."

And they did. He said, "So they took me into the other room where we took this rug off the floor. It is concrete, maybe, and they say there is nothing there." But Shorter—who only stood to get a small percentage of the take anyway—couldn't stop worrying about Mabel Monahan. He told Jack, "'We have got to get this woman to a doctor. She is in bad shape.' I took her pad and copied the phone number off the telephone and stuck the entire pad in my pocket. I told Jack, 'What good is a phone number if I don't have the address? Is there anything with the address on?'"

Shorter then found some bills with the name Monahan and the Parkside Avenue address. "I stuck the card in my pocket and said, 'I am going to call and get some help for this woman.' Nobody said anything. They looked at each other. Jack looked at John, John looked at Emmett, and he looked at me, and the woman looked at me. I knew I had said a wrong thing. I stood a good chance of getting seriously injured, if not killed."

They left the house empty handed. As Shorter rode back to the Smoke House parking lot with Jack, he couldn't contain his anxiety about Mabel. Prompted by his lawyer, Shorter recounted their conversation.

On the way back I said to Jack, "That woman looks awful bad and I am awful worried about her." He didn't say anything for a minute, just looked at me, and he calmly said, "She stopped breathing five minutes ago." I said, "Jesus Christ, that's murder!" He said, "So what?" And all the time we are riding back he is looking at me, and I think he feels maybe he would like to hit me in the head with the gun or maybe shoot me. I know I had cold chills all over me. I asked, "Are you sure that woman's in that bad condition? She is surely not dead. I am going to call anyway." He glared at me and just growled, "I don't give a damn what you do but the woman stopped breathing five minutes ago." When I got back to the parking lot I am shaking so I can hardly walk. Jack sneered, "You're not such a man, are you?" I answered, "I'm not when it comes to a thing like that. I am not really, I don't think."

When they parted company, Shorter drove off to look for a pay phone: "So I headed back to town, looking for a phone all the way. I go down Los Feliz, turned to Vermont and down to Sunset, and pull up by a Standard station and walk back to the phone booth and call for an ambulance."

Deputy District Attorney Adolph Alexander asked, "Where did you phone to?" Baxter Shorter answered, "I dialed the operator and said, 'This is an emergency and send an ambulance.' I gave her the address and hung up."

Shorter's detailed description of the route he took to find that pay phone, its location, and the call he placed to the operator ultimately turned out to be 100 percent accurate.

So he'd actually done something decent. There was just one problem: he told the operator that the house was on Parkside Avenue in Los Angeles. But there was no Parkside Avenue in Los Angeles. The only Parkside Avenue with that address was in Burbank.

The ambulance never arrived.

CHAPTER THREE

Thanks to Baxter Shorter, the cops now had a near-complete picture of how and why the burglary-murder had gone down. Although Shorter knew the men only by their first names—and he hadn't even been sure of that much when it came to the woman—he did manage to give physical descriptions of the men and what they'd told him about their past travels and exploits.

Using that information, the Burbank cops tapped their contacts in the Los Angeles and San Francisco police departments. That gave them their first hit: Emmett Perkins, who lived close by in El Monte. A bony, weaselly faced man with jug ears and beady eyes, his rap sheet alone made him a prime suspect. At forty-four years of age, he'd spent over half his life in custody due to a host of theft-related convictions, such as burglary, auto theft, and bank robbery. He'd been suspected of a robbery-murder in 1931, but the case had collapsed after the sole eyewitness was gunned down.

Their next hit was the man Shorter referred to as Jack. He turned out to be Jack Santo, forty-eight years old. A broad-shouldered, muscular man, handsome in a rough-hewn way, but his cold gaze warned you the good looks were just a mask. Santo was another ex-con, with a mile-long rap sheet that included convictions for attempted robbery, suspicion of kidnapping, assault with intent to kill, and transporting stolen cars over state lines.

The man named John was revealed to be John True—a name that would prove to be the height of irony. True, thirty-eight years old and a deep-sea diver, was small but wiry. His bright-blue eyes and boyish face created a deceptively guileless impression. Unlike the others, he had no prior convictions. True, like Santo, lived up north, near Grass Valley.

Police then got intel on the possible identity of the woman. Perkins had a girlfriend named Barbara Graham who'd come from San Francisco, where she'd gone by the names Barbara Radcliff and Barbara Kielhamer. Her past crimes were almost all misdemeanor-level offenses: drug possession, writing bad checks, and vagrancy—which back then was sometimes a euphemism for prostitution. The only exception was a felony conviction for perjury—more on that later. But notably, there was no hint of violence in any of her records.

While the police believed Barbara and Perkins were still in town— El Monte, to be exact—they didn't have any information on a current location for John True and Jack Santo.

Lieutenant Coveney decided to go back to Palm Springs and talk to Tutor Scherer. If John True really did know him—as he'd told Baxter Shorter—then Scherer should be able to help reel him in. Coveney paid another visit to Scherer's luxury suite and was surprised to find District Attorney Ernie Roll there, dressed for a day by the pool in a Hawaiian shirt and sandals.

Coveney likely took a beat to absorb the unlikely—and questionable— association. But if he was waiting for an explanation, he quickly saw he wasn't getting one. So, he got to the point. Had Tutor driven down to Los Angeles from Las Vegas with someone named John True? Tutor had never heard of the man. Had Tutor ever driven to Los Angeles with a shoebox of cash . . . with anyone? Tutor laughed. Absolutely not. Like he'd said before, he never kept cash in his house, and the story about the shoebox of money was nothing but "pure legend, a complete fairy tale." It was the first of John True's lies to be exposed. It wouldn't be the last.

After the claimed connection to Tutor was debunked, the Burbank police headed up to Auburn, the city near Grass Valley where they knew True had been living before he came down to Los Angeles. With Shorter's statement in pocket, there was more than enough probable cause to bust him. But they worried that if the news of True's arrest got leaked, the other three suspects would go to ground, so they made the trip a clandestine operation, with officers masquerading as civilians on a hunting trip. They spent days talking to one after another of True's known associates, careful not to blow their cover as they tried to find out where he was staying. When the cops finally tracked him down to a small cottage in Grass Valley, they decided to hell with "knock-notice." They barged in; yanked him out of the bathtub, where he was getting ready for a date with his girlfriend; shoved him into a car; and sped out of town, refusing to even tell him why he'd been taken into custody. By April 13, 1953, John True was locked up in the Burbank jail.

This move by the Burbank police was, quite simply . . . crazy. Not to mention illegal and unethical. The cops hadn't just crossed city lines; they'd crossed county lines. This was not their turf, and they had no legal authority to operate up there without the permission of Grass Valley and Nevada County law enforcement. So it was guaranteed to royally piss off both Grass Valley and Nevada County when they found out. And there was no doubt that at some point, they would. The Burbank police knew that. But they needed to buy time to pick up the other suspects.

I imagine if this had been an ordinary case that wasn't making the front page on an almost daily basis—sometimes with more than one story awarded prime placement above the fold—they might've been able to keep it under wraps long enough to bust the rest of the crew. But not when the case was a media sensation like the Monahan murder. Their naive belief that a move like this could fly under the radar for even an hour is a prime example of how ill prepared they were for the unique challenges of a high-profile case.

Don't get me wrong. I sympathize with their effort to control a case that was getting minute-by-minute coverage but was maddeningly difficult to crack. The constant threat of an overzealous press, heedless of the damage they could wreak on a case in the sensitive early phases of an investigation, was an ever-present dilemma in the O. J. Simpson case. In our case, we didn't have the problematic lack of evidence the Burbank police did—we had a wealth of it from day one. But trying to keep the press from compromising witness testimony by feeding them information in the voracious pursuit of headlines was an ongoing nightmare. And then there were the unforced, ruinous errors, like allowing Simpson to walk out of the police station after making a gobbledygook statement that would have landed any other suspect in jail within seconds . . . which led to the now infamous slow-speed Bronco chase.

The analogy isn't perfect. We were dealing with an unprecedented explosion in media coverage, thanks to the very recent advent of twenty-four-hour *televised* news coverage, which turned the case into a soap opera and the trial into a sporting event. The Monahan case, though it attracted a national audience and was the subject of intense media focus, was not positioned at the crossroads of the technological leap that suddenly put minute-by-minute coverage on televisions in homes around the country and the world.

Still, the Burbank police were about to learn a big lesson about the power and the punishment of a cutthroat media culture.

News of John True's unorthodox arrest leaked so fast the clang of the steel jail cell door was still ringing in their ears when reporters started calling Burbank police, demanding to know how and why True had been "secretly arrested." Or as he and his lawyer put it . . . kidnapped.

True's lawyer, Harold Berliner Jr. of Nevada City (who was apparently self-appointed because True told the *Los Angeles Times* he didn't have a lawyer), was furious when he found out what'd happened. He demanded that arrest warrants be issued for Chief Andrews and the three officers who'd spirited True away under the cover of darkness. The press ate it up, and the Monahan case once again landed on the front page: "Police Kidnap Charges Seen, Chief Andrews and Three Aides Accused." And the local police in Nevada County were pissed as hell.

The sheriff openly deplored the "high-handed methods" of Southern Californians. To put it mildly, the stealth arrest didn't quite work out as planned.

And adding insult to injury, True refused to talk. Hoping to entice him into at least naming the others involved, police put him on a polygraph, promising to release him if he answered questions. But although he admitted to knowing Jack Santo (which he'd already done before the polygraph) and repeated the claim that he'd met Tutor Scherer in the past, he insisted he hadn't even been in Los Angeles until three days after the murder and claimed he didn't know anyone named Emmett or Baxter or Barbara. Then he clammed up and demanded to see a lawyer. Although the police did everything but beg him on bended knee, True never did finish that polygraph test.

The police knew he was lying. Not only had Tutor denied ever having met True, but Baxter Shorter had positively identified him in a lineup as one of the suspects.

After True had been held for over seventy-two hours, Berliner—joined by Patrick Cooney, a savvy, well-known lawyer and former associate of famed Scopes trial lawyer, Clarence Darrow—applied for a writ to get True released from custody.

His impending release wasn't a big loss to the police. True wasn't looking like a great witness for the prosecution anyway.

But that was okay. They didn't need to turn him to make the case. After all, they had Baxter Shorter.

CHAPTER FOUR

That is, until someone leaked to the press that one of the perpetrators had been singing. The name Baxter Shorter wasn't mentioned in the story. It just said that an informer who was not in custody had coughed up the names of the perpetrators and details about the crime that only someone involved in the murder would know—like the fact that they'd tricked the victim into opening the door by saying their car had broken down.

It didn't take a rocket scientist to figure out that the informer could only have been Baxter Shorter. Upshaw had backed out well before they finalized the plan for the burglary, and in any case, he'd skipped town and decamped to Mexico. So he wasn't talking to anyone. It couldn't be John True either. Thanks to Cooney's insistence, he'd been allowed to talk to the press, and he'd told every reporter who'd listen that he had nothing to do with the murder. Perkins, Santo, and Graham knew *they* hadn't been talking. So that left only Baxter Shorter. They might as well have put his face on a billboard.

This spelled danger for their star—and only—eyewitness. Coveney and Chief Andrews ran to DA Roll and pressed him to file charges against True and the other three so they could take them all into custody and keep Shorter safe. But Roll refused, saying the case wasn't strong enough. In a statement to reporters, he said that True's arrest was "premature and ill-advised," and that he told "the boys from Burbank" he needed "facts and evidence which they do not yet have."

I agree with Roll. The harebrained scheme to kidnap True had only managed to turn his arrest into even bigger news—and in the process, make the Burbank police look like reckless cowboys. And Shorter's statement—the only evidence they had to prove the identities of the murderers—wasn't even enough for an indictment, let alone a trial. Shorter was an accomplice, which meant his identification of the perpetrators had to be corroborated by independent evidence. They didn't have it.

As for who'd leaked the story, no one really knew. Some suspected it was the district attorney himself, Ernie Roll, angling to curry favor with the press. But Lieutenant Coveney was named as the source of a statement that likewise included the insider information and strongly implied they knew who was responsible for the burglary-murder.

It was never proven one way or the other. But one thing was very clear: the members of the printed press were about as carnivorous as any of today's online keyboard jockeys. They hounded their targets with an unholy zeal, and once they got their teeth into someone, they'd shake them like a rag doll until they got what they wanted. If Roll—having one eye on the polls as most politicians always do—decided to throw them a bone, it wouldn't surprise me.

But regardless of who'd leaked the story, Shorter was now in real danger. Coveney offered him protection, even suggested he move into a secret hideaway. Shorter's lawyer advised him to leave the state. DA Roll told him to go into hiding or at least let them put police around his apartment. But Shorter wouldn't hear of it. He was adamant that he'd be safer out on the streets. If he suddenly disappeared, it'd be a flashing neon sign that he was the snitch. He had a point. Police protection wouldn't last forever, and it was far from foolproof.

But the strategy failed. Just hours after the story hit the street in the evening news, Shorter's wife, distraught to the point of hysteria, called the police and said Baxter Shorter had been kidnapped at gunpoint.

Olivia Shorter said that she and Baxter were watching television in the living room at 8:00 p.m. when someone knocked on the door.

Baxter opened it to find Emmett Perkins standing there. He brandished a gun and said, "Let's go, Baxter." Olivia grabbed the 30-30 rifle they kept in the living room and followed them out into the hall, but Perkins allegedly told her, "Go back in the apartment or Baxter's going to die right here." She claimed she saw Perkins force him into a car, where another man was waiting.

"They'll kill him," she wailed to the detectives. No one disagreed. A police official was quoted as saying, "We'll sure as hell find this guy dead someplace. After all, those men didn't take him out just to talk." Burbank police chief Andrews was equally blunt: "I'm afraid they'll kill him, if he isn't already dead. We told him at noon today to get out of town or they'd kill him."

The story of Baxter Shorter's kidnapping at gunpoint, which called Shorter a "one-time associate of Mickey Cohen," said he'd been taken on a "vengeful 'last ride.'" Based on Olivia's description, it was believed that the car belonged to Barbara Graham. Front-page headlines screamed, "Slaying Figure Victim of 'Last Ride' Kidnapping—Possible Informer in Burbank Killing of Woman Abducted"; "Informer Kidnapped in Ride"; "Murder Suspect Kidnapped—Fear Underworld Vengeance for Reported Squealer."

And with that, the lid blew off. No more waiting and hoping for more evidence. The police immediately issued an all-points bulletin and warrants for the arrests of Emmett Perkins, Jack Santo, and Barbara Graham. The cops had known all along that Perkins and Graham were still in town; they'd been keeping a loose watch on the pair. But now that their identities had been leaked, the police had to act fast. The pair might well go on the run—in fact, they might already be in the wind. And Santo, who'd never been located and had ties to Northern California, could be anywhere in the state. The cops needed to cast a wide net to catch him. They called on multiple police agencies to join in the search.

And the race to find Santo was particularly urgent, because now, he wasn't just wanted for the Monahan murder. On the day the arrest warrants were issued, it was revealed that Santo was also a suspect in a quadruple murder up in Chester, California. Guard Young, his three young daughters (Judy, six; Jean, seven; and Sondra, three), and their friend (Michael Saile, four) were beaten over the head, shoved into the trunk of a car, and left for dead. Only Sondra survived. A suspected mass murderer was at large.

In the midst of this maelstrom, a judge issued the writ ordering John True's release, and Chief Andrews was forced to let him go. Since DA Roll had nixed the possibility of charging True with the Monahan murder, and he obviously wasn't involved in the Shorter kidnapping— because he'd been in custody the whole time—they had no legal basis for holding him. On April 16, 1953, True walked out of jail.

Within twenty-four hours, the cops had lost their only eyewitness and the one suspect they'd had in hand. At that point, they had to accept the very real possibility that they'd hit their final dead end. The whole case was going down the drain.

CHAPTER FIVE

Coveney had maintained that they'd had Perkins and Barbara Graham under surveillance all along. If so, someone had fallen asleep on the job, because now that push had come to shove, it turned out they actually didn't know where to find the two.

That's because they were on the move. And unbeknownst to the cops, Jack Santo had joined them. At first, they'd camped out in Perkins's El Monte gambling house. But like everyone else, the three had been keeping up with the latest developments in the case—easy to do because updates came out daily, in both the morning and evening editions. Perkins wisely deduced that they were "hot." The cops knew about the place in El Monte from past raids. They had to get out of there.

They headed to the Ambassador Hotel, then continued to move until they landed free digs at a dump in Lynwood—courtesy of an associate who worked with lawyer Patrick Cooney. It was a three-bedroom apartment with walls made of pasteboard that'd been converted from an auto shop.

Policewomen who'd been tailing Barbara had spotted her at a shopping area in Lynwood in late April, but they'd lost her in the crowd. Not knowing where else to look, they kept hanging around in the hope of catching her if she returned. Ten days later, she did. This time, they were determined not to make the same mistake. The four female cops tracked her from one bus to another until she led them to the "shabby Lynwood storefront" that detectives figured was their hideout. Within the hour, a posse of fourteen police officers armed with shotguns burst through the flimsy doors and found Perkins lying down in one of the bedrooms, fully clothed, and Santo half-dressed, lying on a mattress in the living room.

But the descriptions of Barbara varied widely as reporters vied for the most sensationalist twist. One claimed she was found "only partly clothed" and appeared to have just injected herself with the hypodermic needle in her purse. Another claimed that police barged in on her as she was "changing clothes in another bedroom." But the winner for the Most Sensationalist claim: that she was discovered standing in the middle of the room "stark naked" after having just scored a dose of heroin. The only consistent detail reported was the fact that she'd dyed her hair blond—though some claimed it'd originally been red, while others reported it'd been brown.

So right from the start, the coverage of Barbara was not only excessively focused on her appearance; it was overtly sexualized, voyeuristic, and deliberately titillating. And not just because she was a woman—though that was a factor since women were almost never involved in such a violent crime. It was also because she was strikingly beautiful. Petite—just five foot three—and a slender 121 pounds, the twenty-nine-year-old Barbara had the looks of an actress, a stark contrast to her purported partners in crime, the forty-four-year-old weasel-faced Perkins and the forty-eight-year-old brutish-looking Santo.

The police had probable cause to arrest Perkins on the spot since Baxter Shorter's wife had identified him as one of the kidnappers—though he adamantly denied it. But Santo and Barbara were another matter. Neither of them had been identified as the second kidnapper. And with Shorter gone, they had no evidence to tie them to the Monahan case. So LAPD had initially been forced to release Santo—a move Burbank PD did not appreciate. They immediately rearrested him on suspicion of murder, probable cause be damned.

But they didn't have to make any risky moves with Barbara. Though she'd denied any knowledge of the burglary-murder, she'd recently passed some bad checks. Those charges would keep her in custody for now. In fact, the cops had set her bail so high—$25,000—those charges would keep her in jail for quite a while. It was a lot of money for petty misdemeanors, and Barbara knew it. In a letter to her husband on May 19, 1953, she said her bail was "ridiculous," but she assured him the talk of a murder charge in the news was false: "I'm innocent and could never commit the horrible atrocities" that'd been reported by the press. She assured her husband she'd be released soon.

At that point, Patrick Cooney, who'd previously represented John True, had taken on all three of them. Cooney filed a writ for Santo that got him released. But this time Compton PD got into the act and arrested him for the misdemeanor of switching the license plates on his car. Nice try, but the police couldn't justify a high enough bail to keep him in. Santo got out again. What finally landed him in custody for good was the reappearance of William Upshaw—Baxter Shorter's buddy.

Upshaw, still in Mexico, had heard from his wife that he was wanted for questioning in the Shorter kidnapping. Upshaw was trying to go straight, and he decided he did not need this grief. The kidnapping might be serious enough to get the Mexican *federales* involved. He flew back and surrendered to the police. But he claimed no knowledge of the kidnapping and refused to take a polygraph test. And with Baxter Shorter gone—most likely dead—the police had no evidence to connect him to either the Monahan murder or the Shorter kidnapping. They had to release him. By May 16, 1953, Upshaw was back on the streets. But the truth was, he had begun to crack.

Two days later, Upshaw asked his lawyer—Tommy Mercola, the same lawyer Upshaw had recommended to Shorter—to get him a deal. With a promise of immunity in his pocket, Upshaw told his end of the story to LAPD chief William Parker and Burbank police chief Rex Andrews. On March 9, 1953, Shorter came to Upshaw's house and told him Santo and True wanted him to come along on a burglary. Upshaw wasn't interested, but he gave Shorter a ride to the meeting place: a drive-in at Laurel Canyon and Ventura Boulevard. They parked next to the car where Santo, Perkins, True, and "the girl" were seated.

Baxter Shorter told him that Santo "had a deal set up in Burbank." John True had said he'd driven down from Las Vegas with Tutor Scherer, and that Tutor had over $100,000 in cash with him. He assured them the cash would be in the Burbank house. Upshaw said he wanted no part of it and told Shorter he'd be a "damn fool" to do it, reminding him that they'd been picked up while casing that house in 1951. In one of the many ironies in this case, they actually hadn't been picked up for casing the house. Upshaw, tricked by his own guilty conscience, was wrong. But Shorter believed him—and didn't care. He was fatalistic. He figured he might as well go along for the ride and get something out of it since he'd probably get blamed for it anyway.

But Upshaw's warning had made him think twice. Shorter told Santo he wasn't sure, and that he didn't like the idea of having a woman involved. According to Upshaw, Santo said he didn't have to worry about her, that she knew what would happen to her if she "squealed." They then drove by the Monahan house. At that point, Santo demanded an answer. Shorter decided he was in.

The next day, Shorter came to see Upshaw. He was shaken. He told Upshaw they'd killed the woman and described what had happened. Upshaw repeated what Shorter told him, and it was exactly what Shorter had earlier told the police—including the fact that it was Perkins, not Graham, who'd pistol-whipped the victim, and how Shorter had tried to get an ambulance for her.

This was all good stuff. Upshaw could identify all the players and describe how they'd planned the burglary. And he wasn't an accomplice, so the prosecution wouldn't need any independent corroboration of his testimony.

But Upshaw hadn't been there when the burglary-murder went down. He didn't have any firsthand knowledge of what'd happened. And even if he testified to Shorter's statement about who'd been involved, that statement was still just the word of an accomplice.

His identification of the others had to be corroborated, and Upshaw couldn't do it . . .

The cops needed more. They needed an eyewitness, and there was only one left. They had to go back to John True.

Luckily, finding John True was easy. It took about ten seconds to learn that he was working in a shipyard across the bay from San Francisco. San Francisco homicide chief Frank Ahern swooped in with an arrest warrant and took him into custody. Later that day, Lieutenant Coveney and LAPD detective Ed Lovold arrived with an indictment for murder in their pockets—ammunition they thought would pry a statement out of him. But True picked up where he'd left off and swore he'd had nothing to do with the Monahan murder. This was bad, very bad. At that point, a grand jury had already been convened, witnesses were testifying, but there was no way they'd get a murder indictment if they didn't put True on the stand. The cops put the pressure on, grilling him for hours at a time, but he held firm.

After two straight days with no sign that True was wavering, they were desperate. They decided to try a different approach. If True wouldn't listen to the cops, maybe he'd listen to his friends. Seth Terry had been a kind of father figure for True and a close friend. He might succeed where they'd failed. Coveney went to work on Terry, telling him that if True talked, he'd get immunity, but if he didn't, he'd wind up spending the rest of his life in prison, along with the others. Terry would be doing him a real favor. Coveney said True was "in a jam." Talking was his only way out.

None of that was true. Not so far—and probably not ever. Although Perkins, Santo, and Graham were in custody, none of them was talking. If John True held firm, the cops couldn't touch him. And although Perkins might go down for kidnapping Baxter Shorter, both Santo and Barbara Graham would walk.

But Seth Terry didn't know any of that. And he had no reason to doubt the word of Lieutenant Coveney, a law enforcement official. Terry agreed to try and make his friend see the light. In private talks with True in his jail cell, Terry and two of True's other closest friends worked on him, believing True would spend the rest of his life in prison if he didn't talk. The following morning, on June 4, 1953, True began to reconsider. But he was no dummy. He wasn't about to roll over unless he got a promise of immunity—one that would stick. "I'm not taking the word of any low-level cop. If the D. A. down there tells me personally he'll guarantee immunity about that Burbank deal, I'll talk."

They immediately put the call through to the district attorney. DA Roll promised True that if his story checked out, he'd personally make sure the indictment against him was dismissed. He told True he'd send his chief deputy and right-hand man, Adolph Alexander, to take his statement. Roll closed the deal, saying, "If you make a complete statement and tell the whole truth, Mr. Alexander is authorized to promise you we will ask for dismissal of this murder indictment. Is that clearly understood?"

True said it was. "You'll stand behind what Mr. Alexander says."

A few hours later, Alexander appeared at the Hall of Justice and took True's statement. That statement, transcribed by an official stenographer, would later become the center of a controversy.

But right now, it was time to celebrate. With John True on board, they had their star eyewitness. And with William Upshaw, they had the key witness who could corroborate his testimony. Less than one week later, True would appear before the grand jury, and for the first time the world would hear a firsthand account of what had happened inside the house on Parkside Avenue.

On the strength of his testimony, the prosecution would charge Emmett Perkins, Jack Santo, and Barbara Graham with murder, burglary, and the special circumstance of murder committed in the course of a burglary. That special circumstance meant all three defendants would face the possibility of a sentence of death.

CHAPTER SIX

Throughout the dealings with John True, the grand jury had been in session, and the prosecution had hauled Barbara, Santo, and Perkins before them. But they couldn't be forced to talk, and they didn't. Santo and Perkins invoked their right to remain silent on the advice of their attorney. Barbara said only that she'd had nothing to do with the kidnapping of Baxter Shorter or the murder of Mabel Monahan, but couldn't remember where she'd been that night—then likewise invoked her right to remain silent on the advice of her attorney.

But the rest of the witnesses were more than willing to talk, so the public had heard about the testimony of Merle Leslie, the friend who'd gone to the poker game with Mabel the night before; William Upshaw, who named all the players and testified to the plan they'd hatched; and the cops who'd responded to the crime scene and described the bloody aftermath of the murder. But since none of them was an eyewitness, no one had heard a firsthand account of what had happened after Mabel Monahan opened her door.

Until John True took the stand on June 9, 1953. Billed as a "deep sea diver" with no criminal record, the press reported only that prosecutors had agreed to ask the judge for "special consideration." The promise of immunity was mentioned in passing and only as a possibility. But of course, the press didn't know about John True's personal phone call with District Attorney Ernie Roll. And the prosecution wanted to keep it that way for as long as possible. Protecting True's credibility was crucial. Because the story he was about to tell would be a bombshell.

True said that he sat in the car with Santo and watched as Barbara knocked on Mabel's door and entered the house. He followed her in seconds later. There, he'd been shocked to find her holding Mabel Monahan by the neck and slamming her in the head with the butt of a pistol "bringing down a gun butt time and time again" with a ferocity so savage that he put his hand on Mabel's face to block the blows. Mabel collapsed, and he went to the floor with her, cradling her head on his lap.

He testified that Barbara then put a pillowcase over her head and Perkins tied her hands behind her back and dragged her down the hall. Santo tied a strip of cloth around her neck—the coup de grâce. The pathologist said Mabel Monahan had died of asphyxiation, strangled by that strip of cloth. True, upset by the violent attack on the victim, claimed he told the others they needed to call an ambulance, that he feared she would die. But when he said that, they all turned to look at him, and he realized he had "said the wrong thing." He waited until they'd left the house, then called an ambulance.

Does that last part sound familiar? That's what Baxter Shorter told the police and prosecutors back in April, before he was "disappeared." Except he'd said *he* was the one who'd demanded to get help for Mabel, and the one who'd called the ambulance. Not John True.

So, who was telling the truth? While Shorter had given a detailed account of how he'd looked for Mabel's address, then gone in search of a pay phone on his way home and described the location of the pay phone he'd used—all of which turned out to be accurate—John True gave no such detail. But he knew someone had called an ambulance, because during the burglary, he'd heard Shorter say they should, and what's more, I think he also knew Shorter's statement had been proven to be correct—because someone told him. And likely even showed True that statement.

That "someone" could only have been one of the cops or prosecutors who were present when Shorter's statement was taken. The press never got to see Shorter's statement, so they only knew what Upshaw told the grand jury, which was that Shorter said he'd called an ambulance. Upshaw never testified that Shorter realized he'd "said the wrong thing" when he suggested getting help for Mabel Monahan. But the prosecutors had the transcript of Shorter's statement. And the near-identical wording in one particular passage between what Shorter said and what True testified to before the grand jury is too suspicious to ignore.

Shorter said that he sounded the alarm about Monahan's condition and that he told the others he was going to make a call and get her help. Here's his quoted statement about what happened next: "They looked at each other. Jack looked at John, John looked at Emmett, and he looked at me, and the woman looked at me. *I knew I had said a wrong thing.*"

Now compare what True said to the grand jury. He recounted how Santo had tied a cloth strip around Monahan's neck, then stated, "The lady was moaning and I said, 'This lady is going to die, you'd better call an ambulance.' Then I realized *I had said the wrong thing.*"

Coincidence? No. I don't think so. And True knew he could get away with taking the credit for calling an ambulance because it was common knowledge—or at least widely believed—that Shorter was dead.

This lie, in and of itself, wasn't a big deal. But what it said about the prosecution was. Witnesses are never supposed to be allowed to read or hear what others have said. Every cop who's ever been to a crime scene knows how important it is to keep witnesses separate. If witnesses hear one another, their memories will be distorted, or they'll lose confidence in their own perceptions, or worst of all, they'll be tempted to lie. And that's doubly and triply true when the witness is an accomplice with every reason in the world to say whatever it takes to please the prosecutor and make himself look good.

For me, this was an early warning signal that someone—either the cops or the prosecutors—was playing fast and loose, bending the truth in order to build up John True's credibility. The motivation was obvious. He was their whole case.

But making John True look like the hero—or at least the only human in that house—was far from the most pressing issue. Of much greater concern was the fact that his was the only testimony that put a gun in Barbara's hand. The only testimony that showed her to be a vicious, pistol-wielding killer—instead of just the decoy who duped Mabel Monahan into opening the door. True's testimony made Barbara the centerpiece of this brutal murder. And since True and Barbara were alone with Mabel for a period of time, only Barbara could've contradicted his story.

But that was never going to happen. And True knew it. By the time he finally spoke to the police on June 4, he knew Barbara had already been in custody for weeks . . . and she wasn't talking. Besides, even if she now changed her mind and gave a statement, it was just her word against his—and who were the cops going to believe? Someone like him, who had no rap sheet? Or Barbara, who had a slew of misdemeanor convictions and a felony conviction for perjury?

Besides, now that True had testified, the prosecution couldn't pull out of the deal with him even if they'd wanted to. It'd look like the prosecutors themselves didn't know who to believe.

The prosecution had to stick with the eyewitness who'd brought them to this point. John True was their star. And he said Barbara was the one who'd pistol-whipped Mabel Monahan. His testimony on that point was key to Barbara's culpability. Without it, Barbara's role was reduced to a decoy and bystander in the whole affair. Even though she'd still legally, technically be liable for the murder (more on that later), the jury would have a hard time convicting her. And there was almost no chance they'd vote to put her to death.

That posed a real problem for the prosecution, because John True was the only one who'd said that Barbara had physically attacked Mabel Monahan, and there was no physical evidence to back up that claim. It's rare for a woman to be that violent—especially toward a stranger, and an elderly victim like Mabel Monahan. In all the thousands of cases I've handled over the years, both prosecuting and defending, I've never seen a woman act out with that kind of brutality against such a vulnerable victim. That takes a special kind of callousness and cruelty.

I wondered: Was Barbara Graham the exception? I had to find out who this woman was.

CHAPTER SEVEN

Barbara Graham, née Barbara Elaine Ford, was born to Hortense Ford on June 26, 1923. Back then, it was widely believed that by nature, all women were meant to be mothers—nurturing, caring, and patient. And kids who were rebellious troublemakers were just bad seeds who were born that way. The word *incorrigible* was used freely to signal that the child was the problem, defective from birth, her parents blameless.

There was little to no awareness that a woman who was a mother could be a heartless, selfish, cruel excuse for a human being. In short, a mother like Hortense.

Hortense's family was one of the many who'd been forced to relocate to the port city of Oakland when San Francisco virtually crumbled in the earthquake of 1906. She was just seventeen years old when she gave birth to Barbara. The father was never in the picture, his identity unknown. Given how hard it was to be a single mother back then, I have to believe she had the baby only because she couldn't get an abortion. Because her utter neglect of Barbara made it clear she'd had no desire to be a mother.

From almost the moment Barbara was born, Hortense began parking her with various friends and relatives—anyone who'd take her. Hortense was determined not to let a baby get in the way of living the life she wanted. But—failing to learn a lesson—she got pregnant again before Barbara was even one year old, giving birth to another baby girl, Claire. Again, no father was on the scene. This time, the authorities took notice. In September 1925, Hortense, then nineteen years old, was branded as "incorrigible" and sent off to the California School for Girls in Ventura, a reform school for "wayward" girls.

The fact that this would mean two very little children (Barbara, just two years old, and Claire, only one year old) would be left homeless apparently mattered to no one.

Barbara and Claire got shuttled between friends, relatives, and total strangers. It's not clear when Hortense was released, but they would've had to let her go by June 12, 1927, when she turned twenty-one. But whatever "reforming" she'd done in that school didn't reform her attitude toward her eldest daughter. The moment she got out, she shipped Barbara off to live with a woman named Mrs. Kennedy. By the age of five, Barbara had been abandoned by her mother twice.

And her time with Mrs. Kennedy wasn't just loveless; it was ugly. The woman had a parrot, and Barbara, maybe half out of curiosity and half out of empathy, opened the cage and let it fly free. For this Barbara was forced to stand in a corner holding a freshly cut onion to her eyes for hours at a stretch, tears coursing down her cheeks. It takes some kind of sadistic creativity to even think of a punishment that cruel. Barbara, recounting her childhood, said every day with Mrs. Kennedy brought "some horror."

For the next few years, Hortense managed to avoid getting pregnant, until she gave birth to a son, Joseph. This time, she married the father—Joseph Wood—and Barbara and Claire took his surname.

Barbara believed he was her real father, and she loved him, called him Papa, and said he was "decent and good." He would visit Barbara at Mrs. Kennedy's to bring her treats and little candies for Halloween, but he must have noticed at some point that Barbara was in bad shape, because he demanded to take her home. Home was just a shack, where the whole family lived with Barbara's disabled grandfather, but at least there Barbara had one source of love in Papa Wood.

Trial by Ambush

Sadly, her time with him didn't last long. He died of appendicitis when Barbara was seven years old. That's when, according to Barbara, things "really got tough."

Not for Hortense, though. For her, Joe's death meant she was free to have some fun, and she took full advantage of it. She was pretty and had a deep bench of boyfriends. The last thing she wanted was to be tied down by a child, and she made sure Barbara knew it. Mistreated children don't have many options when it comes to fighting back. Barbara retaliated in one of the few ways a powerless child could: by running away, again and again.

But Hortense didn't have a lot of time—or any desire—to run after her. Although she got a widow's stipend from the state, it wasn't enough to support them, so she had to work. That meant Barbara and Claire again got bounced around between friends, relatives, and strangers. When those resources dried up, a social worker put the girls in an orphanage, the convent St. Mary's of the Palms in San Jose. Barbara was eleven years old by then; her sister, Claire, was ten.

I'd have thought Barbara would hate all the rules and restrictions of life in a convent. But surprisingly, she loved it. The sisters were kind, and Barbara said those months were the happiest of her childhood memories.

If only she could've stayed there . . . but Hortense took Barbara and her sister home. Barbara said that gave her a "few months of miserable freedom," but at least the family was back together.

Unfortunately, not for long. Apparently Hortense was no happier to have Barbara home than Barbara was to be there. After those few months, Hortense sent Barbara—then just twelve years old—to a convent in the Bay Area, but kept her other two children at home. This convent was no St. Mary's. The Home of the Good Shepherd was a "school for incorrigible girls," and Barbara's stay there didn't last long. She got kicked out for stealing some oranges off the trees in the orange grove behind the school.

49

This, it seems to me, was the first of a few major turning points in Barbara's young life. Nothing says "unwanted" like your own mother throwing you out of the house—especially when she chooses to let her other children stay at home. Barbara had probably sensed it sooner, but she certainly knew then that she was unloved and unlovable. It comes as no surprise that when she was later asked about her childhood, Barbara's frank assessment was that her mother "hated" her and "couldn't stand the sight of" her.

After her release from the Home of the Good Shepherd, Barbara, now thirteen years old, moved back home and enrolled in the eighth grade in a public school. It was a good news–bad news story. She discovered literature, poetry in particular, and was an avid fan of Oscar Wilde, Walt Whitman, and Robert Bridges. But Barbara had turned out to be every bit as pretty as her mother, and she developed early, making her seem older than her years. Boys took notice—and so did Hortense, who reacted by clamping down on Barbara . . . hard. No football games, no dances, no boys walking her home from school.

I'd guess that Hortense, seeing herself in Barbara, was trying to keep her daughter from landing in the same quicksand that'd saddled her with three children, no husband, and no income. But it was way too late to play the disciplinarian, or even pretend to be someone who really cared, since she'd made it very clear from the beginning that she'd never wanted Barbara.

So, understandably, Barbara rejected Hortense's sudden decision to act like a parent. She ditched classes and hung out with a bad crowd, drinking, smoking, and panhandling for money to take the ferry into San Francisco. I'm not judging. I did all that and more. But unlike me, Barbara was starting to look like a woman as a young teen. She ran away to San Francisco and tried to get a job at a bar as a waitress. There, she caught the eye of a man in his thirties—an ex-con. With no money and no place to go, that ill-planned adventure could've landed Barbara in a very bad place. But luckily, he turned out to be a decent guy. When he realized how young Barbara was, he took her to his mother's house and had her stay there.

Hortense somehow managed to track her down and drag her back home, but the ever-defiant Barbara snuck out with boys at every opportunity. She wasn't all that promiscuous; she just reveled in the feeling of being liked and admired—something she'd had precious little of in her short life. But eventually Barbara's delinquency caught the attention of even the not-so-vigilant public school. Whether Barbara got expelled or Hortense was told expulsion was on the near horizon isn't clear.

But it didn't matter. Hortense had had enough. This time, she shunted Barbara off to the California School for Girls in Ventura— the *very same* reform school where Hortense had done time—telling police that Barbara had been "a very bad girl, unmanageable all her life." Barbara begged her mother not to send her away—which moved Hortense . . . not at all.

At that time, these schools were part of a progressive movement that believed troublemaking teenagers were lazy, immoral, "defectives," "morons," and criminals. The girls were routinely branded as "over-sexed." (I strongly suspect the latter claim was a ploy to discredit charges of sexual abuse.) It was believed that what the girls needed was "correction" that instilled a solid work ethic and strong moral values. But the schools were largely unregulated, and all manner of horrific "disciplinary" methods were employed with impunity. The Ventura school where Hortense had done her time—and where Barbara was now incarcerated—was particularly infamous.

By the time Barbara stepped into the jaws of the purgatory that was the California School for Girls in Ventura, it had already been the site of a violent rebellion. In 1921, only four years before Hortense did her time there, the inmates plotted a full-scale revolt and tried to burn the whole place down. More than thirty girls escaped before the sheriff appeared to restore order. But the ringleaders remained to stand their ground and fight. They weren't having any. Hollering that they were wards of the state, not the county, which meant the sheriff had no authority to touch them (a legal theory of dubious validity), they bashed him over the head with a chair and various other pieces of furniture.

That did it. The sheriff called in the cavalry, and the ringleaders were hustled off to county jail, ending what was described as one of the most "sensational riots ever witnessed in any State institution." The girls never revealed the reason for the uprising. But in the past, stories of the school's abusive disciplinary practices had been published in vivid detail by the *Los Angeles Examiner*.

Although the school denounced those stories as salacious yellow journalism (and blamed those stories for the riot), some were certainly—and admittedly—true: such as the school's use of the "water treatment," a form of waterboarding in which they shoved a hose down the girls' throats, or the injection of harmful drugs, or forcing the girls to work barefooted in deep pits, and the prodigious use of solitary confinement for lengthy periods of time. It was reported that a number of employees—nurses, counselors, and a doctor—had quit in reaction to the inhumane treatment meted out to the girls. Indeed, the 1921 riot was said to have been provoked by the departure of Dr. Di Giannini, one of those who'd objected to the extreme "disciplinary" practices at the school.

While the school consistently defended these practices as effective means of encouraging reform, on occasion, they'd agree to stop or at least limit their use. Given the lack of oversight or accountability, it's debatable whether they actually did.

And that's where the just-turned-fourteen-year-old Barbara Graham spent the next two years of her life. According to the school records, she was considered a problem child who needed "lots of attention and correcting," for being "noisy in her dorm room," for "writing on the wall," for being "impudent" and "cutting pictures from books." One entry stated that Barbara had been "kissing and hugging" her pillow. Barbara remembered the gatekeepers telling her she was just like her mother, saying she was a "chip off the old block." Although there's no record of what punishment Barbara suffered for any of these violations, given the school's notoriously abusive reputation, one can easily assume it was draconian.

Reading those records and the petty infractions they described, I wondered what on earth the "teachers" were complaining about. Barbara's violations seemed entirely unremarkable for any teenage girl, let alone one who'd had Barbara's life experience. As any shrink worth the price of a box of Kleenex would know, the need for "attention" and some degree of defiance were to be expected of an emotionally scarred young girl who'd been kicked to the curb and abandoned by her mother practically from the day she was born. And Hortense—by keeping her other children at home—made it very clear that Barbara should take it personally. Had Barbara been able to get the psychological therapy she needed, instead of a hose down her throat, it likely would've made all the difference. Literally—perhaps—the difference between life and death.

But back in the 1930s, shrinks were not a thing. Especially not for minors. Discipline was the order of the day. Kids, it was believed (especially in facilities like these), just needed to be kept busy. The School for Girls really took that theory to heart. The inmates were up at 5:30 a.m., and they worked until lights out at 8:30 p.m.

If only through sheer exhaustion, that probably quashed the rebellious impulses of some girls. Some, but not Barbara. Though she was undoubtedly less criminally sophisticated than most in that facility, she was innately intelligent. With very little schooling, and none at all past the eighth grade (which she only fitfully attended), she was reading at a tenth-grade level. But intelligence, especially when it's combined with the oppositional attitude so often seen in victims of child abuse, can make for a less than pliable subject. Put more bluntly, Barbara wasn't inclined to take any shit.

The school had no fence, so runaways happened frequently. Barbara, of course, was one of them. She escaped three times, hitching rides back to her home in the Bay Area, where she begged her mother to let her stay. Her pleas fell on deaf ears. Time after time, Hortense called the cops and had them take Barbara away.

Ordinarily, Hortense's stubborn refusal to heed her daughter's pleas might've been chalked up to ignorance. Even someone who kept up with the news might not know what to believe about the school. Certainly, the administrators in charge were quick to denounce any charges of abuse as the lies of unruly and unreliable delinquents.

But while the public at large likely wasn't aware of the conditions in that reform school, Hortense had lived there for at least a year, maybe longer. She knew very well what it was like. For my part, even reading about the cruel mistreatment of the girls was heartbreaking. I can't imagine how it felt to be a young girl like Barbara, a victim of that mistreatment, whose mother repeatedly slammed the door in her face and sent her back to hell in handcuffs.

Whatever their intentions, I can't see how those reform schools managed to instill anything but rage, rebelliousness, and hopelessness, not to mention an accelerated education in criminality. Before landing there, Barbara had been running with a "fast crowd." But drinking, smoking, and playing hooky was child's play in a facility that housed gang members, burglars, kidnappers, and forgers. And at barely fourteen years of age, Barbara was one of the youngest—and surely least experienced of the bunch when it came to the world of crime. It seems likely that this school was where Barbara began to learn the tricks of the trade that would later become her means of earning a living: check-kiting, forgery, prostitution, and gambling.

Thankfully, whether the school realized it was fighting a losing battle with Barbara, or she'd somehow managed to convince the powers that be that she was "reformed," they finally let her out on parole in April 1939, when she was two months shy of her sixteenth birthday. She was free. But the law required Barbara to be on parole supervision until she turned eighteen. That meant that until her eighteenth birthday, she'd have to live where the parole authorities dictated and check in on a regular basis so they could monitor her progress.

So many rules for someone like Barbara who had so little desire to follow them. It went about as well as you'd expect. They placed her in a home in Los Angeles, where she did housekeeping for fifteen dollars a day. That lasted about three weeks, after which Barbara—claiming illness—stopped showing up. They then placed her with another couple—presumably for the same deal—but she got bounced out when they went on vacation because Barbara wasn't allowed to be in the house alone. So she got dumped in the LA County Juvenile Hall to wait for their return.

Central Juvenile, where they sent Barbara—known as Eastlake Juvenile when I was assigned there as a prosecutor—was a desolate, miserable place even when it was sort of new-adjacent back in the 1930s. Now there's talk of tearing it down and rebuilding from scratch because it's so dilapidated and unsafe it's virtually beyond repair.

Once again, Barbara escaped. This time, knowing she'd find no mercy at home, she headed south and ended up in Long Beach. Port cities were a familiar refuge for Barbara. She'd been a regular among the groups that hung around the port in Oakland. Those crowds were their own little microcosm, a world where sailors and drifters mingled and no one asked questions. You could be anyone. Pick a name, any name. It was a perfect place to hide, and for a beautiful young girl, an easy place to find . . . friends.

Seagulls. That's what the sailors called the girls who hung around the ports. Not all the liaisons were sexual—though I suspect most were. But some were platonic, just lonely young people looking for a friendly face. In fact, some of those sailors would become Barbara's lifelong friends.

In the Long Beach port crowd, Barbara eventually connected with a girl she'd met during her time in the Ventura School for Girls, and they made their way back up to the ports in San Francisco and Oakland. Authorities had been searching for Barbara throughout this period. Though there'd been sightings of her at various ports—one of the parole officers wrote that fifteen-year-old Barbara had "a fondness for sailors!!!"—they couldn't manage to catch her.

Barbara drifted for the next several months, staying just ahead of the authorities as she moved up and down the coast. When officials came knocking on her mother's door, Hortense told them Barbara wasn't there. There's no indication that she bothered to ask what had happened to her daughter or made any effort to help them find her. As far as Hortense was concerned, out of sight, out of mind. Barbara was no longer her problem.

During that time, she tried to hold down a number of "straight" jobs, working as a dime store clerk, delivering messages for Western Union, and waitressing wherever she could get hired without having to give references. In part because her past record included her stay at the state school for girls, any employer who got a look at it showed her the door.

Eventually, she gave up and headed down to San Diego. Alone in a strange city, with no legally marketable skills, a criminal record, and no money, she took refuge in bars where she could meet men who'd pay for her company. Barbara freely admitted that though prostitution seemed like her only choice, there was "no percentage in playing at the oldest profession in the world" and that "if a girl still has a heart when she tries it, I say it leads to heartbreak. For me, it led to much worse." And so when she got pregnant, likely in the hope of escaping that life, she married the father: a "dull" though nice enough mechanic, Harry Kielhamer. They wound up having two children together (though the second child might not have been his), and I'd imagine that for a time, "dull" was a welcome change from the tumult of her life up to that point. But as Barbara put it, being married to him was like teaming up "a wild mustang and a plow horse." The marriage lasted all of two years before Harry divorced her, leaving her to raise two young children on an income of zero. Thankfully, Harry's mother stepped in to care for them—and once again, Barbara was adrift, though she called it "free."

Remarkably, it was during this time that Barbara made her most serious effort to "go legit" and enrolled in a business college. Some records show it was in San Mateo, but Barbara remembers it being in San Diego. Wherever it was, she actually managed to earn the equivalent of a high school diploma. That could have been another turning point in her life, this time—for a change—a positive one. Sadly, it didn't last. She had a brief marriage to a sailor that she candidly described as a "business arrangement" to take advantage of his allotment. The moment he shipped out, Barbara hit the road again, traveling to Seattle, then to San Francisco, to Reno, and even to Chicago.

In my thirty-thousand-foot view of these years, Barbara seems to have ricocheted from one life to another, her choices dizzyingly impulsive.

Still, up to that point, Barbara's criminal life had been limited to small-time misdemeanors like vagrancy, check-kiting, and low-level narcotics possession, charges that usually ended with a suspended sentence and probation. Predictably, her circle of friends was of a similar ilk, people she'd met in "saloons and gambling houses" who lived on the fringes and the wrong side of the law. But these were the people who treated her kindly, who'd give her money for dinner or rent when income was scarce. Unfortunately, her loyalty to those friends cost her dearly.

In 1948, Barbara, then twenty-six years old, stepped up into the felony leagues with a move that can only be characterized as astonishingly foolish and blatantly self-destructive.

A famous and fabulously successful San Francisco madam, Sally Stanford, was the victim of a home invasion robbery. Two men broke in, pistol-whipped her maid, and attacked Stanford. She ran to the window and screamed, scaring them off. They were caught almost immediately. One of the robbers, who was a friend of Barbara's—but not a close one—asked her to give him a false alibi. Barbara said, "Sure!" She testified at the trial that he'd been with her. It was a blindingly stupid thing to do. She was probably two thousand miles away in Chicago at the time of the robbery. She got convicted of perjury. Barbara's first—and only—felony conviction until the murder of Mabel Monahan.

There is no logical explanation for her willingness to lie under oath. It wasn't as though her robber buddy had paid her to do it, nor was he a particularly close friend. At first, I'd thought that maybe, given Barbara's history of prostitution, there might've been some bad blood between her and the madam. But no. In fact, Barbara later apologized to Stanford, and the madam accepted her apology.

At base, it seems Barbara—in spite of her hard-knock life—was innately softhearted. And although she undoubtedly presented a tough exterior when she had to, even after her perjury conviction, her probation officer said he found her to be "a good natured . . . pleasant and quiet girl." So it's likely that part of the reason she'd agreed to perjure herself was simply her sense of loyalty to anyone she could call a friend. Because she had no real family, friendships were everything to her. She definitely had a sensitive side, as evidenced by her love of literature—the writings of Omar Khayyam would ironically play a part in her downfall during the trial—and she was a big aficionada of classical music and jazz, Gerry Mulligan's West Coast cool jazz, in particular.

And she'd never lost hope of getting the chance to go "legit," as her repeated—albeit failed—efforts over the years had shown. So why would she ignore the obvious risk of getting caught for committing perjury? Maybe, in addition to being able to help a friend, it was enticing to stick it to "the man." To hold up a middle finger to the society that had branded her as a tramp and a lowlife, to throw sand in the gears of a justice system that had been anything but "just" for her. And on a deeper level, a form of revenge against all the authority figures—especially her mother—who'd let her down, broken her heart, and thrown her away.

Whatever the reason, now that she had a felony conviction on her record, it was even harder to get legitimate work. And so she wound up once again working as a casino dice girl. That led to a third marriage and a home in a remote part of Nevada. But life in an isolated town in

Nevada didn't cut it. After one year, Barbara filed for divorce and moved back to California.

This led to yet another turning point, one that could've given her the normal life she yearned for and saved her from descending into the downward spiral that'd been beckoning all her life. Barbara decided to reach out to the two sons from her first marriage: William, who was eleven, and Michael, who was nine. They were living with her ex-husband's mother—their grandmother—in Seattle. Although Barbara had written them letters, she hadn't seen her sons in several years. If she could reconnect, it'd give her a reason to "go legit" and find a stable life so she could be a mother to her young children.

But once again, Hortense stepped in to do her worst. While she'd maintained contact with the boys, she had never helped to care for them. Nevertheless, when she heard about Barbara's impending visit, she took it upon herself to tell the boys' grandmother about Barbara's criminal history, including her conviction for perjury, and even wrote to Barbara's probation officer to tell him she was an unfit mother. Hortense is where irony went to die.

This last betrayal by her mother seems to have been the final straw. The visit now poisoned, her effort to reconnect with her children cruelly thwarted, Barbara cut her visit short, broke off all ties with her family, and refused to report to her probation officer.

Barbara moved back to Southern California—and took her first step on the path that would seal her fate. It began with her discovery that an old friend, Emmett Perkins—and future codefendant—was now living there. When they'd last met in the Bay Area, he'd had dreams of opening a gambling club where there'd be jazz, drugs, and easy money. Nothing came of it at the time, but now, he'd finally made his dream come true—sort of. The "gambling club" was really just a small rented house in El Monte where the only games available were low-stakes poker and dice. Still, dice games were a specialty for Barbara, who'd become an experienced shill—or as they called it, "dice girl"—over the years. When Emmett offered her the job at his so-called establishment, she took it.

Barbara, now in her late twenties, pretty, sexy, and savvy, was perfect for the gig. She'd go to some of the nicer hotel bars and let the men chat her up. When they asked to go somewhere more private, she'd suggest Perkins's gambling parlor, where she'd help them empty their wallets at poker and dice games.

And that's when she met husband number four, Henry Graham, a bartender who made money on the side by helping male customers meet pretty girls—girls, for example, like Barbara. This, of course, worked well for Barbara's job as a shill too. I wouldn't say it was a match made in heaven because I doubt heaven played Tinder for dice girls and quasi-pimp bartenders. But it was certainly a good fit for all concerned. Barbara described Hank as a "gentle little guy" with a good sense of humor. And though she said he was "no movie-star Adonis type," she "fell in love for the first time" in her life.

Barbara was the happiest she'd been in her life since her days at St. Mary's orphanage. Finally, this was her chance to settle down. She'd even begun to make plans to bring her two sons down from Seattle to live with her.

But it turned out the gentle Hank had a not-so-gentle heroin habit. It didn't take long for him to get sucked back down into that tar pit. He started missing work. And though she'd never done hard drugs before, Barbara, too, fell into the quicksand of addiction. A 1951 mugshot taken when they were arrested for misdemeanor possession shows her looking dissolute, her face swollen, one eye bruised, and her hair a mess.

Money was tight with Hank no longer working steadily, and it got a lot tighter when Barbara wound up pregnant, which meant she couldn't work at the gambling house. With no money coming in from either of them, the bills were piling up; she turned to writing bad checks. And Hank still wasn't working when their son Tommy was born in 1952, which meant Barbara was forced to go back to work for Perkins at the gambling house. She'd care for Tommy during the day and shill for Perkins at night. At this point, Hank had stopped even looking for work and was spending all his unemployment checks on drugs. Angry and disappointed, with her dreams of a normal life now shattered, they fought on a daily basis as Barbara pushed him to get off the couch and get a job.

To make matters worse, even though Barbara was still forging checks, the money from the gambling house wasn't enough to cover the bills for the three of them, so she turned to shoplifting. She'd carry an oversize purse and wear low-cut blouses and tight dresses as she flirted with the male employees to distract them.

Barbara was also flirting with serious jail time. She was still on probation in San Francisco for her perjury rap, and between the gambling association, check-kiting, and shoplifting, she'd definitely do jail time if she got busted. But she knew the system pretty well, and she figured that if she lived quietly, the authorities wouldn't bother to go looking for her. That strategy did seem to work. Even though she got arrested for misdemeanor drug possession in 1951, she got released on probation with not a whiff of interest from the authorities in San Francisco.

But that would prove to be the least of her worries. By 1953, Barbara had begun spending the night at the gambling house in El Monte with her baby, Tommy, to avoid her husband and their nonstop fights. And that was when the final piece of the puzzle fell into place, completing the murderous picture of her demise: Jack Santo showed up at the gambling parlor.

A few short months later, Barbara would be arrested—and indicted—along with Perkins and Santo for the burglary-murder of Mabel Monahan.

CHAPTER EIGHT

The day of opening statements was at the height of summer, on August 18, 1953, and Judge Charles Fricke's courtroom in the Hall of Justice on Temple Street in downtown Los Angeles was no match for the ninety-degree-plus temperature outside. I'd handled many a trial in the heat of summer just across the street in what was then unimaginatively called the Criminal Courts Building, and I remember vividly how the heat on the sidewalk burned right through the soles of my shoes. It was enough to make jurors cranky and keep the usual retiree court watchers at home.

But the crowd that was squeezed together on the wooden benches to watch the Monahan murder trial didn't notice the heat. They'd been reading about the case for months, following the twists and turns that seemed to happen on a daily basis. Now, at last, they were about to hear the story unfold firsthand. This was the day they'd been waiting for. The air crackled with tension as reporters leaned in, pens poised over notepads, and spectators stared at the three defendants sitting just feet away—especially the beautiful woman seated in the middle—excited at finally being able to see in person the players they'd thus far only been able to read about.

Chief Deputy Adolph Alexander took in the crowded courtroom as he approached the jury. The sweat under his collar was from nerves, not the heat. This was the biggest case of his career, one of the biggest in the state at that time, if not the country. And although the case in essence was a fairly simple home invasion robbery, it had one very big complicating factor: it hinged almost entirely on the testimony of an accomplice. I can tell you from experience—though I probably don't need to—that any time a prosecutor has to rely on an accomplice for critical aspects of the case, it's trouble.

First of all, the prosecution has to clear a special legal hurdle with accomplice testimony. They have to present some evidence apart from the accomplice's testimony that "tends to connect" the defendant to the crime. For example, the defendant's fingerprint at the crime scene or a neighbor who identifies his car parked nearby. The jurors in this case were instructed as follows: "The corroboration of an accomplice is sufficient if, of itself alone, it tends to connect the defendant with the commission of the offense, although it may be slight and although it, standing by itself, would be entitled to be but little consideration." Another instruction clarifies that one way to determine whether the corroboration is sufficient is to remove the accomplice's testimony and see if the remaining evidence "tends to connect" the defendant to the crime. If it does, the corroboration is sufficient. So basically, the corroborating evidence has to identify the defendant as a perpetrator, but it doesn't have to be enough on its own to prove they committed the crime beyond a reasonable doubt.

But there's one more wrinkle: in addition, the jurors were instructed that "it is the law that the testimony of an accomplice ought to be viewed with distrust." That poses a bigger problem for the prosecution. This instruction gives jurors a lot of latitude in deciding whether to believe an accomplice—even if there *is* corroborating evidence—and it plainly tells them to be suspicious of an accomplice's credibility.

Jurors would probably be inclined to be skeptical anyway—as they should be. Especially in a case like this, where that accomplice, who was right there in the thick of it and not just a getaway driver, got complete immunity, while his crime buddies faced a sentence of life in prison or . . . death. But just in case any juror forgot that an accomplice was no ordinary witness, this instruction reminded them that he had a powerful motive to say whatever the prosecutor wanted him to say—true or not.

Alexander, knowing he faced the uphill battle of persuading the jury to buy John True's credibility, made a grand gesture. In the midst of his opening statement, he said, "We shall ask the Court to dismiss this case as against John True, so that he may testify as a witness." And when he finished his opening statement, Alexander delivered on his promise. Turning to face Judge Charles Fricke, he stated, "Now, if the Court please, at this time, the People respectfully move this Court . . . under the provisions of Section 1009 of the Penal Code of this State for the dismissal of this count against the defendant John True, for the purpose, and solely for the purpose, of using John True as a witness in this case." The judge replied, "So ordered." The prosecutor further stated, "Now, if the Court please, may the record further show he has been released O.R. on Case No. 156,741, along with Count 1 of this indictment?"[4] The judge granted the request, stating, "It will be so ordered."

So what was the point of all that theater? Alexander was attempting to broadcast that John True now had nothing to fear, no sword hanging over his head, and that no matter how he testified, he'd get to walk out of that courtroom a free man. In sum, he had no reason to lie.

But the grand gesture was a sham. What the jury likely didn't remember was that John True wasn't just charged with murder—he was also charged in count 2 with conspiracy to commit murder and burglary. And the sentence for conspiracy to commit murder, both back then and now, is the same as the sentence for murder. Alexander was still holding that charge over True's head, hedging his bet to make sure his "star" witness didn't have a change of heart. And even if the jury didn't

---

4   O.R. stands for "own recognizance," which meant Alexander was asking that True be released on just a promise to appear in court without having to post bail.

remember that he'd been charged with both murder and conspiracy, you can bet John True sure did.

Later, on cross-examination by the defense, when True was pressed to admit that the conspiracy charge was still very much in play, he confirmed it. But he said he understood that charge would also be dismissed, that he'd been promised that "everything would turn out all right," and that he would "not be prosecuted for any offense in Los Angeles County." The unspoken yet obvious caveat was that the promise would only be as good as True's willingness to give the testimony the prosecutors wanted.

Did the jury realize at that point that Alexander had played them when he made his grand gesture of dismissing the murder charge without mentioning that he still had the conspiracy charge up his sleeve? It's hard to know. But even if they did, they surely had no idea that the conspiracy charge alone carried a sentence of life in prison—effectively keeping True on a very tight leash.

The press undoubtedly knew that the dramatic flourish was bullshit, but they gave it—and most of Alexander's opening statement—pretty short shrift. They saved their ink for his graphic description of how Barbara bashed Mabel Monahan over the head with the butt of a pistol, and his coining of the sobriquet "Bloody Babs"—a nickname the press grabbed with both hands and held on to from that day forward.

From the moment of her arrest, the press had seen that Barbara was the only one readers cared about; she was the "get." And before the first witness was called, they'd uniformly declared her guilty. The descriptors *icy* and *cold* were used almost as frequently as her name. But when the trial got underway, the gloves really came off. On the day the prosecution gave their opening statement, reporters trotted out headlines declaring their withering disapproval as they competed to find the most provocative ways to paint Barbara as a callous, cold-hearted murderer. The *Los Angeles Times* declared, "Redhead Accused in Monahan Case—Sits Unmoved at Description of Alleged Beating in Murder Trial." The article went on to claim that the "red-haired"

Barbara showed no emotion as Alexander described the beating of Mabel Monahan, and that she "glared malevolently" at John True, who sat near the prosecutors.

According to the *Los Angeles Mirror*, Barbara "yawned and stretched languorously as she was accused of beating Mrs. Monahan to her knees," and it claimed that as the DA told of the plot to rob the elderly widow, Barbara "studied her lacquered fingernails."

The *Valley Times* joined in with "the attractive blonde never batted an eyelash" as the DA described the vicious, gratuitous beating she'd given the older woman.

While the reporters now couldn't seem to agree on whether Barbara was a redhead or a blonde—I guess as long as she wasn't just a boring brunette, it didn't matter—they had clearly all agreed that she was a bloodthirsty murderess with a heart of stone. Even the head matron of the women's jail, Captain Blumfeld, said she'd never in her life seen a defendant get such negative press.

And the following day gave the press an even better excuse to shine a damning spotlight on Barbara. On her way to court, she'd fallen down the steep, narrow stairs that led from the cellblock to the courtroom. The *Valley Times* reported that the "sultry Barbara Graham" (who, according to this reporter, was a blonde), gave out a "piercing scream" as she tumbled headfirst down the stairs. I can't help but wonder what "sultry" has to do with a fall down a flight of stairs?

The prosecutors decided to pile on as well. Prosecutor J. Miller Leavy—whom I'll say a lot more about shortly—had now joined the team as cocounsel to Chief Deputy Adolph Alexander, and they told the press Barbara's fall was a deliberate stunt. At the time, they declined to explain what she had to gain by it. They saved their speculation about that for later. Suffice it to say, the prosecution was only too happy to give the press more ammunition to trash Barbara. And their snide comments casting her as a scheming manipulator added another layer of iniquity to the persona the media had already created of an unfeeling, hard-hearted villain.

The *Los Angeles Mirror* capitalized on the event in even more sensationalist language, screaming, "'Bloody Babs' Falls; Delay in Monahan Murder Trial." This headline was notable as the first—but by no means the last—to pick up Alexander's creative title of "Bloody Babs."

The *Los Angeles Herald-Express* opened its coverage of the fall saying, "Barbara Graham, icy-calm blonde 'lure' and key defendant in the Mabel Monahan murder trial, fainted or fell down a flight of marble stairs while being taken to court today, thus necessitating temporary postponement of the case." In a follow-up the next day, that same paper said that "pretty Barbara Graham" was "resting easily, wisecracking and flippant . . . after falling down a flight of stairs."

If the coverage of Barbara's tumble down the stairs was overblown, the claim by the *Herald-Express* that she'd somehow become the "key defendant" was simply ridiculous. John True supplied the impetus for the burglary with his dreamed-up story about seeing Tutor Scherer drive down from Las Vegas with a shoebox of cash. Baxter Shorter was the one who knew where Monahan lived. Santo provided the muscle, and Perkins knew how to blow up a safe. Barbara had been drafted only to act as a decoy. But now, apparently, she was the "key defendant." A nifty way to pander to the public appetite for all things Barbara.

And the *Los Angeles Times* got its licks in by reminding readers that this wasn't the first time Barbara had taken a fall. The reporter claimed that when she'd fallen down in her jail cell after the indictments were returned, unnamed "officials" said Barbara had remarked, "When I really get into my act I'm going to make Sarah Bernhard look like a chump." Interestingly, no such remark—or any remark at all—had been attributed to Barbara at the time. And there's a good reason for that: after that fall Barbara had reportedly been unable—or unwilling—to speak at all. So it's highly unlikely Barbara made any comment at all, let alone a smart-ass remark like that. The reporter—for some reason—neglected to mention that.

My guess is, the unnamed "officials" who furnished that supposed quote from Barbara were—once again—prosecutors J. Miller Leavy and Adolph Alexander. And it sounds like their style. The tone of the quote—that shows her to be a lying, scheming manipulator—is very much in keeping with their accusation that she'd faked her later fall down the stairs.

By the way, one outlet—the *Valley Times*—did mention at the very end of the article that Barbara actually was badly hurt after falling down the stairs and had to be carried to the hospital on a stretcher. In fact, the doctor initially diagnosed her possible injuries as "multiple fractures of the spine, pelvis, left shoulder and left arm." It was later determined that there were no fractures, but she was certainly banged up pretty badly. It's doubtful anyone noticed that short squib at the end of the single article that bothered to mention the true extent of her injuries even briefly.

To be fair, Barbara didn't help herself when it came to her own PR. Societal mores dictated that a woman in her position should look demure, pure, and timid. Dress like a librarian, lose the makeup, and soften the expression. Barbara did none of the above. She dressed in tight skirt suits (which, by the way, were in fashion at the time) and high heels, and wore bright-red lipstick, provoking one reporter to write that she looked more like a "showgirl" than a defendant. And her stoic behavior—no doubt a facade adopted by necessity after a life of hard knocks and struggle on the streets—was interpreted by the press as callousness.

I'm sure there were days when Barbara's behavior seemed a little too casual for the occasion. But someone who's being scrutinized for hours a day—and days and weeks on end—is bound to do something that gives someone a reason to take a cheap shot. Especially when that's all they're looking for. Barbara couldn't yawn, smile, or take a breath without some reporter pointing it out as yet another sign of her indifference to the atrocity she'd allegedly committed.

I had a little experience with that myself. Very early on in the Simpson trial, I learned the hard way that I had to be on my guard every minute of the day. In one of the early hearings, well before we'd started to pick a jury, the judge granted a defense request for a pretrial hearing about our DNA evidence that had absolutely no basis in the law and utterly no point in logic. It was a fishing expedition to look for some irregularity in the measurement of the samples collected, a total waste of time. The judge never should've allowed it.

And as the hearing dragged on for hours and then days of meaningless, tail-chasing cross-examination, I sat there, jaw clenched, thinking about how much work was piling up on my desk. On one of those days, our DNA expert, Lisa Kahn, joined me at the counsel table. Brilliant, and hilariously funny, she was a welcome ray of sunshine. Her muttered asides about the absurdity of the hearing gave me some sorely needed comic relief. I hid my few little laughs from the judge by turning toward the jury box, which was empty. Unfortunately, I'd forgotten that there was a camera secreted behind the wall of the jury box, and it picked up every smile and chuckle. TV watchers called in, outraged by my cavalier attitude. Someone nastily called me "Giggles Clark." Which was—I admit—kind of funny. But I learned a big lesson that day: no matter how mundane the hearing or how small my reaction, every move would get noticed—and graded.

I don't know whether Barbara's lawyers advised her to tone down the look and wear a chastened expression at all times. But even if they had, I doubt it would've changed anything. The reporters had their knives out, and they were going to find a reason to write about the ice water running through her veins no matter what she did. If she'd openly wept, they would've accused her of faking it.

And that reality aside, Barbara probably wouldn't have taken the advice. She didn't need to be told that a scrubbed face and demure expression was the look that was expected—more, *demanded*—of her. It was the '50s; everyone knew how a woman was supposed to act.

Not that things have changed all that much today. For anyone who doubts it, I have two words: Casey Anthony. And what helped enormously was the fact that Casey Anthony, who was acquitted in the 2008 murder of her little daughter, Caylee, despite damning evidence, knew how to play the game. When it was time to pick a jury, she traded in her short shorts and cling-wrap tank top for high-neck collars and a librarian bun, kept her face bare of makeup and her eyes downcast.

Barbara wasn't as savvy. Oppositional, rebellious, and self-destructive, she'd spent her whole life stepping on rakes of one kind or another. She either couldn't or wouldn't stop now. But there was an upside to the societal expectations of the '50s. Back then, murderous females existed only in Raymond Chandler's imagination. Especially if the woman was beautiful. The idea that someone like the petite, pretty, young Barbara could commit a murder as vicious as the one True had described was going to be a tough sell to a jury in 1953, no matter how the press trashed her.

I'm not saying the media's damning, vilifying coverage—which the prosecutors were happy to encourage with nasty tidbits of their own—wasn't helpful to the prosecution. It was. But it ran counter to society's belief about pretty young women, so it couldn't be counted on to last. It's a truism in trial work—especially criminal trial work—that the more time a jury spends in court with a defendant, the more likely they are to see her as a human being. Sitting in the courtroom day after day with a beautiful young defendant like Barbara, and trying to square that image with the vicious murder of Mabel Monahan, could soften hearts and minds.

And the visual impact of that Beauty being flanked by the two Beasts—Perkins and Santo—at the counsel table would, over time, only magnify the contrast between the woman they saw and the hideous acts she was accused of. Those men might've done it. They looked like the lowlife bottom-feeders they were. Barbara certainly didn't.

And that's probably why, throughout the trial, Perkins and Santo got very little ink. Reporters largely ignored them. But Perkins inspired the more unflattering descriptions. A reporter for the *Los Angeles Mirror*, mastering the obvious, said Perkins provided a "sharp contrast to the attractive Barbara," and went on to detail his "high balding forehead" and "hair streaked with gray." He had "deep-set, ferret-like eyes" that "peered down his long nose" and a "dimpled chin." He often wore "funny expressions" that looked like "a perpetual grin or . . . grimace."

Rounding out this lovely picture was the observation that he had a "prominent Adam's apple" that "bobs as often as a nerve on his neck twitches." And on that particular day, he'd dressed for success in a "loud sports shirt" and khaki pants that were likely jail issued. One reporter dubbed him "the Weasel."

Santo drew far less attention for his looks, but his photographs depicted a dangerous-looking thug. The adjectives used to describe him in the few articles that bothered to take note called him "stone-hard," "husky," and "tall and bespectacled, with graying, bushy hair and a thin mustache." But the one that best captured the man I saw in the photos was "brutish." This was not someone you wanted to bump into in a dark alley—or even a brightly lit one.

The jury wouldn't have any trouble believing these two had done exactly what they were accused of . . . and then some.

Sitting next to them, Barbara looked like a Botticelli angel. And the press wasn't immune to the effects of daily exposure to the lone woman in the dock either. So there was an ever-present possibility they could always turn, decide Barbara might after all be innocent, and sic their poisoned pens on the district attorney's office. That could spell doom for the prosecution's chances of convicting her. It's worth remembering that it only takes one holdout juror to cause a deadlock that ends in a mistrial.

All of this is to say that while the press was momentarily happy to trash Barbara, and she, to a certain extent, played into the prosecution's hands with her refusal to capitulate à la Casey Anthony, convicting her of murder still posed a very real challenge.

CHAPTER NINE

So the prosecutors had their work cut out for them. With an accomplice who was gum deep in the murder as their mainstay and a young, pretty woman for a defendant, they had two Achilles' heels to contend with.

Now prosecutors are always under pressure to win. It's expected of them, and not just by the victim's loved ones—by everyone. If a case has been filed, that should mean there's proof beyond a reasonable doubt that the defendant is guilty. Of course, things can go wrong, and on occasion prosecutors file weak cases or—more commonly—over-file, with more serious charges than the evidence warrants. But usually, prosecutors take cases to trial only if they're pretty damn sure they have a win in the bag. And usually, they do.

But that typical pressure ratchets up to an eleven when the case is in the news, and the more high profile it is, the greater the pressure. That pressure comes from all sides. Beyond the victim's family and friends, it comes from the district attorney, whose electability is always on the line. It comes from the cops, who don't want their hard work to go down the drain—or get slammed as sloppy and subpar. It comes from the public, who want to be reassured that the justice system works. And it comes from their peers. Any loss gets noticed around the office; egos and reputations get bruised—sometimes ruined. But add the fact that the case is high profile to the mix, and all of the above is magnified a hundredfold. An acquittal that would be devastating even when there's no press becomes that much more painful when the whole world is watching. I have some experience with that feeling.

The problem is, all this pressure can lead to a win-at-all-costs mentality that tempts a prosecutor to push the legal and ethical envelope. Most resist it. Some do not.

The prosecutors in this case were no strangers to the stresses of a high-profile case. Adolph Alexander, who was also chief deputy—a position that's second in power only to the district attorney himself—had been assigned as the lead prosecutor from the beginning of the investigation and was involved in the interrogations of Baxter Shorter and John True before the case even got filed. He was an experienced prosecutor and a heavy hitter. But he wasn't the star of the team.

That title went to J. Miller Leavy, who was brought into the case after the indictments were returned. Leavy was a celebrated figure in the LA DA's office, where I was a prosecutor for fourteen years. Though he left the office long before either I or any of my contemporaries were even in law school, we all knew about him. He was legendary. Whenever one of us lost a case, the standing response was "J. Miller Leavy could've won it." We said it as a joke, but deep down, we believed it. I know I did.

Leavy had an impressive string of convictions, and he put thirteen of those defendants on death row. One of them was Caryl Chessman—the notorious kidnapper and rapist dubbed the "Red Light Bandit." Leavy had also handled the case against L. Ewing Scott—who'd murdered his wife but nearly escaped justice by disposing of her body. The Scott case was the first established no-body homicide in the state, and it was a notable win for Leavy. It's hard to get a conviction in those cases, because the defense can point to the possibility that the victim isn't dead, just missing.

And Leavy was my inspiration when I had my own no-body homicide case. Unlike the murder victim in the L. Ewing Scott case—a wealthy society woman—the victim in my case had been a fringe character whose semilegal and flat-out illegal activities involved frequent travel to Thailand

and other Southeast Asian countries. It was a perfect setup for the defense, who could—and did—argue that the victim wasn't dead; he was simply hiding out from the law. We got a first-degree murder conviction, in large part by proving that a spot of blood found in the undercarriage of the driver's seat of the defendant's car was a paternity match to the DNA of the victim. When we won, I thought of J. Miller Leavy. I hoped I'd done him proud.

Although Leavy wasn't a particularly large man, those who knew him said he was a big presence with a commanding voice and a pit bull, take-no-prisoners style. When he walked up to the podium, he radiated power. Judges and juries alike sat up and took notice. And he possessed that rare combination of skills that blended a thoroughgoing knowledge of the law with the gift of a natural storyteller. It's no easy thing to make it simple for the jury without sounding condescending and at the same time weave a story that plucks on their heartstrings. By all accounts—at least according to office lore—Leavy did it all.

Whether our intra-office lionizing was deserved is hard to say. A winning lawyer isn't always a great one. Sometimes it's just a lucky one, or more to the point, a cherry picker who's careful to ferret out the winners and avoid the uphill climbs. And stories of great courtroom moments are often overblown. In fact, Leavy himself dispelled the myth of one particular anecdote that'd been attributed to him. In the closing arguments on that no-body homicide, the defense attorney had dramatically proclaimed that the jury couldn't find his client guilty, because they'd never know whether the victim was really dead. Pointing to the courtroom door, he thundered, "The victim could walk through that door any minute!" The jury couldn't help but slide a glance in that direction.

As the story goes, Leavy acknowledged the dramatic moment on rebuttal, but said, "When defense counsel pointed to that door, I saw everyone in this courtroom turn to look. All except for one: the defendant." Because he knew the victim was dead. A great line that made for a terrific war story. And Leavy never uttered a word of it. To his credit, he admitted as much to the reporter for the *Los Angeles Times* who'd later interviewed him.

So whether he was as masterfully skilled as office lore would have it is hard to say. But there's no question he was considered a force to be reckoned with.

When I decided to write about the Barbara Graham case, I was excited. I'd actually get to see—via the trial transcripts—my icon in action. But when I finally got those transcripts—all four thousand plus pages of them—I saw that I'd have to wait. Alexander was first up, and since it was his case to begin with, he presented the biggest witnesses for the prosecution: William Upshaw and John True.

By the time John True appeared at trial, his statements to the grand jury had already been publicized, so his testimony held few surprises. Still, it did flesh out a few things. One of those things was how he wound up palling around with a rough player like Jack Santo. He testified that they'd met in January 1953, up north in Grass Valley, and spent a lot of time together. Santo had said he was in the construction business.

Sounds pretty mundane, right? Except I learned that wasn't really the whole story. As I mentioned, John True had given a statement to Alexander on June 4, 1953, when he was in custody up in San Francisco. That statement had never been given to the defense, and although the defense knew Alexander had contacted True, they never knew he'd given a formal, transcribed statement detailing his involvement in the crime.

And since that statement was never produced in discovery or entered into evidence, it was never made part of the official record. So, when I got the official transcripts of the trial, it wasn't included. But I knew it existed because I'd read letters written in 1958 and 1959 between Ed Montgomery, a reporter who collaborated on the film *I Want to Live!*, and the film's producer, Walter Wanger, that made multiple references to a transcript of that statement. Wanger had managed to get the transcript to help with the research for the film. But what were the odds that they'd kept it? That was almost sixty-five years ago.

I was frustrated and depressed, figuring I was out of luck. But it turned out that Walter Wanger had kept a collection of documents that'd been gathered during the production of the film. And I was thrilled to see that he'd kept the transcript too. Gotta love those Hollywood producers—and the wonderful folks at the Wisconsin Historical Society who kindly sent me a copy. It proved to be a gold mine. And it painted a very different picture of John True. What I'm about to share with you is information the jury never heard.

In his June 4 statement, True said that shortly after he and Santo met, Santo asked him if he knew how to "open a box," meaning crack a safe, and also quizzed True as to whether he knew any gold miners or had any experience in buying and selling gold. Apparently, none of this sounded any alarm bells for True. He told the friend who'd introduced them that Santo was a "pretty right guy." In fact, True said they'd become fast friends, and went hunting and fishing together.

Sounds a little different than True's trial testimony that Santo merely said he was in the "construction business." And that's not all.

True, a deep-sea diver, told Santo about how he and his friend Seth Terry planned to get into the logging business. Santo offered to put up money in return for a share of the business, so he'd be able to show a legitimate source for his income—which he admitted at that point consisted of stolen gold. If he could unload it on the black market, he'd be able to invest a substantial amount of money in True's enterprise. True was all in, saying, "Well, it was none of my business how he got rid of it or how he come by it."

So True certainly knew Santo was a dirty player right from the start. Santo's supposed "construction business" was a load of garbage. If the jury had heard all that, they might've had a somewhat different view of John True.

As for Perkins, True claimed they first met in Los Angeles, a few days before the Monahan burglary-murder.

Not so. In his June 4 statement to Alexander, he said he met Perkins up north in Auburn at least a month—maybe more—before the burglary. That's also what he said when he testified at the grand jury hearing. But at trial, he claimed it was a mistake, that he hadn't met Perkins in Auburn, and that he'd told the prosecutors he'd been mistaken. Why lie about that? Because the more distance he could put between himself and Perkins and Santo, the less he'd look like the collaborator and crime partner he really was.

The discrepancies got more notable as the events leading up to and including the murder came into focus. True testified at trial that he drove down to Los Angeles with Santo in "early March" or the first of March, because Santo said he had some business to conduct there and True had a diving job he wanted to do with his nephew. True claimed he didn't know about any plan to commit a burglary and thought Santo was just working on the gold deal they'd been discussing up in Grass Valley. In fact, he claimed at trial that he didn't hear about any plan to do a home invasion robbery until the day of the crime, March 9, when he, Santo, and Perkins met William Upshaw and Baxter Shorter at a drive-in. During that meeting, Santo asked whether True knew a man named Tutor Scherer. True claimed that was the first time he realized that there was a plan to rob the owner of the house in Burbank where Tutor was known to visit.

But in his June 4 statement to Alexander, True said Santo introduced him to Perkins and talked about doing a "caper" involving a burglary shortly after they arrived in Los Angeles—days before the murder.

With regard to Tutor Scherer, True testified merely that he had met Tutor in Los Angeles, and knew he had a casino in Las Vegas. But in his June 4 statement to Alexander, he said that he and Tutor were "on a very friendly basis," and that Tutor had invited him to his wedding in Las Vegas.

Now, the prosecution knew very well that Tutor Scherer had denied knowing True or even recognizing the name John True. Mysteriously, at trial, his supposedly "very friendly" relationship with Tutor turned into only a terse mention that they had "met." If the defense had known of True's June 4 statement claiming to have danced at Tutor's wedding,

Marcia Clark

they would've put Tutor Scherer on the witness stand in a heartbeat to counter that bald-faced lie. And in the process, not only would Tutor tell the jury he'd never met True, but he'd also let them know he'd told the cops months earlier that he didn't know the man.

When it came to the events on the night of March 9, the conflicts between True's testimony and his June 4 statement grew even sharper. True testified that they met at the Smoke House Restaurant in Burbank and drove by the Monahan house earlier in the evening to scope it out. He claimed Santo told him no one lived there, that Tutor Scherer had been hiding "black money" from Las Vegas in a safe, and that Baxter Shorter would know how to open it. True claimed he didn't want to do the burglary unless they knew no one would be home and that Santo had repeatedly assured him no one would be there.

The notion that True thought no one would be home is utter nonsense. In fact, in his June 4 statement, he'd said the only reason they brought Barbara along was because they *knew* Mabel Monahan would be home, and that Baxter Shorter had said they'd need a frontman to get Mabel Monahan to open the door. Santo had initially recommended they use True to get Mabel to open the door, because he didn't have a record, so his fingerprints wouldn't be on file. But True said he refused because he "would not take a gun and rob anybody." Shorter said Mabel Monahan wouldn't open the door to a man, and Perkins then recommended Barbara, saying, "It would have to be a woman. And I've got the woman who will do it."

With their plan—if you can call it that—complete, True testified that they set out for the Monahan house in the evening, around 7:30 p.m., and Perkins gave True a gun, telling him, "Take this gun and don't come back without it." True thought it was a .38 or .45 automatic. True—who'd said on June 4 that he "would not take a gun and rob anyone"—took the gun and prepared to rob Mabel Monahan.

They parked around the corner from the house on Orchard Drive. Santo gave Barbara and True their marching orders. Barbara was to ring the doorbell or knock and, if someone was there, detain them until the others could arrive. True was to follow right behind Barbara. Santo instructed, "The minute she goes through the door, you walk on in. You go in behind her." Barbara, who was wearing a long coat and gloves but not carrying a purse, went to the front door. True, wearing gloves and carrying a gun, did as he was told and followed her to the house "about a minute" after she went in.

The account of what happened next inside the house came from only one source: John True.

True testified that he found the door partially open. When he entered, Barbara was just inside the front door, standing next to Mabel Monahan and holding her by either the neck or hair or shoulder with her left hand while hitting her with the gun that was in her right hand. He thought she hit Monahan two or three times, and said that Monahan was bleeding from the face and head. True claimed he told Barbara not to hit her anymore. He put his hand between Mabel's face and the gun, and as he did so, Monahan sank onto the floor. True said he went down to the floor with her and had her head on his lap. Barbara then put a pillow cover over her head. At that point, Santo, Perkins, and Shorter had already entered the house.

But now check out what he told Alexander in his June 4 statement. True said that upon entering and seeing Barbara strike Monahan, he ran up, pushed Barbara back, grabbed Monahan by the face, and said, "Lady, tell them anything they want but don't resist them." Mabel then fell to the floor, and True sat down and put her head in his lap. At that point, *Perkins* entered and ripped up some sheets and used the strips to tie her hands behind her back, and then *Perkins* put a pillowcase over her head and dragged her down the hallway, away from the front door. Later in his statement, True changed that claim to say Barbara had been the one to put the pillowcase over Mabel Monahan's head. But that later accusation was brief, unlike his initial, more detailed description identifying Perkins as the one who'd put the pillowcase over Monahan's head. Whether True was merely sloppy or lying about who'd done what is hard to tell.

In his trial testimony True reaffirmed the statement he'd made before the grand jury that Santo then tied a cloth strip around Mabel Monahan's neck, which the autopsy surgeon would later identify as the cause of death: asphyxiation. According to True's testimony, he remained with Monahan and held her head up because she kept trying to turn it down toward the floor, and that he used his knife to cut a hole through the pillowcase to let her breathe. True then left her and went to search the house with the others. He went to the kitchen, "fooled around, looked in the icebox, killed the time," and then searched the dining room before joining the others, who'd gathered in the den. When he returned to Monahan, he saw that she was still alive and moaning. Contradicting his earlier testimony, he said that later point was actually when he cut a hole in the pillowcase, pulled it off her head, and cut the cloth strip off her neck. He claimed Shorter then said, "Stop that racket [referring to Mabel Monahan's moans] or I'll stop that racket."

On June 4 True claimed he told the others, "This lady is going to die if we don't do something," and one of the men replied that he hoped she did die. True said he then cut a hole in the pillowcase with his knife, but after Santo tied the cloth strip around her neck, he didn't remove it or cut it off, he "loosened it." True and the others left the room and continued to search, but at some point, he heard someone—he thought it was Barbara—say, "She is moaning. Knock her out." He then heard someone strike Mabel Monahan. When he went back, he saw that Monahan was bleeding and told Shorter to call an ambulance.

Setting aside for the moment the obvious conflicts with Baxter Shorter's statement, True's description of events—both in his trial testimony and in his June 4 statement—is strange in two respects. True paints himself as the only one concerned with Monahan's well-being. Yet, although he claims to have cut a hole in the pillowcase to let her breathe, he says nothing about removing the garotte around her neck until *after* he'd gone to search the house with the others, and "fooled around." And whether he ever actually removed the garotte is highly debatable. In his June 4 statement, he never said he removed it, only that he "loosened" it.

But people don't die of ligature strangulation in a few seconds. It takes a while, at least three and possibly as long as five minutes, to choke the life out of someone. John True had to have left that garotte untouched for a while because—as the forensic pathologist testified—Mabel Monahan died of asphyxiation. So although True tried to leave the impression that he'd "loosened" or removed the cloth strip shortly after Santo tied it around Monahan's neck, in reality, he couldn't have done it that soon—if indeed he ever did it at all. The more likely scenario is that he left her, gagged and choking to death, to go search the house, and by the time he got back, she was already dead.

By True's estimate, the whole tragic sequence of events took just fifteen to twenty minutes. Twenty minutes—to take an innocent life and leave empty handed.

True's testimony about what happened during the actual burglary and murder stands alone. No one else could testify to those events. That means that for those critical minutes, the jury was stuck with the story he told on the witness stand. They never got to hear about the prior inconsistent statements he made to Alexander on June 4, 1953.

The prosecution is—and was back then—constitutionally obligated to provide the defense with any and all statements made by the witnesses they present. It's a fundamental aspect of a defendant's right to a fair trial. The jury can't make an accurate assessment of a witness's honesty and credibility unless they have all the facts. And the prior inconsistent statement of a key prosecution witness is a prime example of such evidence. The prosecution's failure to provide the defense with True's prior statement to Alexander was an egregious violation of due process. As he was the key witness in the case—and an accomplice—John True's credibility was of utmost importance. Even minor discrepancies can make a difference in the impression a witness makes on the jury. And an inconsistency like the claim that Barbara put a pillowcase over the victim's head versus the prior statement that Perkins had been the one who did it is far from minor.

Alexander would later claim that he had given True's statement to the defense, but the record unequivocally disproves that. At the end of his direct examination, Alexander asked True whether he remembered having "a conversation" with him and Captain Ahern and Lieutenant Coveney of the San Francisco Police Department on June 4. At that point, Barbara's attorney, Jack Hardy, objected to any further testimony about the contents of that "conversation" on the ground it was hearsay.

And the reason he objected was because he didn't know what that so-called conversation entailed. The judge agreed, because he didn't know, either, saying, "I don't think the conversation itself would be admissible unless something more appeared." By "something more" the judge meant some indication whether it was a statement about the case—especially if it was a prior inconsistent statement, which would definitely have been admissible—as opposed to simply a chat between True and Alexander about who was buying dinner. This was Alexander's chance to clarify that it was indeed a statement about the case, and provide it to the defense. Alexander did no such thing. He simply moved on and said to True, "Now, after I had a talk with you, you were brought back to Los Angeles, is that correct?" True confirmed that was correct.

In doing so, Alexander deliberately misled the defense. A "talk" or "conversation" is a very different thing than a forty-three-page interrogation about the murder, transcribed by an official stenographer. Had Hardy known any of that, he'd have demanded that the statement be produced on the spot. But thanks to Alexander's slippery wording, Hardy couldn't know that. And it's very clear that Hardy never saw that statement, because in closing argument he told the jury that he assumed Alexander had told True he'd "turn [True's] rotten hide loose" if he said the "right thing," but as for what else was said in that conversation, Hardy stated, "I don't know and I have no way of knowing."

And that June 4 statement wasn't the only thing the jury never got to see.

CHAPTER TEN

I read Baxter Shorter's statement early in the process of researching this case. A few months went by before I managed to get access to John True's trial testimony, and it took even longer to get hold of his June 4 statement.

So when I finally got to read that statement and compare it to his trial testimony, I went back to have another look at what Baxter Shorter had said. I was immediately struck by how much more detailed—and clearer—Shorter's statement was. Unlike True, who—during his June 4 statement—needed prompting, guidance, and even suggestions from both the prosecutor and the police, Shorter spoke in a free narrative, his account both detailed and graphic as he described the events and his horror at the treatment of Mabel Monahan.

And in the process, I noted an important discrepancy. Shorter described how he, Santo, and Perkins had gotten nervous as they waited in their cars after Barbara and True entered the house. John True should've had the older woman under control within a minute. But it'd been several minutes with still no sign from True that the coast was clear. So Santo gave Perkins his gun and told him to go inside and see what was going on.

I stopped right there as I remembered that Shorter had also said there were only two guns between them. He was very specific about that, recounting how Santo had asked Shorter whether he had a gun, and that when Shorter said he didn't, Santo remarked that left them "short." True testified that Perkins gave him a gun on the way to the Monahan house—a .38 or .45 caliber. True took that gun into the house when he followed Barbara. That accounted for one gun. Then, when Santo told Perkins to go inside and see what was taking so long, he gave Perkins a gun. That accounted for the second gun.

So where did the gun True claimed Barbara had used to pistol-whip Mabel Monahan come from, and what happened to it? There were only two, and both were accounted for. Neither of them in Barbara's possession. Although Shorter had said he'd seen Barbara put a .38 caliber gun into her purse, he didn't say *when* he saw that. And True testified that Barbara didn't take her purse into the house. In fact, he never saw her with a gun at all until he got inside the house.

Then I remembered that on the drive to the Monahan residence, Shorter had been in the car with Jack Santo. Perkins had followed in his car with Barbara and True. Putting it all together, a clearer picture emerges: Perkins took that gun out of Barbara's purse and gave it to True on the way to the house. After all, they didn't plan to have Barbara do any strong-arming. Her only job was to get the woman to open the door. True was supposed to take it from there.

There's another reason to believe Barbara didn't have a gun. Baxter Shorter said Mabel Monahan was moaning as she lay on the floor. According to True, Shorter said she was making too much noise. (It seems more likely Santo or Perkins said that.) But both Shorter and True stated that Barbara then said, "Go ahead and knock her out." Perkins then pistol-whipped her. Barbara had no need to tell someone else to knock her out if she herself had a gun.

Here's one more very simple reason why I don't think Barbara could've had a gun. If she'd had one, she would've pointed it at Mabel as soon as she got in the door. It's the easiest way to take control of the situation. Not for one second do I believe that elderly woman, who walked with a limp, would've even thought to struggle with Barbara if she'd had a pistol pointed at her face—if indeed, she ever struggled with Barbara at all.

And apart from all that, even if she did have a gun, True's claim that he found Barbara pistol-whipping Mabel Monahan when he entered the house is fraught with logistical problems. True said she was standing next to Monahan—not behind her—holding her by the back of the neck with her left hand, while wielding the pistol with her right. Barbara's lawyer, recognizing the awkward choreography, made True reenact the scene, with True playing Barbara and Hardy playing Mabel Monahan.

But True and Hardy were men, both much bigger—and stronger—than either of the women who were actually involved. The scenario makes even less sense when it's remembered that Barbara was just five foot three, 121 pounds, and she was supposedly controlling Monahan, also five foot three, but 158 pounds, with just *one hand* on the back of her neck while she wielded the gun with her other hand. Granted, Mabel Monahan walked with a limp, but she certainly wasn't "partially paralyzed" as represented in one of the typically hyperbolic tabloid articles.

Controlling someone, even an older woman like Monahan, with just one hand to the back of the neck is no easy thing. I had a hard time envisioning how a normal woman who wasn't a weight lifter or a trained fighter could do it. So I decided to do a little experiment of my own. I'm not a particularly big or muscular person. I'm five foot four and 125 pounds. I asked a female friend who is three inches taller, has a third-degree black belt, and is a lot stronger than me to play Barbara. I stood in for Mabel. She grabbed me by the back of the neck. And I pulled out of her grasp in less than two seconds. It was easy. Why? Because the position True described gave Barbara very little leverage. It's hard as hell to hold on to someone by the back of the neck with one hand in *any* position, let alone while standing next to them—especially for someone like Barbara, who was small and not particularly strong.

There's one more salient fact to bear in mind, and it's a fact that's undisputed: at Santo's command, and by John True's own account, True was right behind Barbara when she walked into the house. That meant she had very little time alone—no more than seconds—before True walked in. Yet there was a considerable lapse of time after he entered when he was alone with Barbara and Mabel Monahan. So much time it made Perkins nervous about what was taking so long. Plenty of time for True to do the pistol-whipping and take the victim down.

Beyond that, True's description of his own behavior was a ridiculously obvious whitewash job. Witnesses usually do want to make themselves look better in front of the jury. But an accomplice who needs to please a prosecutor has a much bigger incentive to color his actions in a rosy glow. And John True's testimony about his actions with Mabel Monahan was a 180-degree departure from reality.

First of all, if this deep-sea diver who was described as a "muscular" man was so appalled by Barbara's actions, then why didn't he just push Barbara down? Or grab her gun? Or grab her hand? Or point his gun at Barbara? Remember, he admittedly had a gun. That he instead merely put his hand on Monahan's face, then cradled her head in his lap when she collapsed, is the most illogical reaction—and the least effective. Putting a hand on Monahan's face would only have resulted in True getting his hand bashed straight into her cheek, since according to him, Barbara was in the process of repeatedly striking her with the butt of the gun.

Secondly, Baxter Shorter's statement shows that, far from being outraged or upset by the assault on Monahan, John True was—at best—indifferent to the woman's suffering. Contrary to True's testimony, he wasn't "cradling" Monahan's head in his lap, he was holding her down. And when Baxter Shorter insisted that John True "take that gag off her," True looked up at Santo and said, "Shall I do what he said? What's the difference? She's not going to give us any more trouble."

So if True ever did take the garotte off Monahan's neck—an open question—by the time he got around to it, she was likely already dead. As Santo had told Baxter Shorter when he was anxious to call an ambulance.

Putting True's June 4 statement and testimony together with Baxter Shorter's statement, it seems clear that True's story merely swapped out identities to depict himself as the most innocent player. So he claimed Barbara was the one who pistol-whipped Mabel Monahan while he was the horrified onlooker when it was almost certainly the other way around. And he took over Baxter Shorter's role as the one who protested the brutality of the assault on Monahan, even though Shorter's statement makes it clear that True was actually the one who was actively restraining her at one point and then left her to choke to death while he searched the house, removing the garotte only after getting Santo's permission.

Now, neither the press nor the jury ever got to hear that statement by Baxter Shorter. He'd disappeared and was most likely dead. Nor did the press or jury get to hear about True's June 4 statement to Alexander. Undeniably, those unseen sources reveal a much darker picture of John True, one that seriously undermines his credibility. But the obvious flaws and inconsistencies in True's trial testimony alone provided plenty of reasons to doubt his credibility.

Yet the press coverage was bafflingly credulous, swallowing True's claim that Barbara was a cold-blooded murderess hook, line, and sinker, and that he was a naïf who unwittingly got caught up in this ugly plot and the hero who came to the "rescue" of Mabel Monahan.

Gossip columnist Florabel Muir of the *Los Angeles Mirror* was among the nastiest, though she was only one among several contenders for providing the worst, most distorted coverage of Barbara, writing, "That monster disguised as a woman, Barbara Graham, 29 year old blonde gun moll, must be a pleasant little trick to meet in a dark alley. True said . . . Barbara did some fancy work with the handle of her gun on the victim's graying head. Isn't Barbara the same dame who was accused by San Francisco police of sticking up Sally Stanford, well-known femme about the Bay District, and letting her have it over the head with the gun butt? Let us hope Barbara will be restrained from ever pulling her rough little capers again."

Of course, Florabel was wrong about the incident with Sally Stanford, the famous madam. Barbara had nothing to do with that robbery—other than giving her buddies, the actual robbers, a phony alibi. But accuracy didn't matter; readership was the only thing that mattered, and heaping more sordid accusations on Barbara was a sure-fire way to get it.

On the other hand, True was now hailed as an innocent bystander who somehow got ensnared in the plot and was now bravely testifying though it put his life in danger. The *Valley Times* led with the headline "11 Guards Watch True on Stand," security precautions that the *Los Angeles Times* said "rivaled those accorded the President of the United States."

Actually, both Upshaw and True had been the subject of death threats. There'd been rumors of an offer to pay $1,500 to "rub out" William Upshaw, who'd testified after True. The deputies who guarded the courthouse had been patrolling the hallways from the first day of trial, but after word of that threat on Upshaw, they stepped up their routine security watch and kept a closer eye on all spectators who'd come to watch the proceedings.

And there'd even been reports of bomb threats, one of which involved two confederates of Santo's who'd allegedly planned to turn John True into a "human torch" by smashing him with a "napalm bomb." A letter referring to the plot was found in the room of one of the would-be bombers. Another rumor reported that a woman planned to hurl a "finger bomb" in the courtroom. No particular target was mentioned. Backing up that rumor was a report that a "woman in grey" who'd been "displaying some nervousness" had asked to be seated near the exit, and when she was refused, she'd left the courthouse. A search failed to locate her, but after that, the security was dialed up, and for the duration of the trial, all spectators—especially women—were given a thorough once-over before entering the courtroom.

So, there was reason to have concern for True's safety. But that didn't guarantee his honesty. The fact that someone wanted him dead didn't mean his word was gospel. The press, however, didn't see it that way. The *Valley Times* article described True as though he were an Eagle

Scout: "Under questioning by prosecutors, True came forth with a clear-cut and extremely courteous recital of the brutal events leading to the March 9 murder . . ."

"Courteous"? Based on what? He knew how to say *sir*? And more to the point, that's now—at least implicitly—supposed to be proof of honesty?

The reporter then went on to recount without a hint of skepticism True's claims that he'd had no idea anyone would be in the Monahan house, though it'd been reported ad nauseum that Barbara was only invited to come along because she stood a better chance of getting Mabel to open the door: "The deep sea diver said he agreed to go along 'providing the house was unoccupied and no one would get hurt.'"

The *Los Angeles Times* likewise gave True a pass on his nonsensical claim that he didn't expect to find anyone in the house, and even subtly applauded the fact that when confronted with the inconsistency on cross-examination, he "snapped back in clipped accents" that he "more or less went to her rescue." It was a nonanswer that made no sense. But it did make True look good, and that seemed to be the order of the day for the press.

This fairy tale that featured John True as the savior and hero was also repeated in the *Progress-Bulletin* of Pomona, which told of how John True "tried to save the wealthy widow from death at the hands of fellow members of a robbery gang."

But the press did manage to take a break from their hero worship to squeeze in another swipe at Barbara. The *Valley Times* reporter who wrote uncritically of True's claim that he didn't know anyone would be at home also wrote that when True saw Barbara in the courtroom, she "returned his gaze with a half-hidden smile."

Barbara smiled at True? Pigs would've flown in private jets before that happened.

Worst of all, lost in all this was the fact that this so-called savior was an accomplice who was testifying under a grant of full immunity. And even more importantly, that much of True's testimony about what had happened inside the Monahan house was uncorroborated.

The cops could corroborate the fact that the house had been ransacked. The forensic pathologist could corroborate the fact that Mabel had been beaten and died of strangulation. And Upshaw could corroborate the fact that Santo, Perkins, and Barbara were in on the planning of the burglary.

But none of them could corroborate True's testimony about what he had done inside that house, or his most damning claim about what Barbara had actually done that fateful night.

The fact that the press blithely overlooked all these warning signs to heap praise on an accomplice to a brutal murder is a testament to the dire consequences of groupthink, and a graphic example of what happens when everyone jumps aboard a train moving a hundred miles an hour down the wrong track.

CHAPTER ELEVEN

Meanwhile, though only a few were aware of it at the time, a lot had secretly been going on behind the scenes, and it all reached a peak in the last few weeks before the trial began.

It was about Barbara's alibi. From the moment Jack Hardy was appointed to represent her in July 1953, Barbara had insisted she'd had no part in the burglary. But she was "iffy" about where she'd been that night. She at first thought she'd been with someone named Mr. Logan, but when he failed to back that up, she thought she must've been at home, fighting with her husband, Hank. They'd been doing a lot of fighting back then, because they were in dire financial straits. Hank had lost his job and wasn't interested in looking for another one. All he wanted to do was get high. If Hank could say he'd been with Barbara on the night of the murder, that would've given her at least a semblance of an alibi, although as her husband, he was hardly a neutral witness. But even that didn't pan out. Hank was a junkie. Days and dates meant nothing to him. After talking to him, Jack Hardy determined his testimony would be "valueless." Hardy kept pushing Barbara for any detail that might give him a thread to pull, some lead on a decent witness, but she couldn't come up with anything else. Exasperated, she asked, "Do you know where *you* were on March 9th?"

Hardy found Barbara's seemingly cavalier attitude about it perplexing. In one of his earlier letters, he wrote, "As I told you, I feel your chances are very slim unless you can account for your time that night by some better means than your own uncorroborated testimony. So please think as carefully as you can. Surely there must be something, or someone, who can verify the facts as you state them." But as the trial date drew near with nothing but Barbara's claim of a fuzzy memory, Hardy really began to sweat. In personal visits and letters, he begged her to give him something to work with, threatening Barbara that "I don't remember" would send her straight to death row.

You might be wondering why there was so much pressure to come up with an alibi. Why couldn't Barbara just say, "I was there, but I never hurt Mabel Monahan"? The reason she couldn't do that was because she'd still be held liable for murder. As long as she was involved in the burglary when the murder went down, she was equally guilty as the actual killer, even if all she did was tell Mabel to be quiet while True bludgeoned her.

In California—actually, in a total of forty-eight states—there was, and still is, a rule that holds everyone liable for a homicide that occurs in the course of certain serious felonies, whether they had anything to do with the actual killing or not. If they were involved in the felony—such as robbery or burglary—and someone gets killed in the process, they're liable for first-degree murder. Even if it's an accidental killing. It's called the felony murder rule.

And if the prosecution chooses to add the special circumstance charge of murder in the course of a serious felony, it makes the defendants eligible for the death penalty as well. Today, the law in California limits first-degree murder liability for those who were not the actual killers. But at the time of the Monahan murder, it didn't matter whether a defendant was the actual killer or just a getaway driver. And the prosecution had charged all three defendants with a special circumstance of murder in the course of a burglary, so they were all eligible for the death penalty. That's why having an alibi was so crucial—and why Barbara's inability to come up with one was driving Hardy up a wall.

No matter how hard he tried to drive home what was at stake, Barbara didn't seem to understand her peril. In phone calls and letters, he begged her to give him something to work with, telling her that if "you got on the witness stand and said simply that you weren't there but you didn't know where you were that you would probably be headed for the gas chamber." At one point, he even had his cocounsel, Benjamin Wolfe, join him on the phone to emphasize her dire straits. But Barbara remained adamant. She didn't know where she'd been that night.

Enter Donna Prow. In the months leading up to the trial, she and Barbara had become close . . . very close.

Donna's origin story bore some general similarities to Barbara's. Born on November 9, 1932, Donna was just under four years old when her mother divorced her father and moved to Los Angeles from Casper, Wyoming. Donna somehow came to the attention of the LAPD Juvenile Division when she was fourteen and a half, for having sexual relations with one J. C. Twigg. How the cops managed—or why they even bothered—to prove that a teenager was having sex is an interesting question.

Be that as it may, they took action. Claiming Donna "lacked parental supervision," they made her a ward of the court. Theoretically, that should've required some probation officer or social worker to step in and provide that lacking supervision. But less than two years later, when Donna was in eleventh grade and still on juvenile probation, she got pregnant, got married, and dropped out of school. The man she married was Jack Prow. They tied the knot in Yuma, Arizona, though it's not clear whether he was actually the father. However, it was clear that they wound up with two children, Sandra and David.

Jack worked at the Wilshire Manufacturing Company in Los Angeles, while Donna worked as a carhop at Bob's Drive-In in Burbank. But their connubial bliss came to an end in the spring of 1952, when Donna filed for divorce, claiming infidelity, physical abuse—specifically that Jack once shot her through the foot—and mental cruelty. She took the kids and moved out.

There are some indications that Donna was no angel herself. The court ordered both exes not to "harass, molest or annoy" one another.

That may have been a standard order, but Donna wasn't alone for very long—if indeed she ever was. When she separated from Jack, she moved into the Valencia Apartments in Burbank. Coincidentally, one Graydon Burnam—a multiply convicted thief and ex-con—lived there too. He turned out to be Donna's boyfriend. She claimed that they didn't live together, and that she had her own apartment. But she admitted Burnam was giving her forty to fifty dollars a month, and Burnam's father was kicking in small monthly amounts as well. So . . . draw your own conclusions.

Just a few months after she hooked up with Burnam, the tragic event happened that would ultimately bring Barbara and Donna together. On the afternoon of September 3, 1952, Donna—whose driver's license had been suspended for an accident she'd caused three months earlier—tossed back some of the phenobarbital pills sent by her doctor that morning (prescribed for "menstrual difficulty"), washed them down with a copious amount of booze, then decided to take her boyfriend's convertible for a spin.

She managed to drive a mile or two before colliding with a lamp-post and a parked car at Avocado Street and Rowena Avenue, then headed down Los Feliz Boulevard—a heavily trafficked main artery that runs through the Griffith Park area—turned down a side street, and struck two more parked cars. When a witness tried to stop her, she drove up onto the curb, crossed the sidewalk, and turned back onto Los Feliz. Prow then careened onto Riverside Drive, in Burbank, another heavily trafficked boulevard within a stone's throw of all the major studios. She flew down Riverside, tires smoking, left front fender dragging, then veered into oncoming traffic, where she finally smashed head-on into a Mercury sedan carrying a family of five.

The front seat passenger in the Mercury was slammed into the dash with such force it fractured her legs, crushed her rib cage, and shoved her stomach up into her chest. She was taken to the hospital but pronounced dead on arrival. The back seat passenger had his jaw nearly torn off, and all four survivors suffered leg fractures, punctured lungs, broken arms, and chest injuries.

But Donna? She limped off with nothing more than a dislocated kneecap and a scratch on her arm. Though she claimed she'd only had "one drink," the officer who responded to the scene smelled a strong odor of alcohol on her breath and found two cans of beer in the car. When she was examined in the hospital forty-five minutes later, her pupils still failed to react to light. Donna got carted off to jail, but she immediately bailed out and ultimately pleaded guilty to one count of manslaughter.

Though she'd decimated an entire family, who were forced to mortgage the house to pay the medical bills that weren't covered by insurance, Donna got a sweet deal: one year in county jail and seven years' probation. But the probation officer who wrote up the report was clearly no fan of Donna Prow—or her ex-felon boyfriend, Graydon Burnam—stating,

> The defendant and Graydon Burnam made a number of unconvincing statements as to the defendant's present social and economic situations as well as to the defendant's activities and physical condition prior to the time of the offense . . . Their chief concern appeared to be about her own nervousness and her own physical injuries due to the accident. The defendant's concern for the people she had victimized seemed superficial, and her remarks about them were spoken with an attitude of cold expediency rather than with a feeling of genuine and extreme remorse. She shed no tears except when talking about her own affairs. The probation officer is of the opinion that this defendant is a very unstable person, that the prognosis for her future rehabilitation is indeed poor, especially if she continues her association with her present boyfriend.

Nevertheless, the probation officer recommended that in light of Prow's young age—she was just twenty years old—a grant of probation was appropriate, provided she first serve a "substantial period" in the county jail, that she surrender her still-suspended driver's license, and that she "cease all association with Graydon H. Burnam."

Donna's lawyer surely went over that report with his client before the sentencing hearing. But guess who Donna brought to court on March 18, 1953? The redoubtable Mr. Burnam. Judge Mildred Lillie—one of the very few female judges back then—took note and gave her own assessment of Donna Prow's character, stating that Prow "shows no apparent remorse or grief for her actions." But the judge followed the probation officer's recommendation nonetheless and granted probation conditioned upon serving one year in jail.

Donna landed in the Los Angeles County Jail on March 18, 1953. Barbara would join her there on May 4, 1953, initially booked for writing bad checks to keep her in custody until the prosecution had enough evidence to file the murder case.

According to Donna, they first met in the sewing room. Donna took an immediate liking to Barbara, and she wrote her an affectionate note, telling her she was pretty. They grew their relationship primarily through letters from June through August, writing to each other at least once a day—and sometimes more. But Donna didn't just send notes; she sent Barbara money and candy and even knitted her some socks, promising to knit her a dress to wear to court, as well. (I guess back then they weren't worried about female inmates using those needles as deadly weapons. I can't imagine that'd fly in any jail today.) Soon, their letters became more intimate. Donna said she liked Barbara "very much" and wanted to help her, that she understood how people might make mistakes. Barbara agreed about the mistakes but said she was innocent of the charges that'd been made against her. (By then she'd been charged with the murder. She had no quarrel with the check-kiting charges.) She told Donna that although she couldn't remember where she'd been on the night in question, she knew she hadn't been at the scene and that she'd had nothing to do with the burglary.

But those letters revealed that Donna and Barbara were more than just friends. Barbara called Prow "baby" and closed by saying, "Nite for now. Stay as sweet and pretty as you always are." In another, she made their amorous connection even more explicit:

> Hi Baby,
> Your note was so sweet, honey, but I want you to be sure of your feelings or I wouldn't want to start something we couldn't finish. You are a very lovely and desirable woman, honey and I want you very much.

So, yeah. Donna and Mrs. Graham had a thing going on. But as the trial date loomed, Barbara got more and more anxious. Her lawyers' fears had finally penetrated her armor of hope. Were they right? Was she doomed without an alibi?

Barbara confided her fears to her bestie, Donna. Her lawyers were saying she had to have an alibi, but she couldn't remember where she'd been. In a letter to Donna, she said, "Hi sweets, my attorney wrote me a letter. He told me I was facing the gas chamber because he couldn't locate two people. So I guess you could call it 'the short happy life of B. G.'"

Barbara said she knew she was either at home or at the home of someone named Logan, but since her attorney said she hadn't been with Logan, she thought she must have been home. It would've helped if her husband could confirm it. But they'd split up around the time of the burglary, and he'd never responded to the letter she'd written him back in May. His mother, who was taking care of Barbara's little son, Tommy, said Hank had moved out of state.

Donna rode to the rescue. She knew someone in the underworld, a man named Vince. For a price, he could give Barbara an alibi. Barbara, now desperate, agreed to let her put out feelers. In a subsequent note to Donna, she wrote that her lawyer had been by to see her and that he was disgusted with her for not having any better recollection of her whereabouts. She said she had told him to hang on for a while, but said nothing about the plan, and asked, "Have you heard from your friend again? Sure hope so. The way things are now, without this, I can't think of a thing."

Donna came through. The man had agreed to meet with Barbara and put together a story. Barbara just needed to think of a password so they could identify each other. She chose a line from the *Rubaiyat* and wrote to Donna: "Baby I thought of a password—it is from Omar Khayyam—Hope your friend doesn't think I am too weird—but then we can be sure. 'I came like water and like wind I go.' Do you think he can remember that? If not, you can use something else and let me know."

But the day before their meeting, Barbara was terrified: "Donna, hon, I don't know what to say . . . I'm so afraid there may be a slip-up. A slip-up could be the end, probably would be anyway. It's so hard—almost impossible—to trust anyone."

That had to be one sleepless night for Barbara. Even though Donna very likely did what she could to reassure her girlfriend, it wasn't her life on the line. When, the following day, a matron came to tell Barbara she had a visitor, she probably got the shakes. This was it. If this man refused to help and walked away . . . her psyche recoiled, unable to finish the thought.

They each gave the password, speaking through a wire mesh screen, and the tall, darkly handsome man confirmed that he had been sent by Donna's connection, Vince. He asked whether Barbara's lawyers knew about him. She said they didn't, that they wouldn't like this setup, but she reassured him that if they wouldn't call him to testify, she'd get other lawyers. He asked who else was involved in the case, and Barbara named John True and Jack Santo but not Perkins. I don't think she intentionally left him out in an effort to protect him. Everyone knew he'd been charged. I'm guessing it was just an oversight, an indication of her anxiety and distraction. He asked about Baxter Shorter, stating that he'd "heard the police have him hidden away until the trial starts." Barbara told him not to worry about Baxter, that he wouldn't be at the trial.

The man—whose name was Sam—asked if it would "clear" her if he said they were out of town, staying in a motel together, for two or three days between March ninth and the eleventh or twelfth. Barbara said that would be wonderful.

They met two more times to work out the details, and on their last meeting, Sam brought a registration card and receipt for a motel in Encino that showed they'd stayed there for a span of three days. That more than covered the night of the murder. Barbara asked him to contact her lawyers and tell them what he was going to say so they could prepare to present his testimony. He agreed to call that day.

They were all set.

CHAPTER TWELVE

Two weeks later, on August 27, 1953, the prosecution was ready to call the last witness in their case in chief. J. Miller Leavy hadn't been involved in the early stages of the investigation in this case and only officially joined the team a week before trial. But he'd been feverishly working behind the scenes in preparation for this day, when he'd get to present the part of the case that was his brainchild. His and Lieutenant Coveney's, that is.

Leavy knew he was about to deliver the knockout blow and the biggest headliner of the trial. He must've relished the moment as he took his place at the lectern, his body tingling with the electric anticipation of the shock waves that were about to spread throughout the gallery—and the country.

Leavy told Judge Fricke the next witness was on his way, then turned and watched as the handsome, dark-haired Sam entered the courtroom and moved to the witness stand. Sam Sirianni, the man who'd concocted the false alibi with Barbara, was a cop. I can only imagine the utter heart-clutching panic she must've felt as she watched him take the oath and tell the jury that he was a police officer for the Los Angeles Police Department. She'd been had—and in the worst way possible. Not only had he taken notes of their meetings, but he'd also worn a hidden wire and recorded them.

This kind of trial by ambush could never happen today. Prosecutors are required to hand over discovery of all witness statements, including any statement by the defendant, well before trial. But back then, discovery in criminal cases was a matter of judicial discretion, meaning the trial judge had the right to decide whether and when the prosecution was required to show the defense what they had. In particular, prosecutors were routinely allowed to withhold a defendant's confession or any statement made to the police under the misguided theory that letting them see it before trial would encourage them to lie. Actually, the opposite is true. In any case, back then, it was perfectly kosher to spring Barbara's statement on the defense in the midst of trial.

So although at first when I read this part of the transcript, I practically jumped out of my seat and even yelled, "Object! Damn it, object!" at the defense attorneys—who, for some reason, didn't answer me—a quick search on Lexis told me this was par for the course in those days.

But kosher or not, it was a bombshell of epic proportion that exploded through the courtroom and every news outlet.

This was one of the rare occasions when the press bothered to take note of Santo and Perkins. The *Daily News* said the pair "reared galvanically in their seats" and "looked in amazement at the 29-year-old woman beside them." The *Valley Times* reported that Barbara leaned toward them and started to say something, but according to a sheriff's deputy who was nearby, Perkins cut her off, saying, "Don't give us that." One of them said, "This is what we get for having a woman in on it."

But naturally, the main attraction was Barbara. Throughout the trial, the press had strained to embellish descriptions of Barbara's reactions, saying she'd "glared" at the witness or "smirked" or "frowned angrily" at one person or another. But invariably, the accompanying photographs contradicted those accounts, showing nothing more than a neutral, occasionally contemplative, expression.

This time, I suspect the prose was closer to the mark. The *Los Angeles Times* wrote that Barbara's "jaw fell in dismay" when Sirianni took the stand, and that although she regained an "icy composure," she was "somewhat pale of face and tight lipped" throughout his testimony.

The *Daily News* also zeroed in on Barbara's face, claiming her "heavy jaw fell" when Sirianni "strode" through the courtroom and that "fear widened her eyes and she clutched the arm of her chair" as he recounted their conversations. The *Los Angeles Mirror* reported that "she turned crimson, bit her lip and muttered profanely in an undertone when she saw her alibi witness revealed in the court . . . as an undercover police officer."

The only ones in the courtroom more stunned than Barbara were her lawyers. This time, even *their* reactions made the news, with articles that said they were "visibly shocked." And Hardy reportedly "nearly swooned" in his chair as Sirianni detailed his encounters with Barbara.

Hardy had good reason to swoon. Sirianni testified in agonizing detail about how he and Barbara had concocted an elaborate alibi, including times, dates, and locations for their fabricated vacay that placed them out of town for three days—and notably in a motel together on the night of March 9. An adulterous affair wouldn't have been my first choice for a cooked-up alibi. But considering Barbara was already charged with murder, the stain of an extramarital hookup was a hit worth taking.

Sirianni explained that Lieutenant Coveney was the mastermind of this operation. At his direction, Sirianni met with Donna Prow on August 7 before going to see Barbara that day. When he met with Barbara, he gave the agreed-upon password, "I came like water and like wind I go," and confirmed that he was the "Sam" identified by Donna. He and Barbara met again on August 10 and 12. Although Sirianni had worn a wire at all three meetings, the recorder hadn't worked on the seventh and tenth. So he read from the notes he'd made on those first two days. While the meeting on the twelfth did record their conversation, the recorder, a crude device called a Minifon, picked up so much ambient noise of the jail that it was virtually unintelligible when they played it for the jury. So Sirianni had to read from the transcript of that meeting.

From their first conversation on August 7, Barbara made it clear that this was an act of desperation, saying, "Without you as an alibi, I'm doomed to the gas chamber."

Under the guise of making sure no one could contradict the false alibi, Sirianni repeatedly grilled Barbara about the murder. It quickly became clear that he had two main goals: to get Barbara to admit she was at the Monahan house that night and to find out what she knew about Baxter Shorter's disappearance. Over and over again, Sirianni pushed Barbara to admit she'd been with Perkins and Santo on the night of the murder, claiming he needed to make sure no one else could come forward to say they'd seen her that night and expose his lie.

Barbara initially resisted and told him not to worry, she was sure no one else had seen her, saying, "I was home most of the night, Sam." His demands got increasingly forceful as Barbara failed to give him the answers he wanted: "Now, then, you were with Perkins, True and Santo that night?" Barbara's answer was inaudible. Sirianni pressed her again: "Now, listen, I want to know everything down the line. Now, for Christ's sake, don't hold anything back here because this is it. This may be the last meeting, OK?"

Barbara answered, "I'll speak with my attorney."

Sirianni: "OK, and then you can go ahead and tell your attorney what you want. I want it straight down the line or I'm quitting as of now."

Even then, Barbara continued to hedge. But Sirianni kept pushing.

Sirianni: "All right, now, I want to know where you were that day, because if anyone—I don't care where it is—if anyone saw any of you they'll be in court and I don't mean perhaps! Now, Perkins, True, Santo—how about Bax? Was he there that night? If he was there that night that will make four of them?"

Barbara: "Uh-huh."

Sirianni: "You were with those four guys on the night of March 9th when everything took place. Now, then—were you?"

Sirianni testified that Barbara was visibly nervous at this point. Now, with the threat that he'd abandon her hanging over her head, Barbara finally cracked:

Barbara: "I was with them."

He'd gotten what he came for: she'd finally admitted she was there that night. But just to make sure, he hammered the point again:

Sirianni: "All right, you were with Perkins, True, Santo and Bax on March 9th—the 9th of March. That was the day that we have to make alibi for. Is that right?"

Barbara: "Uh-huh."

Sirianni: "You know all these men?"

Barbara: "Uh-huh."

And then again:

Sirianni: "If you will assure me that you were with these four men that we named before—"

Barbara: "I was, and not another soul saw me that night."

Sirianni pushed Barbara almost as hard for information on Baxter Shorter. He again hid his true reason behind the claim that he was worried Shorter might show up and say he'd seen Barbara. Barbara said only that she knew he wouldn't be there, but that she didn't know where he was. As Sirianni continued to ask about Shorter's whereabouts, Barbara was forced to get more definitive, saying, "If I wasn't sure that he wouldn't show up I wouldn't say this. So you can use your imagination . . . I say he won't be here."

But Sirianni continued to push, and again asked her for reassurance that Shorter wouldn't be there, saying, "That boy worries me."

Barbara: "He won't be here."

Sirianni insisted that the newspapers said "they had him hidden away and that they were going to produce him in court."

Barbara: "Every time I read it, I laugh."

Sirianni: "You do? You know what happened to him?"

Barbara: "Uh-huh."

Sirianni: "You do?"

Barbara: "Uh-huh. Just don't worry. He won't show up."

Sirianni: "I more or less take your word, but do you know where he's at?"

Barbara: "Definitely."

But her most incriminating response to the questions about Shorter wasn't captured on tape. Sirianni testified from the notes he'd taken after their meeting. In an effort to bait her into divulging what she knew about his whereabouts, he again said he'd heard the police had Shorter hidden away until trial. Barbara—doubtless afraid he'd back out—went further. She said that wasn't true, that she could give her word he wouldn't show up, and that he is "well taken care of." Sirianni asked, "Well taken care of?" Barbara replied, "Yes, been done away with. I assure you he won't be at the trial."

Sirianni also testified that the motel receipt he'd produced to back up the alibi was prepared by Lieutenant Coveney.

Sirianni's testimony effectively decimated Barbara's defense. It was a one-two sucker punch. Her admission that she'd been with Santo and Perkins shredded her alibi, and the confidence of her assertion that Shorter wouldn't appear, showing her knowledge that he'd been killed, solidified the truth of that admission.

Take away either one of those damaging statements and the lawyers would've had something to work with. Without Barbara's assurance that Shorter had "been done away with," the lawyers might've been able to argue that Barbara had been pressured into saying she was at the Monahan house—even though she really wasn't—frightened by Sirianni's threat to back out of the alibi. Or take away her admission to having been with Perkins and Santo and the lawyers could've argued that she'd only said Shorter was "done away with" to reassure Sirianni, that she suspected something had happened to him, as had many others at that point, but that she didn't really know anything. But the combination of her admission that she'd been at the crime scene and her obvious awareness of Shorter's demise was an insurmountable hurdle.

The moment Leavy finished his direct examination of Sirianni, the lawyers rushed to the bench for a sidebar. The phony-alibi scheme wasn't just a devastating blow to the defense; it also posed an ethical dilemma for Barbara's lawyers. If the judge believed they'd been in on it, they could be disbarred. Hardy, still in shock from the unexpected bombshell, asked the judge to relieve him as counsel of record: "I admonished my client . . . repeatedly during my interviews with her that if she in any way told me any lies or deceived me or any misrepresented any facts relative to her defense, that I would ask leave of Court to withdraw . . . [in view of her statements to Sirianni] I feel that I have been deceived and misled; and under those circumstances, I would like formally to ask leave of the Court to withdraw as attorney."

Actually, there was no reason for Hardy to panic. Sirianni had testified that Barbara made it clear her lawyers knew nothing of their scheme. In fact, Sirianni testified that he'd told her he wanted to wait until the last minute to contact them so they wouldn't have a chance to check out his story.

Judge Fricke, predictably, denied the lawyer's request to be relieved: "I think it is a matter of rather common knowledge among those of us who have practiced law for a period of time, that the instances in which a client tells his attorney the truth, the whole truth, and nothing but the truth, are scarcer than those in which the converse is true."

Cross-examination of Sirianni at that point was limited. The defense needed time to regroup and prepare for this last-minute bombshell witness. But Hardy did have one burning question for Sirianni: Who the hell was Donna Prow? Sirianni answered that she was a "girl that is now in the County Jail," who was not a member of any law enforcement agency.

Hardy asked whether she was currently incarcerated there. Sirianni confirmed that she was.

And on that note, with Sirianni's damning testimony ringing in the jury's ears, the prosecution rested.

CHAPTER THIRTEEN

So "the pretty Donna Prow," as reporters almost uniformly called her, Barbara's lover and devoted supporter, was a plant.[5]

The idea for the setup with her was hatched by Lieutenant Coveney. Jail deputies who'd been monitoring Barbara's mail showed him Hardy's letters warning her that she was facing the gas chamber if she didn't firm up an alibi. The moment Coveney saw those letters, he realized it was a golden opportunity. Here was the hook they needed, and he just happened to have the perfect bait for it.

They say there's no such thing as coincidence. But I'm not so sure. Because Donna's landing in jail at just the right time was one hell of a coincidence, and a truly diabolical twist of fate. Coveney had known Donna for some time before she wound up in the county jail. He testified that he first met her in September 1952, in connection with a non-support matter related to her divorce from her ex-husband, Jack Prow.

That would mean Coveney and Donna had only met near or after the time of the fatal collision that led to Donna's conviction for manslaughter. But that definitely wasn't true. First of all, there was no

---

5   At that time, the use of an informant at this late stage of the case, after an indictment had been handed down, was still legal. The United States Supreme Court put a stop to this practice in 1964, in Massiah v. United States, holding that the interrogation of an indicted defendant without the presence of an attorney was a violation of the Sixth Amendment.

nonsupport filing for Donna Prow in any court records. In fact, there was no reason why Donna would've sought out Coveney's help with child support. Although the judge had ordered her ex—Jack Prow—to pay seventy dollars per month in child support, Donna failed to allow him the court-ordered visitation for several months, so the judge refunded him the money he'd paid into a trust account and struck the order for child support. Bottom line: there was no order for child support. And in any case, there's no indication Jack ever failed to make his support payments.

Second of all, in her post-guilty-plea statement to probation, Donna said that she'd known Coveney before the drunk-driving fatality collision. She told the probation officer that she would call on Coveney whenever she was feeling "unwell" and that she'd called on him again shortly after the collision. Donna said nothing about consulting Coveney about any nonsupport issues. So she'd known Coveney for a while before the collision—and apparently felt they were close enough to expect that he'd come to her aid whenever she was feeling "unwell." Since Coveney wasn't a doctor, I can only guess what Donna thought he might be able to do for her—but I'm pretty sure it didn't involve a prescription.

Third of all, according to the *Daily News*, Coveney had met Prow back when she'd been a carhop at a drive-in eatery. And Donna told a reporter they'd met when he was a customer at a restaurant where she worked as a waitress. So Coveney's claim that he met her in an official capacity to help with her nonsupport claim doesn't match up with any of the known facts.

One source stated they had a romantic relationship. While that couldn't be corroborated, it was clear this was not an ordinary "cop to citizen" connection.

Lovers or no, they were certainly buddies, because on May 10, 1953, Coveney trusted Prow enough to recruit her to help him take Barbara down. Her mission was to get close to Barbara, gain her trust, and tell her that she had underworld connections who could "help" her out. Prow was to say her friend "Vince" could take care of Barbara. "Vince" was the code name for Coveney. Coveney testified that he gave her explicit orders: "To find out the truth as to where Barbara Graham was on the night of March 9th, to find out exactly what had happened to Baxter Shorter, if she could, to find out what she knew and could tell about her associations with John True, Jack Santo, Emmett Perkins and Baxter Shorter."

Prow was quoted as saying that when Coveney told her about his plan, she thought it was "a crazy idea." But she was willing to go along with it.

In fact, she threw herself into the task with inordinate zeal, pursuing Barbara relentlessly. I doubt Coveney anticipated Donna would go so far as to engineer a romantic connection, but I'm sure he was very pleased with his little informant when she let him know they'd been exchanging love letters. He told her to turn them over, and Donna happily complied.

Barbara, totally unaware that her letters were being read and collected by Lieutenant Coveney, didn't keep Donna's letters. Inmates weren't allowed to pass notes, and if the guards found any in her cell, she'd get punished, so Barbara threw away the letters Donna had written to her. Of course, Donna had no such worry. After all, she was working for the Man. But she didn't give Coveney all the letters Barbara wrote, because—according to Coveney—Donna said they were "of such an amorous nature she would be embarrassed to have me read them."

Or maybe it was because those missing notes from Barbara made it too clear that "the pretty Donna Prow" had been the one to suggest the fake alibi. That would've been a critical piece of evidence. If Barbara had been the one who'd come up with the idea and asked Donna to help find someone who'd be willing to testify to a false alibi, that would be one thing. Whether the move was born of desperation or not, it would've been a move Barbara made on her own. But if Donna, guided by Lieutenant Coveney, had been the one pushing the alibi, and Barbara—under increasing pressure from her lawyers, not to mention the threat of the death penalty—had finally broken down and agreed to the scheme, it would look significantly different.

There was good reason to believe it was the latter. In her statements to the press the day after Sirianni revealed her involvement in the case, Donna boasted about having gained Barbara's trust, and said Barbara had then confided that she was worried because her lawyers hadn't been able to come up with any witnesses to back up her alibi. Of course, Donna already knew that. That's why Coveney had enlisted her in the first place. It was the opening Donna had been waiting for, and Coveney had primed her with the answer. She told Barbara she had an underworld friend, "Vince," who could get someone to fix up an alibi for her.

As a matter of fact, she proudly claimed that she'd managed to lure Barbara into the trap all on her own, that although she hadn't met with Coveney for three weeks, when he finally came to see her, she'd had it "all wrapped up." That, actually, was a lie. Coveney never even left her alone for three days.

The testimony from jailers established that he'd been Donna's constant visitor from May 21 right up until the day before Donna got released, August 27—when he actually visited her twice. The record of his official visits alone shows he saw her fourteen times in that period. But those were just the official visits, the ones that took place on the thirteenth floor, where records were kept that showed who the visitors were, which inmate they saw, and the dates they visited. There were other unofficial visits that took place on the tenth floor that were not recorded anywhere. The jailers had special orders to keep everything regarding Donna Prow "confidential" and not to keep "any records of any visits that transpired on the tenth floor." Meaning, Coveney visited Donna *at least* fourteen times, but probably many, many more.

So, no. Donna wasn't left on her own for anything close to three weeks. Coveney kept her on a tight leash. I'm sure he was unhappy with the fact that the press had gotten hold of her, and that she'd talked about how she'd ensnared Barbara—which was likely what tipped off the defense to the importance of her role—but once she was out of custody, there wasn't much he could do about it. But the real question was, Why was she out of custody when she had another six months of her already-light one-year sentence left? The answer: because out of custody and out of reach was where Coveney and Leavy wanted her to be.

Now, the defense had never so much as heard the name Donna Prow until the day Sirianni took the stand. But the moment they heard it and saw her statements to the press, they knew she'd be a crucial witness. Those statements alone showed that she'd been the one who suggested the false alibi. If the jury got to hear how, at Coveney's behest, she'd manipulated Barbara and deliberately lured her into the trap by planting the idea of putting on a phony alibi, that would change the picture—or, as they say, "flip the narrative." It wouldn't be a story of "Barbara, the lying schemer." It'd be a story of how an innocent woman's understandable desperation was cruelly exploited by cops, prosecutors, and even fellow prisoners. It could significantly undermine the impact of Sirianni's damning testimony—or at least, soften the blow.

The defense started searching for Donna the moment Sirianni finished his first day of testimony on August 27, 1953. She'd still been in custody when he began testifying that day, so it should've been easy to find her. But the defense quickly realized it wasn't going to be so simple. The very next day, on August 28, 1953, Donna gave a statement to reporters. That meant she'd been released. The race was on. The defense had to get her into court before the case ended, or the jury would never see her. They gathered as much information about her as they could and fired out a subpoena.

A judge signed the subpoena that same day, August 28. It included an affidavit that listed the names and address of her parents, and the address Prow had given to probation of 6348 Longview in Hollywood. The subpoena ordered Prow to report "immediately" to Judge Fricke's courtroom, Department 43.

But it came back undeliverable. In the return, dated August 31, the deputy sheriff who'd tried to serve the subpoena stated that "after diligent search and careful inquiry, I have been unable to find Donna Prow—unable to locate at either address given. No longer living at Longview address. Not in at Marsh St. address. State they have no knowledge of her whereabouts."

Jack Hardy, having exhausted his resources, turned to the judge for guidance, at which point the following exchange took place in front of the jury:

Hardy: "May it please the Court, we have here a subpoena for Donna Prow which we have made every endeavor to serve, unsuccessfully. I wonder if the Court could give us any assistance in serving this subpoena on her. We desire to call her and I have checked with several people who should know her whereabouts and apparently don't. I don't know how we are going to get her . . . it is important we get her here."

Court: "I don't know how I can give you any assistance. I know nothing about the witness or the whereabouts of the witness."

Prosecutor J. Miller Leavy: "I thought the Sheriff was supposed to subpoena witnesses for the defendant."

Mr. Hardy: "It doesn't make any difference who serves her as long as we can locate her."

Prosecutor Alexander: "This is a surprise to me, your Honor. This proceeding I didn't know it was coming up here at all."

The Court: "I don't know why the Court should be called upon to serve a subpoena for the defense."

Mr. Leavy: "The law says that the Sheriff is supposed to serve subpoenas for the defense without charge."

Mr. Hardy: "Apparently she is hard to locate."

Hardy undoubtedly thought Leavy understood the sheriff *had* tried to serve Donna Prow, but had failed. And I'd guess Leavy likely *did* know that. As his remarks show, he knew the sheriff's department was the only source available to the defense to serve subpoenas. So when Hardy said he'd been unable to serve Donna Prow, the most obvious explanation was that the sheriff had tried but was unable to find her.

The Court: "I don't know as it is my duty to leave the bench and serve it for you."

Judge Fricke was being sarcastic. Judges have never had a duty to serve a subpoena.

Mr. Hardy: "I thought I might have the assistance for the D.A.'s office of some sort."

The Court: "I don't know anything about the situation."

Mr. Alexander: "I suggest Mr. Hardy first ask the D.A.'s office for some assistance."

That last remark by Alexander was reportedly sarcastic. Of course it was. Because Hardy had just done exactly that.

The judge then pronounced that none of this should've been done in the presence of the jury: "I think you are talking about something that has no place in the case at all. The jury is to entirely disregard the discussion between Mr. Hardy and the District Attorney and myself. You may proceed."

And so the jury was ordered to not even think about the fact that the defense was unable to locate a key witness. A witness/snitch who'd seduced Barbara to gain her trust and likely been the one to suggest the fake alibi to begin with. This meant that the prosecution got a win-win: they got to ambush the defense with Sirianni's testimony *and* keep the jury from even thinking about the fact that the stool pigeon who'd set it all up was in the wind.

There wasn't much Hardy could do about it, but he tried. Later in the proceedings, he called Coveney back to the stand to question him about his relationship with Donna, and he brought in the jail deputies to testify to all the visits he paid her—both official and unofficial. And during the defense case, in front of the jury and all counsel, Hardy read the sheriff deputy's affidavit stating he couldn't find Donna Prow. Leavy and Alexander stood mute and made no response. Their attitude—and intended message to the jury: this was a defense problem. It had nothing to do with them.

Everything about the way the prosecution handled this was disturbing. Donna was a key figure who'd been an important part of the plot to trap Barbara. The fact that they were acting like she didn't exist, and their total lack of concern that she'd blown off her obligation to provide a valid address to the probation department when she got released, only heightened my suspicion. And the more I thought about it, the more it jangled my nerves. Something about this was off, very off. As I pored over page after page of trial testimony—and then all one thousand plus pages of the clerk's transcript—I hoped I'd find some answers. I even went back to the books, newspapers, and magazine articles, praying that there was something I'd missed. But there was nothing. And there was no one I could interview about it. Everyone involved in the case was dead. Upset, but stymied, I realized I had to let it go. There were bound to be limits to what I could uncover about a case that was over seventy years old. I had to accept that reality and move on.

Then, I got lucky. At that point I'd finished reading everything I could find about the trial and was busy churning through the sources I'd plumbed for posttrial information. One of them was the Walter Wanger Collection, which largely consisted of letters between Walter and others, and a few letters from Barbara to various people. And there, purely by accident, I discovered a report prepared by Carl Palmberg for Barbara's appellate lawyer, Al Matthews. It turned out to be a treasure trove of information on Donna Prow. Meticulously researched, Palmberg's report drew almost exclusively on documentary evidence, making it a source that was both neutral and reliable. And there I found the evidence I'd been searching for. As it turned out, I'd been right.

Those prosecutors—and most certainly J. Miller Leavy—had known very well where Donna was. And Leavy had made sure Donna would never be located. On Sirianni's first day of testimony, J. Miller Leavy—unbeknownst to the defense—requested an emergency hearing for Donna before Judge Mildred Lillie, the judge who'd sentenced her to a year in jail and seven years' probation for killing one and maiming four in the drunk-driving collision.

Donna hadn't been due to be released from jail until the following March in 1954. But thanks to Leavy, she got out on August 28, 1953, the day after Sirianni's first day on the witness stand, having served just five and a half months of her one-year sentence. Leavy put Donna on the stand before Judge Mildred Lillie and had her describe how she'd helped law enforcement trap Barbara into hiring an undercover cop to give a false alibi. And then, to make sure the judge understood she needed to issue Donna her "Get Out of Jail Free" card immediately, Leavy claimed Prow's life was in danger if she remained in custody because she'd been threatened by another inmate for having cooperated with the police. The threat allegedly stated, "If I could get hold of some poison I'd put it in her grub." It was attributed to an unnamed "female prisoner."

It was a load of bunk. First of all, Donna's involvement had only been revealed on August 27, when Sirianni took the stand. And news accounts of his testimony didn't come out until the following day, August 28. But according to Leavy, that supposed threat had already been made by the time he brought Donna to court on the morning of August 28. There was no way on earth any prisoner could've even *learned* of Donna's dirty work by then, let alone have issued a threat—and one that just happened to be found in time to bring to court that *same* day.

Nor could any of the inmates know Donna was working for Coveney before the press found out. I don't think Donna was any kind of genius, but it didn't take a Mensa membership to know it might not be a great idea to blab about being a snitch in a jail full of cop haters. I'm also sure Coveney would have sworn Donna to secrecy—if not for her own safety, at least to ensure Barbara didn't find out that she was working for him. And Donna could certainly count on Barbara not to talk. But Judge Lillie never asked to see any proof of the claimed threat against Donna. Why would she? A celebrated prosecutor—an officer of the court—had given his word.

This early release was obviously Donna's payoff for helping Coveney set the trap, though they all tried to deny it. Donna told the press she'd agreed to be Coveney's plant because it was her "duty" and that she'd only done it for the sake of "justice." J. Miller Leavy said she'd cooperated "willingly"—an artful dodge that didn't deny they'd promised to get Donna out of jail in exchange for all that cooperation. But Lieutenant Coveney used no such sleight of hand. He flatly denied having made Donna any promises. When he was asked on cross-examination whether any promises or "inducements" had been given to Donna to secure her cooperation, he stated, "No. None whatsoever." Confronted with the fact that she'd been released the day after Sirianni's testimony, Coveney confirmed it but claimed he "had nothing to do with that."

This was technically true, but essentially a flat-out lie. It was true that he didn't take Donna to Judge Lillie, or fabricate a threat against her from another inmate, or plead for her immediate release. Leavy did all that. But there is no way on earth Coveney didn't approve every bit of it—and well in advance. This move had been orchestrated from the very start. "Pretty Donna" hadn't spent weeks seducing Barbara with love notes, money, and knitted goods for the fun of it.

And that's not all Coveney and Leavy did. They knew that even though the sheriff had been unable to serve her, the defense was continuing to search for Donna. Hardy had issued subpoenas demanding the transcript of Donna's hearing before Judge Lillie and the jail visitor passes for Donna that showed who'd visited her and when. The transcript might reveal the addresses she'd given to justify her release on probation, and the jail visitor passes might show who Donna could've run to. Leavy could easily have known about those subpoenas because—as required—they'd been filed with the court. But by then, it was early September, and the trial was winding down. Coveney and Leavy knew the defense was running out of time. All they had to do was keep Donna out of reach a little while longer.

So on September 11, 1953, while Hardy was still waiting for someone to respond to his subpoenas (and it appears no one ever did), the district attorney's office and the Burbank Police Department made arrangements to let Donna move out of state to be with her relatives. Obviously, the prosecution *did* know how to find Donna—when they wanted to. At that point, the trial was still in session. Hardy could've put her on the witness stand if Leavy or Coveney had simply given him the address they'd had for her. They didn't. I guess Coveney—if asked—would've said he had "nothing to do with that" move either. But Hardy never got a chance to ask him, because the clock had run out. On September 15, 1953, both sides rested their case. The jury would never hear from Donna Prow.

Would her appearance on the witness stand have made a difference? Quite possibly. With Donna Prow on the witness stand, the defense could've shown the jury that the whole alibi scheme was her idea, that she'd seduced and manipulated Barbara into going along with it, and that Coveney, the puppet master, had been pulling Donna's strings all along. That would've put the whole scheme—and Barbara's complicity—in a different light.

But of course, the prosecution knew that, and they weren't about to let it happen. What they did was a legal and ethical violation of the highest order. To deliberately hide any witness, let alone one of such critical importance, is a Constitutional violation of the right to a fair trial, the right to present a complete defense, and the right to the effective assistance of counsel. While the rules of criminal procedure back then were far more lenient for prosecutors, this was one violation that would never have been tolerated.

Hardy certainly suspected there'd been some kind of foul play, though he couldn't prove it. In the closing argument, he said, "We tried to find [Donna Prow]. We had no law enforcement agency. We tried to use the Sheriff's office and they . . . couldn't find her. Why didn't the State produce Donna Prow? No, that would have been a little too risky, the truth might have won out . . . I would be awfully suspicious of that kind of a prosecution and that kind of a State's case."

And Hardy returned to the point later in his argument: "Now I'm very sorry that we weren't able to locate Donna Prow because she might have helped us a great deal, but she was not available for various reasons, as you know. It's very interesting that Mr. Sirianni who testified on the 27th of August, [and] on the 28th of August Donna Prow's probation was modified and she was released from the County Jail. Think that over." And he pointed out that Donna had only served five months on her yearlong sentence.

So Hardy had a feeling something untoward had taken place, and if he'd had a little more time, he might've been able to prove it. Nevertheless, it is worth noting that even without knowing what the prosecutors had done to hide Donna Prow, a federal district court judge who reviewed Barbara's habeas petition would later remark that the method of gathering evidence against her was "distasteful."

What's even more upsetting is the reason Leavy could get away with this. Back in those days, when counsel was appointed by the court, they didn't get paid. That not only meant the lawyers were working for free; it also meant they had to go out of pocket if they wanted to hire an investigator. That alone undermined a defense lawyer's ability to do a good job, because investigators are a necessity. They're the ones who find the witnesses—especially slippery ones like Donna Prow, who don't want to be found. Although it's true that sheriff's deputies were tasked with serving subpoenas for the defense back then, the sheriff's department really didn't have the time or the manpower to beat the streets for defense witnesses. It's remarkable the deputy on this case accomplished as much as he did. But there was no way he'd have been able to find someone who deliberately gave false addresses and whose location was actively being hidden by police and prosecutors.

This alone hobbled Hardy's ability to act as an effective adversary. While the prosecution in this case had access to multiple law enforcement agencies—Leavy and company got help from LAPD, Burbank Police, and the Department of Justice—the defense had only . . .

themselves, Jack Hardy and Ben Wolfe, the lawyers. This was a fact Hardy specifically lamented on the record during his closing argument.[6]

Now, it's true that back then, in recognition of the hardship this created for the defense, the prosecution would sometimes volunteer one of their investigators to help out the defense. And notably, on one or two occasions, the prosecution did lend Hardy an investigator—to find *other* witnesses. But not to find Donna Prow.

Postscript on "the pretty Donna Prow": after skipping town in September, she didn't turn up again until December 12, when a probation officer asked to modify the terms of probation to allow her to live out of state. I'm not sure why the probation officer bothered. Donna was obviously going to live wherever the hell she pleased no matter what anyone said. But anyway, since the probation officer claimed she was reporting regularly, the request for modification was granted.

Except it turned out Donna actually hadn't been reporting regularly. A probation violation hearing was scheduled for May 19, 1954, because her new probation officer said she hadn't reported since October 1953. Donna's father, George Ewald, who lived in Scotts Bluff, Nebraska, wrote to the probation department that Donna had left his house in October. His note said, "Heard from her Feb. 28, 1954. No return address." According to Donna's mother, Anna Walton, she was living in Fairbanks, Alaska, with her now-husband . . . wait for it . . . Graydon Burnam, the ex-con thief. It was also reported that she might be living in South America. When Judge Lillie read this report, she finally threw up her hands and declared, "I guess love will find a way," and took the matter off calendar.

So Donna, who actually had killed someone, got to go off to Rio. And Barbara got to face the gas chamber.

---

6   Though his vow to fight for the right to get financial assistance from the state for the defense in indigent cases didn't produce immediate results, it did eventually bear fruit. Now—at least in California—it's well recognized that the Sixth Amendment right to counsel and a fair trial requires that the government pay for a lawyer and provide the necessary funds to conduct an investigation for indigent defendants.

CHAPTER FOURTEEN

By the time the prosecution rested, they'd presented a host of witnesses, ending with the coup de grâce of Sirianni's testimony and the recording of Barbara's voice admitting she'd been with Santo and Perkins. From what the jury could see, the case was more than proven.

The prospect of a death sentence now hovered more closely than ever. It was up to the defense to show why Barbara shouldn't be convicted—or at least why she should be allowed to spend the rest of her life in prison. But Barbara was charged with felony murder, which meant she couldn't claim she didn't know Santo et al. were going to kill anyone, or that she got pressured into acting as the decoy. The only defense to felony murder was alibi; i.e., she wasn't there. Having failed to come up with any witnesses who could say where *else* Barbara might've been that night, Hardy realized he had no choice. He had to put Barbara on the stand.

Now, maybe that was their plan all along. But I'm betting it wasn't. Because it's so rarely a good idea to let a defendant testify. Even when the defendant has a solid story, they still have to sell it to the jury—and that's no easy thing. By the time they get up on the witness stand, the jury's been listening to days—and sometimes weeks—of incriminating testimony. Most defendants aren't great orators to begin with, and the pressure of knowing this is their one chance to "say it ain't so" often ends in a crash and burn. The witness stand is a scary place even for an ordinary citizen—let alone a defendant who's on trial for their life—because the person testifying has zero control. And that loss of control gets exponentially more painful once the prosecutor gets his shot at them on cross-examination.

But what choice did Hardy have? And besides, how much worse could it get? Barbara had already been publicly branded by the press as a liar who'd even been convicted of perjury, not to mention as a deviant who wrote love letters to other women. The '50s wasn't exactly an era known for its "live and let live" philosophy when it came to any form of homosexuality. With all the obstacles Hardy was facing, Sisyphus would've realized he'd had it easy. I'm guessing the defense figured they had nothing to lose by putting Barbara on the stand.

And so Barbara was the first witness called by the defense. The personal challenges she faced were daunting. She had to admit to her less than virtuous life (four marriages and three divorces), her past criminality—and in particular her prior conviction for perjury, a real credibility killer—explain her relationship with Donna, and most of all, why she'd agreed to solicit a false alibi. And somehow in the process, she had to convince the jury that in spite of all that, she was innocent.

On top of everything, she'd just suffered the blow of finding out that Donna, supposedly her lover and ally, had betrayed her in spectacular fashion, cruelly luring her into a trap that could cost Barbara her life. And as her letter to Donna showed, Barbara had a vivid memory of how her last appearance on a witness stand had ended with a perjury conviction—a frighteningly possible harbinger of things to come. Barbara was also likely aware that the reporters who'd cracked open a thesaurus at every opportunity to find new ways to demean and deride her were now packing the gallery, eagerly awaiting fresh ammunition to fire into their afternoon and evening editions.

So . . . pressure? What pressure?

At that point, the only hint the press had given that Barbara might have a human side was a photograph and short blurb buried at the bottom of a page that showed Barbara's eighteen-month-old son, Tommy, in a perambulator with her mother-in-law, Anne Webb, who'd brought him to court to see his mother. The caption explained that the judge had turned her away because he'd banned minors from the courtroom (possibly to shield them from exposure to the proceedings, but more likely to avoid disruption). Apparently, the sight of her baby brought tears to Barbara's eyes, because one reporter had written that "Barbara's eyes glazed with moisture when she was told her baby had gone." But that short squib was a raindrop in the hurricane of cruelly derogatory coverage in nearly all the other articles.

Now, the *Herald-Express* presaged her appearance on the witness stand with a description of her past that spared no adjective in an effort to denounce it as rife with sordid excesses: "In the wreckage of Barbara Graham's past, littered with broken marriages, smashed hopes and three children . . . lay the story of how she faces the gas chamber today with icy composure . . . She easily slipped from truancy to highpowered crime. From various sources, including the reports of police and probation officers in San Francisco, where she has a considerable police record, the biography of a bawd who stumbled along the primrose path from being 'very promiscuous sexually' to association with the 'bigtime' crooks she so admired, can be developed in all its sorry detail."

"Considerable police record"? Other than the perjury conviction, Barbara's record was a model of—pardon the expression—chickenshit: low-rent misdemeanors like check-kiting and possession of marijuana. And Barbara had certainly "stumbled" into an association with "bigtime crooks" when she hooked up with Perkins and Santo, but there's no indication she'd done so before—or that she'd "admired" Perkins or Santo or any other "bigtime crook."

The following day, the *Herald-Express* put out a two-column-size close-up of Barbara's lips, with a caption that read "The Lips of the Icy Blonde." The lede announced that "shapely Barbara Graham, the blond iceberg 'lure' in the Mabel Monahan slaying case, today indicated she intends to come up with a few surprises herself next week in her defense at the murder trial already chockfull of sensational surprise evidence."

Utter nonsense. Barbara indicated nothing of the kind—because she couldn't talk to the press, and even if she had, she certainly wouldn't have said she'd come up with any "surprises." She'd maintained her innocence at every bend and turn, and there was no way she'd say anything different now.

But the *Herald-Express* in particular refused to be constrained by any notions of fairness or accuracy. The day Barbara took the stand, the reporter went all out, starting with a graphic punch. They ran a two-column-size close-up of her hands on the front page with a caption that said, "Barbara Graham's hands. They are the hands that cruelly pistol-whipped Mabel Monahan, according to the Prosecution."

Nice touch, adding, "according to the Prosecution," at the end, like an afterthought. The article carried through on theme: "As a matter of fact, her strong hands gripped the arms of the witness chair as she tried to convince the jury that she certainly could not have had any part in the murder. That was the first time that she had displayed the strong fingers which, the state contends, wielded the murder weapon in the senseless murder of Mabel Monahan. She made one mistake. After admitting she was the mother of three children; she crossed the left hand over a shapely thigh and there was no wedding band on the third finger of that hand."

The "mistake" being that she'd revealed she wasn't married though she had three children. Actually, she was still married to Hank Graham. She probably wasn't wearing a ring because the jailers wouldn't let the inmates keep any jewelry. But this, according to the *Herald-Express*, showed Barbara was a killer. Sure, because obviously, being divorced and a mother is well known to be a sign of homicidal tendencies. So, I guess if Barbara *had* worn a wedding ring, this reporter might've decided she hadn't "wielded the murder weapon"?

The article went on,

> She kept her hands tightly knit while she declared in a voice
> that is as metallic as her character and her features, that she

had never seen Baxter Shorter, the missing man. The reason he is missing, according to the state which hopes to send the bronzed Barbara and her co-defendants, Emmett Perkins and Jack Santo, to the last seat in the gas chamber at San Quentin, is because he has been eliminated by one of the unholy trinity or their friends. Barbara Graham wore the same tight-fitting summer weight suit that she has worn during the trial but she did not impress the ladies of the jury, notably Juror No. 5, who goes in for white blouses and a general appearance designed for comfort more than chic. Juror No. 5 even looked down her nose at the woman who potentially could be the most beautiful victim that the gas chamber will ever have claimed. Miss Barbara Graham, when it was apparent that time was running out, kept drubbing the palms of her hands, using up two handkerchiefs in the process. A newspaperman gave her the third, a blanket size comparatively speaking just before Judge Fricke called a recess.

So much to unpack here. First of all, the lack of even a semblance of objectivity, not to mention the gratuitously critical tone of the article, was shocking. And the searingly personal nature of the attacks is stunning. It made me wonder whether this reporter had been one of the pathetic saps who'd followed Barbara to the El Monte gambling house in hopes of a romantic liaison and lost his shirt instead.

As for the supposedly "bronzed" Barbara, a woman who's been incarcerated in the county jail for months sees about as much sun as a mushroom. And it seems highly unlikely the bailiff would allow anyone to get within range to so much as throw her a kiss, let alone pass her a handkerchief. And by the way, what on earth does "a voice as metallic as her character and her features" even mean?

As for the straitlaced "Juror No. 5" in the high-necked blouse who looked down her nose at Barbara, that kind of juror would've been a problem for any female defendant—especially a pretty one. The '50s was a tough time for women. *Misogyny* was not a word anyone knew outside the field of psychology, let alone used, and judging a woman's looks was not only accepted; it was celebrated like a blood sport. The Nielsen ratings for the Miss America, Miss Universe, and Miss World pageants were in the double digits, and the most popular feature of those telecasts was the swimsuit competition, which required women to strut up and down the runway half-naked and in high heels with the camera following every move to make sure the audience—and especially the judges, who had a ringside seat—got a good look from all angles.

This societal acceptance of objectification created an atmosphere of competition. Women were expected to covet and fight for the title of prettiest in the room, and they largely internalized this misogynistic culture. So they were often the harshest critics of their own gender. The young, beautiful, and sexy Barbara was bound to inspire resentment among plainer, less glamorous-looking women like Juror Number 5. I'm sure the prosecution was counting on it. Just as I know for a fact that the prosecutors worried about getting the opposite reaction from the male jurors.

And to that latter point, a few news outlets were more charitable toward Barbara. In fact, the contrast between their own stories about her first day on the witness stand and their past descriptions of her as an "icy blonde" siren with a shockingly cavalier attitude was remarkable.

Painting a very different picture than the *Herald-Express* article's depiction of Barbara's "metallic" features and murderously strong hands, the *Daily News* reported, "Barbara, her blond hair drawn tightly and fastened in a bun in back, lost some of the icy composure that has marked her previous court appearances as she strode quickly to the witness stand when attorney Jack Hardy opened the defense. Her hands were constantly in motion, clutching the microphone in front of her face, grinding handkerchiefs into damp, wrinkled balls. But always she kept her face and her voice under control."

The *Los Angeles Times* coverage was downright sympathetic: "With her hair drawn back into a neat bun and wearing a trim beige-colored suit, Mrs. Graham presented a picture of primness on the witness stand. Her eyes dropped demurely when, in the course of questioning, she admitted indiscretions such as narcotics, working as a shill for a gambling game operated by co-defendant Emmett Perkins and writing bad checks."

The *Valley Times* almost cast her as a victim: "Forlorn but still pretty, Barbara lost herself in the big witness chair as she measured every word which she hopes will save her from death in the gas chamber."

And interestingly, another reporter from the *Herald-Express* had a strikingly different take than his sneeringly critical colleague:

> Blonde Barbara Graham, fear in her eyes and a tremor in her voice, opened her fight for life in the Mabel Monahan murder trial today with a denial that she ever saw the slain woman and a startling confession on the witness stand that she was a gambling shill for her two co-defendants in a floating poker racket game. The icy calm of the pretty mother of three children melted a bit as she walked on high heels to the witness stand in a dead silence. The jammed confines of Superior Judge Charles W. Fricke's court were soundless as she raised her hand to "tell the truth, the whole truth, and nothing but the truth." Within five minutes she had virtually told her life story, entered her denial and declared she wasn't even with the two ex-convicts on trial with her, Emmett Perkins and Jack Santo, the night Mrs. Monahan was bludgeoned and choked to death in her Burbank home last March 9. Black circles ringed her eyes and she looked hesitantly at the jury only once or twice in her recitation. Her lips trembled and her voice came low and soft, barely audible. Her hands nervously clutched at the microphone.

I noticed that no other reporter commented on Barbara's "metallic" voice and character as described by the reporter for the *Herald-Express* the day before.

This marked disparity between articles exposes a stunning degree of subjectivity, distortion, and cynical manipulation that deprives truth-seeking readers of any reliable source to which they could turn. The only thing that mattered was selling newspapers, and the only way to outsell the competition was by grabbing the public's attention with flamboyant claims and floridly graphic descriptions. No newspaper that reported "the facts, ma'am, just the facts" could survive. Although I think reporters today are a little less reckless, the reliance on exaggeration and sensationalism in the pursuit of patronage is still very much in evidence in the clickbait stories that are flung online with little to no concern for accuracy and a vigorous rejection of nuance.

So to put it mildly, taking the witness stand was no easy thing for Barbara. Hardy had her step through her life history with little embellishment, hitting the highlights—or rather, the lowlights—in just enough detail to show she wasn't trying to hide or whitewash her less-than-stellar past. As Ralph Waldo Emerson put it, "In skating over thin ice, our safety is in our speed." A smart way to create an impression of honesty without harping on the downsides of her mistakes and transgressions. Hardy had Barbara begin with a thumbnail sketch of her life, acknowledging her brushes with the law along the way and ending with the description of how she'd met Perkins in San Francisco in 1950 and become his shill in the gambling house he ran in El Monte. She met Santo in that gambling house in 1952 or 1953.

Then they moved on to the alibi. Again, Hardy made a wise strategic choice. He had Barbara give her alibi as much specificity as possible without piling on details that could later be used to trip her up. Barbara said she had no knowledge of the Mabel Monahan murder, and that when she'd previously been asked about her whereabouts, she hadn't been able to remember where she was because nothing spectacular had happened.

But now, she remembered that on the evening of March 9, she'd been at home with her husband, Hank, and they'd been fighting. Nothing unusual for them because she was upset that he wasn't working or even looking for work. Hank had declared he was leaving and started putting clothes into the trunk of his car. A friend named Croff came over to help him move out. Barbara and Hank continued to fight, and at one point, Hank threw a cologne bottle at her, which hit her on the knee and broke. That made the baby cry and made the whole house smell. They continued to fight throughout the night as Hank packed his things.

Her husband came and went in the next few days, but Barbara had had enough. She asked Perkins to help her move out, and he temporarily settled her in the El Monte house. In early April, Perkins heard John True had implicated him in the Monahan murder, so they moved to the Ambassador Hotel. Barbara went with him because she had nowhere else to go—the rent on her own house was only paid up until April 1. Not long after that, she read in the papers that she, too, had been implicated in the murder. Barbara was still on probation for her perjury conviction, and she'd written some bad checks, so she needed to keep a low profile. But she wound up getting arrested on May 4 for those forgery charges and taken to the county jail.

When she later met with Hardy and said she didn't know where she'd been on the night of the murder, he'd explained the importance of an alibi and finding witnesses who could corroborate her whereabouts. He told her on more than one occasion that if she told the jury she couldn't remember, they'd send her to the gas chamber. She at first thought she'd been with a man named Logan, but he'd said he only saw her on March 10. At that point, Barbara still hadn't been able to remember anything about the night of March 9 and hadn't recalled the fight with Hank until very recently.

So Barbara's testimony about her alibi had its strengths and weaknesses: the strength lay in the fact that she'd always been uncertain of her whereabouts—that although she'd initially thought she might've been with Logan, she'd always had the lingering belief that it was more likely she'd been at home with her husband; the weakness lay in her sudden recovery of the memory of a particularly heated fight they'd had that night. That was about as good as it was going to get. If her husband or Croff could back her up, it'd help. But prospects that the former might come through seemed dim. Hank was an addict with a memory about as reliable as a politician's promise. And Croff . . . who knew? He was Hank's buddy, and as they say, birds of a feather . . . Hardy moved on to the much more difficult, and likely more intriguing, subject for the jury: Donna Prow.

Barbara first met Donna when she approached Barbara's cell and slipped her some candy through the bars along with a note that said, "Here is some candy, and if you need anything else—I heard that you didn't have anything—let me know; and please don't take this the wrong way." Shortly after that, Donna wrote her another note saying her sister, who was a waitress, said she'd waited on Barbara at a restaurant in Hollywood and again asked if Barbara "needed anything." Barbara wrote back that she didn't recognize the sister's name and told Donna to keep her money. In spite of Barbara's lack of interest, Donna wrote to her again and sent her money and a couple of things she'd knitted. Barbara testified, "I would see her as I passed into the dining room on the way to breakfast and on the way back from dinner at night. She would always speak to me, and it was generally trying to build up a friendship, you might say."

After that point, Donna's notes became more "serious." She told Barbara that she liked her "very much" and that she wanted to help Barbara. She realized people made "mistakes" and asked how Barbara's case was coming along. They started exchanging notes daily. Barbara testified that they'd write "little insignificant things about the jail and maybe about the girls; and then [Donna] would—now and then she would mention my case and would say something about mistakes and things like that; and it didn't dawn on me at first that she was leading up to anything. And I had written and I told her, I says, well mistakes or not, I said I'm innocent of this thing." Donna wrote back saying she was going to knit some stockings for her and that she'd like to knit a dress for Barbara to wear at trial.

Barbara wrote back that she didn't need her help, because she was innocent and that she was sure things would work out. In whispered conversations during their time in the TV room—the only time they could talk in person—she again told Donna she was innocent, that she was never at the scene of the crime, and although she couldn't prove that, she believed it would all work out somehow. Barbara admitted she was a little puzzled by Donna's repeated offers, but she merely thought "it was kind of her."

But Donna was insistent, and during their TV room time, she suggested she could "do something" for Barbara, but Barbara put her off, saying, "Well, let's not talk now. I would rather watch television." She testified that "it didn't strike me at the time . . . since all this come up, how she was always so insistent upon talking. Then—but all along she was putting in little, you might say, insinuations that she could help me."

This back and forth went on for almost a month, with Donna pushing and Barbara pushing back, but then Barbara opted out of the trustee line. Barbara and Donna had both been trustees, an elevated status that gave inmates more freedom and more opportunity for personal contact. But it came with a heavier workload that exhausted Barbara. When she dropped out, their opportunities for personal contact dwindled to the point that notes were practically their only source of contact.

Barbara, knowing she'd get disciplined if she was spotted with notes, threw Donna's away. Donna kept Barbara's notes—at least, *some* of them—and passed them along to Lieutenant Coveney. Whether Barbara knew that at the time she testified isn't clear, though based on the way the prosecution operated, I'd guess she didn't.

As time passed and the trial date drew closer, Donna's notes grew more persistent as she stepped up her campaign to "help" or "do something" for Barbara. The truth—though Barbara clearly didn't know it—was that by early August, Donna was starting to sweat. Time was running out. Jury selection was due to start on August 14, 1953. Coveney was pressing her to get Barbara to buy into the fake-alibi scheme. But now Barbara was also feeling the pressure. Hardy visited her on August 5, and again pressed her to come up with witnesses who could give her an alibi, but she still had no memory of where she'd been on the night of the murder. When Barbara told Donna what the lawyer had said, Donna was ready with the solution. She had a connection, someone from the underworld named "Vince."

Barbara testified, "This Vince she was telling me about, she said he was the head of Tiny Naylor's or some such thing. I think that is a restaurant. That he had a friend that would help me if I could not remember where I was; and she said something about, well, 'If you are innocent, I'd hate to see anything happen to you'; and at the time I told her—in fact, I think I wrote it. I says, 'Well, things look kind of bad for me because I just can't prove where I was. I can't remember. My attorney says if I don't have sort of support, I would probably go to the gas chamber, because people—well, just up here without any proof, it looks funny.'"

Barbara testified that Donna wrote back saying she "definitely could get in touch with this party if I wanted her to, that she could furnish the money until I got out—she was coming into some sort of an inheritance or something when she was 21—and she said that she and this Vince would guarantee the money, she would go good for it if I wanted some help, someone to come on the witness stand for me." Barbara, frightened as she was by the dire warnings of her lawyer, was still "leery" of the idea: "I knew it wasn't right, I myself had gone up as a witness once before and I knew how wrong it was; and I know that you can't get away with things like that. I was just frantic."

Still, Barbara came up with the password for their meeting: "Like water I come, and like the wind I go." But on the morning of her meeting with Sirianni, she continued to have serious misgivings. Donna— the ever-faithful supporter—reassured her: "I know Sam personally.

He is a good friend of mine, and he will be all right. You can tell him anything." Barbara wrote back, saying that she was still afraid, but she'd take a chance.

Barbara's testimony about her meetings with Sirianni largely tracked what he'd said. But she made it very clear that the only reason she'd admitted to being with Santo and Perkins on the night of the murder was because he'd threatened to back out. Sirianni was her "last chance," and "he gave me the impression that if there were people who had seen me, that he was going to back right out and leave me. So I thought, well, the only way I can make him think that no one has seen me is to say that I was with them. Then that way maybe he will stay with me." For that same reason, she'd told him Baxter Shorter would never show up. She denied ever having met Shorter, but she'd read that he'd been kidnapped and hadn't been seen since, so she surmised he'd been killed.

Hardy then had Barbara recount how, on August 12, she'd told him that she'd found an alibi witness and that a man named Sam Sirianni would call him that day. But he never did. And he still hadn't made contact by the day the trial started, on August 14, 1953. It looked like her only alibi witness had quit on her. But five days later, after she'd fallen down the stairs on her way to court, she had time to think as she was lying in her hospital bed, and she'd remembered that there might be a witness who could give her an honest alibi. Her neighbor's young daughter, Corrine Perez, who lived in the duplex next door. She could always hear what was going on in Barbara's apartment. The walls were thin, and the fights between Barbara and Hank were loud. When Hardy came to visit Barbara in the hospital, she told him to see if Corrine remembered hearing them shouting that night. Barbara had also remembered that Hank's friend, William Croff, had come to help him move out around that same time.

At last, Barbara had come up with a real alibi. Maybe. It would certainly have helped if she'd thought of it sooner—before trying to dream up a false alibi with Sirianni. Now, it was a much more challenging proposition: in order to convince the jury this alibi was the truth, she'd have to convince them she'd only gone along with the Sirianni gambit out of desperation. It was a lot to hope for, but it wasn't impossible. Sirianni had admitted he'd pressured Barbara with threats to back out of the deal if she didn't say she'd been with Santo and Perkins. And Hardy had Barbara recount how he himself had repeatedly warned her of the dire consequences if she didn't give him the name of a witness who could support her alibi.

Under Hardy's questioning, a door had opened to the possibility of Barbara's acquittal. But now, it was the prosecution's turn. The smart move for Barbara would've been to speak softly and slowly, look nervous—even a little frightened—and let the prosecutor come off as a bully. Whether Hardy and Wolfe tried to give her that advice, I don't know. Whether it would've mattered even if they did . . . seems unlikely.

Since J. Miller Leavy had been the architect of the trap that ensnared Barbara in the false-alibi plot, he'd won the right to do the cross-examination. He knew—as did everyone—that his questioning of the star of this trial would be the most dramatic moment yet. He strode up to the podium, loaded for bear, and went straight at Barbara's recently recovered memory of her whereabouts on the night of March 9, 1953:

Leavy: "Was it last week, the first time that you suddenly remembered where you were on the night of March the 9th of this year?"

Barbara: "Would you explain what you mean by 'suddenly'?"

The back-and-forth went on for some time as Leavy came at Barbara again and again in an effort to force her to admit that she'd known when the murder occurred all along and yet had only realized where she'd been within the past week or so. But Barbara wouldn't be strong-armed into giving him the answers he wanted, and at one point, in frustration, he asked, "Well, was last week the first time you thought back and were able to remember where you were on the night of March the 9th? You're hesitating."

Barbara answered, "I am trying to think."

Leavy's editorial about Barbara's hesitation provoked Hardy to object, "Well, just a moment. Now, I submit the witness is certainly permitted to hesitate without any comment of the district attorney. It is self-evident whether she hesitated or not. She is entitled to think her thoughts." The judge—as he often did—pushed aside Hardy's objection, saying the jury would decide if Barbara had hesitated. To which Hardy replied, "I think the courtesy to the witness requires a little better treatment than that."

Indeed it does. Leavy might've been permitted to make a comment, such as, "Let the record reflect the witness has hesitated." Many judges wouldn't even allow that and might well sustain Hardy's objection, telling the jury, "Folks, it's up to you to decide whether you think she hesitated." But directly accusing a witness of trying to avoid or delay an answer simply because they hesitated is a form of badgering the witness.

It wasn't a huge moment, but it was prophetic, setting the stage right off the bat for one of the most confrontational and aggressive cross-examinations I've ever seen by a prosecutor. Or, as the press would call it, "scathing questioning" and "slashing cross examination." This could've worked to Barbara's benefit if she'd been able to show a touch of fear, let her voice tremble a bit, and show the jury that this powerful, experienced prosecutor was beating up on a vulnerable woman. Juries don't mind it when cops or other professional witnesses get a tough grilling, but average citizens—and especially women—are a different matter. It comes across as bullying, and juries seldom go for that.

But after a life of hard knocks, Barbara had grown her own set of brass balls, and for much of Leavy's relentless—and often caustic—cross-examination, she held her own. She didn't have the schooling or the training Leavy did, but Barbara was no dummy, and she wasn't about to be pushed around. Still, she wasn't made of steel, and at times, she broke down under the strain.

After hammering Barbara over and over again about her faulty memory and failing to shake her testimony that she'd been at home with her husband, Leavy moved on to what—according to my research—had been one of his favorite tactics.

Reminding Barbara that prior to trial, she'd been called to testify before the grand jury, he pointed to the transcript of the hearing and said, "On June the 9th of this year, when Mr. Alexander was questioning you, did you give this answer to this question: 'Do you know where you were on March 9, 1953?'" Leavy then read Barbara's answer: "I refuse to answer on the grounds it might incriminate me."

Leavy asked, "Did you give that answer to that question at that time and place?"

Hardy's cocounsel, Benjamin Wolfe, strenuously objected, stating that this use of Barbara's lawful right to exercise "her privilege under the California Constitution . . . is incompetent, irrelevant, and immaterial."

The defense established that Barbara had not asked to testify before the grand jury—she'd been compelled to take the stand. And she'd been advised by Alexander that "any testimony you may give will have to be free and voluntary on your part; that if you refuse to answer you may do so on constitutional ground, such as it may tend to incriminate you."

Barbara never voluntarily consented to testify before the grand jury, and when Alexander questioned her, she stated she did not want to answer any further questions, but he continued to question her anyway. Barbara then objected and said she hadn't had time to confer with her attorney. At that point, the district attorney himself, Ernie Roll, advised her that the only ground upon which she could refuse to answer questions was by asserting her right against self-incrimination and dictated the language she'd need to use. Barbara then repeated verbatim what he'd said, stating, "I refuse to answer the question on the ground the testimony might tend to incriminate me." Now, Leavy was trying to use her invocation of her Fifth Amendment rights as proof of her guilt.

After considerable legal argument, Judge Fricke overruled Wolfe's objection.

Leavy repeated the question, "What is your answer?"

Barbara replied, "Did I give that answer? Yes I did."

Leavy then repeated this show five times, reading each question posed to Barbara at the grand jury hearing regarding her whereabouts on the night of March 9, 1953, and each time repeating Barbara's answer in which she invoked her Fifth Amendment right against self-incrimination.

This tactic, called the "comment rule," had been banned in federal courts in 1893 (*Wilson v. United States* (1893) 149 US 60). But it was still allowed in state courts, and specifically, in California, until 1965, when the United States Supreme Court declared the comment rule must also be prohibited in all state courts as a violation of a defendant's Fifth Amendment rights in the landmark decision *Griffin v. California* (1965) 380 US 609. In strong language, the high court denounced the practice, stating that it was "a remnant of the 'inquisitorial system of criminal justice'" and "a penalty imposed by courts for exercising a constitutional privilege. It cuts down on the privilege by making its assertion costly."

The counterargument in favor of preserving the comment rule was that it was natural to infer guilt when a defendant refuses to answer a question that only asks for information he should know. But to that claim, the court responded, "What the jury may infer, given no help from the court, is one thing. What it may infer when the court solemnizes the silence of the accused into evidence against him is quite another." In so holding, the court quoted from *Wilson v. United States*, the earlier Supreme Court decision in 1893, that outlawed the "comment rule" in federal trials. In that case, the court explained why it was constitutionally unfair to ask the jury to infer guilt from a defendant's silence: "It is not every one who can safely venture on the witness stand, though entirely innocent of the charge against him. Excessive timidity, nervousness when facing others and attempting to explain transactions of a suspicious character, and offences charged against him, will often confuse and embarrass him to such a degree as to increase, rather than remove, prejudices against him. It is not every one, however honest, who would, therefore, willingly be placed on the witness stand."

This is a truism known to all defense counsel.

But *Griffin* hadn't yet been decided at the time of Barbara's trial, so Leavy was allowed to flog Barbara with her invocation of her Fifth Amendment rights again and again. Much as I hated it, I got that he was only doing what the law allowed back then. But prosecutors in particular have to think a thousand yards ahead. Just because you can doesn't mean you should. It's a lesson I learned the hard way.

I was prosecuting a truly heinous child molester. Although I'd only been able to file charges for one ten-year-old victim, I'd later learned that there was another little girl, this one just nine years old, who'd also been a victim of that predator. She didn't want to come forward, but she did give a statement—yet another harrowing tale of abuse very similar to the one my witness had told. I turned over the statement to the defense with the warning that I might ask permission to let her testify if she changed her mind. Evidence of uncharged crimes has legal restrictions, and although I thought her testimony would probably be admissible, I'd seen cases reversed on appeal for improperly allowing that evidence, so I decided I'd only chance it if my witness got too shaky. But my witness came through with flying colors. I decided I could spare at least one little girl the trauma of taking the witness stand and having to face that monster. I rested my case without calling the other victim.

Then, the defendant testified on his own behalf. Predictably, he denied having molested the victim. But his attorney took it one step further and ended his examination in a booming voice with the question: "Have you ever molested a child in your life?" The defendant sat up straight and answered firmly, "No, never."

I sat there, stunned. Did he just say what I think he said? I asked the court reporter to read back the exchange. "No need!" thundered the attorney. "I'll ask it again." He then proceeded to ask the same question—with the same oratorical flair as before—and the defendant answered in the same triumphant voice: "No, I have never molested a child in my life."

I didn't even realize I'd been holding my breath until it sank all the way in: the defense had just handed me the right to call the other victim on a silver platter. I wouldn't need to jump through any legal hoops to justify the admission of her testimony now. This was a bright-line issue. I could call her to testify as direct impeachment of the defendant's lie.

When it was time for rebuttal, I put the other little victim on the stand. As long as I live, I will never forget the way her jaw trembled as she testified with her eyes trained on me—as I'd recommended—and described with heartbreaking detail what he'd done to her. The memory is so searing I tear up every time I think of it. The defendant got convicted after one of the shortest jury deliberations I'd ever seen.

One year later, I got the call. The court of appeal had issued its opinion. They'd reversed the defendant's conviction for ineffective assistance of counsel. The court held that no reasonably competent attorney, knowing the prosecutor had another victim in the wings, would have opened his client up to such damaging impeachment. I was devastated as I wondered what I was going to say to the victims. How do you explain to these brave little children that this was justice? That even though everyone believed what they'd said, their tormentor might go free?

The reversal allowed me to retry the defendant, but the little girls couldn't go through that ordeal again, and I didn't blame them. Ultimately, the defendant pleaded guilty to a lesser charge, a charge that required him to register as a sex offender. It was cold comfort. I could only hope he'd get busted for failure to register and get locked up as soon as possible, because I knew he'd never stop abusing children.

I'd learned my lesson. Just because you can doesn't mean you should. Leavy had to know he was pushing the envelope by hammering Barbara with her invocation of the Fifth Amendment. Because even then, there was plenty of talk that the legality of the "comment rule" was coming into serious question. But it seemed typical of Leavy to go for the jugular with extreme tactics. This was just one more example. And at least it was technically legal—unlike the deliberate effort to hide Donna Prow.

Leavy then moved on to ask Barbara whether she remembered her first cellmate in the County Jail after she'd been arrested. Did the name Shirley Olson ring a bell? It didn't. In fact, at first, when Leavy showed Barbara her photograph, she still didn't recognize the woman. Then she remembered that Olson was always talking about all the robberies she'd committed and that Olson used to follow her around all the time. Barbara thought Olson was odd and didn't trust her. She certainly never talked to her about the case. Leavy then read statements Olson claimed Barbara had made to her.

Leavy: "Did you tell this Shirley Olson the only thing that had you worried was that if certain things come to light you'll be a cinch for first degree? Did you make that statement?"

Barbara: "Definitely not . . . I never made that statement to anyone."

Leavy then asked whether an inmate said it'd been reported in the newspapers that Santo had been picked up, and that Barbara had remarked, "'Jesus, maybe I'll be smelling that cyanide yet.' Did you make that statement?"

Barbara: "I hardly think so."

Leavy: "Did you make the statement . . . that you were worried, 'because if anything goes wrong and certain facts come to light, I'm a cinch for cyanide'?"

Barbara: "I don't think I ever said a thing like that, Mr. Leavy. Most of our conversation was pretty one-sided. In fact, I would have to ask her to be quiet so I could go to sleep." (It was actually a twisted—and deliberately more incriminating—version of what she said. Barbara would later tell a reporter she said, "I'm a cinch for cyanide if I don't get an alibi.")

Asked how long Olson had been in the cell with her, Barbara couldn't remember, but she did remember that Olson had said she was a fugitive from Utah, or "some state up there." Leavy then cut in, asking, "You thought she was a prisoner, didn't you?"

Barbara snapped back: "Just a minute please. May I finish?"

Leavy backed down. "I beg your pardon."

Barbara then explained that Olson had nothing on her property slip, which was strange, and that she was always following her around, which made her feel that Olson was "put there on purpose."

Leavy posed other questions about statements Barbara had supposedly made to Olson, one of which was a boastful claim: "You only know about the checks and what the papers said about the murder and kidnapping, but I'll tell you something tonight that'll prove just how big this all is." Barbara categorically denied having said that: "No, I never had that much conversation with that girl."

Leavy: "Your answer to my question is 'No'?"

Barbara: "Is 'No.'"

What the big "something" was that Barbara had supposedly promised to tell her was never revealed. And Barbara likewise denied making any of the other incriminating statements the mysterious Olson had attributed to her. But Leavy wouldn't let it go, and his relentless efforts to shore up Olson's credibility veered so deeply into the minutiae of the times, dates, and places where they'd supposedly interacted even the prosecution-minded Judge Fricke eventually sustained defense objections to Leavy's questioning as irrelevant and immaterial.

So, of course, Shirley Olson was a cop. And a truly lousy undercover operator if Barbara's description of her "moves" is to be believed. Leavy later called her to the stand on rebuttal, where she repeated the claims about statements Barbara had supposedly made during the five days she spent in the cell with her.

I obviously wasn't in the courtroom when she testified, but based on the transcripts of her testimony, she didn't come off as particularly credible. The statements she attributed to Barbara were so arch and contrived, they felt like they'd been lifted out of a cheap '50s detective novel. And unlike Sirianni, she hadn't worn a wire. She claimed to have taken notes to memorialize what Barbara said, but she couldn't do it while Barbara was around, so the notes weren't even contemporaneous. It occurred to me there were other forces in play here. It was 1953, female cops were a rarity, and the few who made it were under a hell of a lot of pressure to deliver. Olson needed to show she'd managed to get something good out of Barbara or she'd be back to making coffee. So I can imagine she did a little embroidering to show she'd made a big score. Just a thought. In any case, if I'd been on the jury, I'd have taken her testimony off the table.

But to me, what was most notable about Olson's testimony was what Barbara *didn't* say: she never once mentioned a worry about not having an alibi, nor did she mention any desire to find a person who could give her one. Nor did Olson ever say Barbara had expressly admitted being involved in the Monahan murder. In fact, the only crimes she did admit to were writing bad checks.

Leavy then moved on to what he'd clearly planned as the centerpiece of his cross-examination: Barbara's liaison with Donna Prow.

CHAPTER FIFTEEN

It was a twofer for the prosecution. Barbara's willingness to set up a false alibi plus the fact that she had a romantic relationship with a woman gave Leavy all he could possibly hope for: evidence that not only showed Barbara's willingness to lie and her consciousness of guilt but also showed her to be a "sexual deviant." If anything, Barbara was more likely bisexual than a lesbian, but no one back then drew a distinction between the two. There was zero tolerance for any kind of same-sex liaison. It branded her on a purely personal level as a subhuman, and that—coupled with her criminal past—was bound to alienate the jury. But even if the jury was inclined to take a charitable view of Barbara's involvement with Donna Prow, there was a horde of reporters who were definitely not so inclined. The ugly yellow journalism then in vogue had the power to drive public opinion, and that in turn put pressure on the jurors to fall in line. What the press condemned, the public condemned, and the jury couldn't help but feel it. This alone ensured that the deck was stacked against Barbara.

So her romantic connection to Donna Prow was a boon to the prosecution. Even better, the proof was in Barbara's own handwriting. And Leavy wielded those letters like a battering ram.

He started with the letter in which Barbara suggested they use the password that was the quote from Omar Khayyam's *Rubaiyat* and made a point of asking, "Did you end the letter here, 'Nite for now, stay as sweet and pretty as you always are. I'll be thinking of you. Love'?"

Barbara, faced with the actual letter, confirmed that she had. He then homed in on the picture he wanted to paint for the jury:

Leavy: "Weren't you attempting to gain Donna's confidence?"

Barbara: "Well, she had already written to me."

Leavy: "Were you attempting to gain Donna's confidence?"

Barbara: "Well, how do you mean?"

Leavy: "You answer the question. If you can't understand it, you say so and I will reframe it."

Barbara: "Would you reframe it, please?"

Leavy: "Were you attempting to get Donna to do anything for you?"

Barbara: "No. She had already put herself at my disposal."

Leavy: "And were you willing to further her willingness?"

Barbara: "I don't know how to explain that."

Leavy: "Explain it any way you believe you can, if you can."

Barbara: "Well, the way she presented herself to me, she was so aggressive that I didn't have to further anything, it was laid there for me if I wanted it."

Leavy: "Did you tell her you didn't want it?"

Barbara: "Didn't want what?"

Leavy: "Her help."

Barbara: "Yes, I told her many times."

Leavy was hoping to show that Barbara the seductress had used her wiles to ingratiate herself with Donna so she could persuade Donna to give her a false alibi. If he could get the jury to buy that scenario, it'd keep the jury from seeing the truth: that Donna had been the seductress, the one who'd initiated the relationship, and the one who'd originated—and then pushed—the idea of putting on a false alibi.

But the letter he'd just read said only that a meeting to set up an alibi had already been arranged. And while it showed a romantic relationship between the women, it offered no basis to believe Leavy's spin that Barbara was the temptress-spider who'd lured the sweet, naive Donna into her web.

He ended the court session that day by reading the letter Barbara wrote after her last meeting with Sirianni. Barbara said he'd promised to call her lawyer right after their meeting, but he hadn't come through. Leavy asked if she'd written the following: "And although we had everything all set he refused to talk with [my attorneys] about anything and said he would be out of town until Tuesday."

Barbara: "That is correct."

Leavy: "So you went on to say in writing to Donna—you called "Baby doll," is that right?"

Barbara: "Yes, it is."

Leavy: "You say then, ' . . . if he backs out now I will be left high and dry.' Is that right?"

Barbara: "That is correct."

Leavy: "Didn't you go on to say, 'Oh well, then, I know for sure now that the DA is really out for blood. We won't be needing S [Sirianni] for quite a few days but I hope he doesn't fail us.' Did you say that?"

Barbara: "Yes."

Leavy: "Then did you say, 'If he does, guess I'll just have to sit up there and look pretty.' Is that right?"

Barbara: "Well, that was just conversation with her."

Leavy: "Did you write that?"

Barbara: "Yes."

It was—as they say—like shooting fish in a barrel. How necessary it all was is a different matter. Sirianni had already testified and played a recording that left no question about the fact that she'd hired him to give her a false alibi. And in case that wasn't enough, she'd just admitted it on the witness stand when being questioned by her lawyer. So was it simply a matter of overproving the point that she'd agreed to concoct a fake alibi? Or was it an effort to drive home the romantic nature of Barbara's relationship with Donna?

If it was the latter, the press definitely got the point—as Leavy no doubt intended. The *Valley Times* ran with the front-page headline—above the fold, no less—"Jail Love Notes Thaw 'Icy' Blonde." The article stated that "news of the sensational notes leaked out to a long line of spectators in the hallway and caused hub-bub among the crowd hoping to get in on the trial later in the day." The *Daily News* reported that Barbara's "passionate nature" only surfaced when Leavy questioned her about "the pretty prisoner," Donna Prow, as Barbara insisted she'd only gone along with the false-alibi scheme because she was feeling "kind of panicky . . . kind of desperate." And the *San Francisco Examiner* observed that the sight of her notes to Donna Prow "seemed to weaken her cool composure."

Nearly all the articles quoted the love notes verbatim, and at length. This was one time the reporters didn't bother to embellish the story. They didn't need to. The words themselves were enough to do the job.

The next day, Leavy detoured from the letters and embarked on a meandering cross-examination regarding what newspaper articles Barbara had read about the kidnapping of Baxter Shorter and her movements between the time she left the house in El Monte and arrived at the converted apartment in Lynwood, where she was arrested.

But he came back to the letters with an abrupt turn, pointing to a drawing: "And is the figure which is drawn on there yours?"

Barbara: "Yes."

Leavy: "What is that, a candy cane?"

Barbara: "Yes, it is."

Leavy: "What does it say up above; 'Too much, huh'? Is that right?"

Barbara: "That's what it says on the paper."

Leavy: "What is this figure that appears partway down towards some other writing? Is that intended to be a candy cane?"

Barbara: "It is."

Leavy: "And the rest is in quotes: 'Sweet Candy Pants'; is that right?"

Barbara: "It is."

Leavy: "You meant Donna when you said, 'Sweet Candy Pants,' and wrote what you did there; didn't you?"

Barbara: "It was not meant as her name, no."

The relevance of that drawing and cutesy nickname to any actual issue in the case was nil. But it served two purposes: it underlined the lesbian affair, and it made Barbara seem frivolous and unconcerned. Point being: to show Barbara wasn't driven to go for a false alibi out of sheer desperation—she was just inclined to do so because she was a criminal who'd always choose to lie and cheat given the chance.

Leavy moved on to ask whether Donna had questioned her about Baxter Shorter. Barbara couldn't remember but thought she might have. He then presented another letter she'd written on August 4, 1953, which was a few days before she'd met Sirianni.

Leavy: "You said, 'And honey, you do not have to worry about that—' and you underline—'other party showing because it won't happen—' and you underlined that, and 'won't happen' is underlined three times, is that right?"

Barbara: "Yes it is."

Leavy: "Who did you have reference to when you said, 'Don't worry about the other party showing because it won't happen'?"

Barbara: "Offhand, I can't remember."

Leavy: "Not Baxter Shorter, of course?"

Barbara: "It could have been. Have you ever been desperate! Do you know what it is!"

Leavy: "Was it or was it not Baxter Shorter?"

Barbara: "I don't know offhand. It probably was."

The heated exchange was—of course—featured in the press. Up to that point, the press had said that Barbara, although clearly nervous, had managed to remain fairly composed. But now, the hours of grilling had taken their toll. She finally lost her composure. The *Los Angeles Times* reported, "She gave vent to emotional outbursts for the first time in bitter exchanges with Deputy District Attorney J. Miller Leavy. Her eyes appeared damp, though no tears flowed." Barbara's outburst expressing her anguish was too real to doubt—even by a press that'd usually viewed her with a jaundiced eye. And it flared up again when Leavy pressed her to admit that she'd referred to Sirianni in another letter:

Leavy: "Sam Sirianni was the man you hoped would see you and he would either arrange with you or go to your lawyers and for you to come up here and give false testimony, is that right?"

Barbara: "It was false, I admit that."

Leavy: "That was your plan at the time you wrote this letter, is that right?"

Barbara: "Yes, it was. Have you ever been in a position like that?"

Leavy: "You can't ask me questions, Mrs. Graham."

Barbara: "I think if you were that desperate, you might do the same thing."

At Leavy's request, that answer was stricken.

These outbursts told Leavy he'd drawn blood. Barbara's self-control was rapidly crumbling. He got her to admit that even by her own account, she'd lied repeatedly: she'd lied to her lawyer by telling him she'd been with Sirianni that night, and she'd lied to Sirianni when she told him she'd been with Santo and Perkins—though only because she was afraid he'd refuse to testify. It was a classic "Were you lying then or are you lying now?" This was certainly fair game. It was a weak spot in Barbara's story, and any prosecutor who missed the opportunity to go after it would be incompetent. Barbara could claim desperation drove her to make the deal with Sirianni, but she couldn't deny that her story showed she'd lied to everyone involved.

But Leavy then went in for a sucker punch with yet another letter to Donna. Leavy—as required—showed it to her before beginning to question her about it. Barbara saw that it was a love letter.

Leavy: "You told Donna at this time—"

Barbara: "Mr. Leavy, do you have to read that?"

Leavy, ignoring her plea, plowed on.

Leavy: "This was before Sam first visited you on August 7th, isn't it?"

Barbara: "This could have been written any time from the time I started to write to her."

Leavy: "You told Donna, whenever you wrote this letter: 'Your note was so sweet, honey. I do love you, but I want you to be very sure of your feelings as I wouldn't want to start something I couldn't finish. You are a very lovely and desirable woman, sweetheart, and I want you very much. I know how sweet you would be. Maybe one of these days I will be able to show you how I love you. If the time does come, I am sure I can make you happy.' Did you write that to Donna?"

Barbara: "I did."

Leavy: "Were you doing that to encourage or further her help?"

Barbara: "No, Mr. Leavy, I didn't. She wrote to me thusly first, and there is so little affection or anything up there as it is, that you kind of just—"

Leavy: "Did you mean what you said, as I read in the letter you wrote to Donna?"

Barbara: "I might have at the time."

This exchange in particular—from the moment Barbara pleaded, "Mr. Leavy, do you have to read that?"—made my stomach clench. I thought, *Stop it. Just stop it.* This was overkill. Now, Leavy was simply humiliating her for the fun of it.

Leavy's only legally relevant use for these letters was to show that Barbara had deliberately seduced Donna to enlist her help in cooking up a false alibi. But Barbara had repeatedly made it clear that she hadn't needed to do any coaxing. Donna came on to her, not the other way around. And in any case he'd long since beaten that horse to death. Either the jury bought his story or they didn't. The persistent brandishing of love letters that offered no new information about who'd seduced whom was an ugly and obvious effort to turn the jury—and the public—against Barbara.

What maddened me even more was the fact that by this time Leavy knew full well that Donna had already bragged to the press about how she'd pursued Barbara in order to win her trust. So whatever Leavy might've initially believed about who was the driving force in the relationship, by the time Barbara took the stand, he certainly knew he'd been wrong. Donna had been the instigator all along, not Barbara. But Leavy also knew that unless Hardy could put Donna on the stand, he'd never get to present her boasts to the jury. Her statements to the press were hearsay and therefore inadmissible.

Leavy next pivoted to questions about what Barbara knew of her husband's whereabouts. A neat little segue to remind the jury that while she was playing footsie with Donna, she was still a married woman. I'm not sure a jury in today's world would've cared, but back in 1953, they sure did.

Barbara said her last contact with Hank was sometime after March 10, when he moved out and went to stay in a hotel. Leavy asked whether she'd written to her husband after she got arrested, and she said she had. She'd written to him on May 19. Did she ask him in that letter if he remembered where they'd been on the night of the murder? Barbara didn't believe she had. She'd only written to him that one time, and he never wrote back. When she tried to find him, his mother said he'd left town. But Barbara had always believed she'd been home on the night of the murder.

Leavy produced the May 19 letter, which had been turned over to the cops by her husband. Leavy's intent was to show that she hadn't bothered to ask in that letter whether her husband could remember where they were on March 9. And that—Leavy believed—was evidence that she knew he wouldn't give her an alibi. Fair enough. By that I mean, it was at least a valid legal point. If she thought she'd been at home, fighting with him, it would've been logical for her to ask whether he remembered that.

But the problem with that logic—as that letter plainly revealed—was that at the time she wrote it, Barbara had only been formally arrested on check-kiting charges and she'd written that she was sure she'd never get charged with the Monahan murder. Leavy showed her the letter, but when Hardy asked him to go ahead and read it to the jury, he refused, saying, "I don't care to take the time."

Well, of course he didn't. Because if he read the letter, the jury would see very clearly that it offered no basis for the belief that she didn't ask her husband where they'd been on March 9 because she knew they hadn't been at home together.

The letter, as later read to the jury by Hardy during redirect examination, said in relevant part:

"Hi hon. Would have written sooner but circumstances prevented it. Anyway I'm as well as can be expected in here. Things are working out nicely, as you must know by now the murder charges here has been dropped. Burbank still has a hold for suspicion of murder but it is a formality. My attorney was up again last night [the attorney was Patrick Cooney at that time] and brought very good news. He is going to try to get Burbank to drop the charge so I can bail out . . . I bet you were really surprised to read all those terrible things that were said about me but you know that I'm innocent and could never commit the horrible atrocities. They dropped charges against Jack and as I said before the only thing is the checks."

Clearly, at the time she wrote that letter, she had no idea she needed an alibi.

Leavy then pivoted back to another letter to Donna. This one was written on August 5, 1953, just two days before Barbara met with Sirianni. As Leavy proposed to read it, Hardy remarked, "I understand you said for the interests of time you didn't want to read the letters." Leavy—now busted for cherry-picking only the incriminating evidence—said, "I didn't want to read the [May 19 letter to her husband]. I am allowed to conduct my cross examination as long as it is proper as the Court sees fit."

Well, the short answer is yes. You do get to present the evidence in the order and manner you choose as long as the judge doesn't stop you. The problem with that MO is the judge doesn't see the evidence until the prosecutor decides to show it to the jury. So Judge Fricke didn't know what was in that letter. He couldn't know that Leavy had deliberately prevented the jury from seeing that Barbara had no reason to raise the subject of an alibi with her husband at that point. Now, even if he had known, Judge Fricke might've let Leavy get away with it and simply told Hardy to go ahead and read the letter when he questioned Barbara again on redirect examination. Which is what Hardy did.

But by the time Leavy finished his cross-examination and Hardy had the chance to read the letter out loud, the jury might well have lost the whole thread. Dates, times, places, and characters were flying around the courtroom fast and furious. As smart as those jurors might've been, it's a lot to expect from laypeople who aren't accustomed to evaluating evidence—or tracking how a prosecutor is presenting it. And Leavy knew that. Indeed, he was counting on the jury to forget what the point was by the time Hardy got to question Barbara again. While I admit Leavy's move was legal, it was also sleazy—a deliberate effort to mislead the jury.

Leavy again returned to his favored theme—Barbara's love letters—saying, "Let's see if I can get in focus here again." He began to read the August 5 letter to Donna: "'Hello Sweet, my attorney was up for a few minutes today and he is really disgusted because he feels he can't do anything for me. He says the way things are now there is just nothing he can do. So I told him to hold on for a while, but said nothing.'" Leavy asked, "Is that what you told Mr. Hardy? And is this what you wrote?"

Barbara: "That is correct."

Leavy continued reading: "'Have you heard from your friend again? I sure hope so.' Did you write that?"

Barbara: "I did."

Leavy read on: "'The way things are now, without this, I can't think of a thing.' Is that right; you wrote that, didn't you?"

Barbara: "I wrote that."

Leavy: "'The way things are now'—by that you meant that you had no alibi witness for the night of March the 9th; isn't that right?"

Barbara: "That meant knowing I was at home I still didn't know—I mean, I wasn't quite sure what to do. I couldn't—it didn't occur to me to send Mr. Hardy out to the neighbors."

Leavy: "Well, you knew then at the time you wrote this letter you were at home; is that what your testimony is now?"

Barbara: "In my mind, Mr. Leavy, I always thought I was at home. I just hadn't been able to prove it. When he told me I had not been at Mr. Logan's, it never occurred to me I was anyplace but home."

Leavy: "When you wrote this letter [the August 5 letter to Donna], you didn't tell Mr. Hardy at that time you were at home; you told him to just hold on, and said nothing; isn't that right?"

Barbara: "I had told Mr. Hardy all along I was at home, but he told me without someone to support that evidence that it would be very unlikely that anyone would believe my story that I was just at home."

Leavy: "What did you mean when you said: 'The way things are now, without this I can't think of a thing'? What did you mean when you wrote that? . . . What is your best memory now on what you meant about it at that time you wrote this [letter to Donna]?"

Barbara: "About that time, all I could think of was if someone didn't prove I was at home, I was going to the gas chamber; and I knew I was innocent and I didn't want to die for something I hadn't done."

Leavy went on to ask if she'd also written in that letter, "Being in here really ties one's hands. If only this charge had a bail on it, then I could take care of myself, but no can do."

Barbara confirmed that she had written it.

Leavy: "What did you mean by that, if the charge you were in on was bailable and you were outside you could take care of it, what did you mean by that?"

Barbara: "Well, exactly I don't know. Might have been able to find my husband—I really don't know, Mr. Leavy, my mind is in such a turmoil anyway."

Leavy: "Was your mind in a turmoil when you closed, 'Many kisses and much love, Bonnie'?"

Barbara: "Yes, it was."

And on that snide, gratuitous note, Leavy told the judge this was a convenient time to let the jury break for lunch.

That afternoon, Leavy again returned to the love letters. This one was written on the morning of August 7, the day before Barbara was to meet with Sirianni for the first time. Leavy read it aloud. It began, "Damn—honey, I don't know what to say about tomorrow. I'm so afraid there may be a slipup. I would really like to do it but it's such a chance." Leavy asked, "Did you write that to Donna?"

Seeing that Leavy was once again going to use the tactic of drawing out the process by stopping after each line and asking her to confirm that she'd written it, Barbara tried to short-circuit him by replying, "I wrote the whole thing and told her that I didn't think it was a good idea all the way through, but I was desperate there."

But Leavy was not to be deterred from plumbing his gold mine.

Leavy: "Did you write that to Donna?"

Barbara: "I wrote the whole letter to Donna to tell her I didn't want to."

Leavy bulldozed on.

Leavy: "Well, after you wrote, 'but it was such a chance,' didn't you write, 'You can believe that I want to, in fact I should, but a slipup would be the end.' Did you write that?"

Barbara: "Yes, I did. I did not want to commit perjury again, believe me, but I didn't know what else to do."

Leavy: "Then you went on after, 'but a slipup would be the end,' you wrote 'Probably will be anyway.' Didn't you?"

Barbara: "I didn't want to get her in trouble or her friend."

Leavy: "Did you write what I just read?"

Barbara: "Yes."

Leavy continued to read: "Did you write this after 'probably will anyway,' now, read on—'It's very hard, almost impossible to trust someone on anything like that.' Did you write that?"

Barbara: "Because I knew it was wrong."

Leavy: "Did you write that?"

Barbara: "I wrote that."

Leavy: "Then you went on, 'Do you understand, baby? I want to, but I know what you or anyone else would have to go through if a leak came out and it's very rough.' Did you write that?"

Barbara: "Yes, I was referring to having done it once myself."

Leavy: "Did you then go on, 'Most men can take it—I know I can because I have.' Did you write that?"

Barbara: "Yes, referring to my previous perjury conviction."

Leavy: "And you went on, 'Anyway, as a friend it isn't even fair of me to subject you to such a thing. You think it over and if you think you should mention it to your friend, feel him out cautiously first.' Did you write that?"

Barbara: "Yes. She had written about Vince and I had kept telling her I didn't think I should do it, and then finally, as I told you before, I was getting so close I didn't know what to do, I didn't know which way to turn. I told Donna, well, if she wants to go ahead and try it, maybe I would too."

Leavy read the rest of the letter in the same line-by-line manner, which largely repeated the same expressions of desperation and fear.

Leavy: "Then you closed the letter: 'Well, sweetheart, I am sleepy. Stay pretty and sweet as you are, and remember that I miss you.' And you ended the letter. Is that right?"

Barbara: "That's correct."

As I read that testimony, it struck me again and again how heavy handed and blatantly personal this was. And it wasn't as though Leavy, frustrated by Barbara's truculence, lost his temper. This was a cold, calculated effort to browbeat and defame her, fueled by an animus and hostility that had nothing to do with obtaining the conviction of a guilty defendant.

Leavy had exceeded the point of achieving any valid legal goal with those letters hours ago. To the extent he hoped to show that the false alibi was Barbara's idea, the letters never proved it one way or the other. They certainly didn't refute Barbara's testimony that Donna was the instigator all along. Especially since Donna's letters to Barbara were never produced. But if that point were Leavy's main purpose in reading the letters aloud, he could've skipped most of the terms of endearment. It took only a few lines to establish that Barbara and Donna were more than just friends. There was no need to emphasize every romantic word and phrase—the least relevant aspect of the letters—as Leavy did. It was just an ongoing opportunity to poison the jury's opinion of Barbara on a personal level, a constant drip, drip, drip of character assassination that had nothing whatsoever to do with her guilt for the crime. Please bear in mind, when I use the words *character assassination*, I'm referring to Leavy's tactic of pandering to the negative attitude toward gay and lesbian relationships in the '50s. In today's society, not only would a jury likely be repelled by a stunt like that, but also no judge would allow it.

The letter campaign continued. Leavy next launched into a series of questions about a letter in which Barbara described her meeting with Sirianni and expressed concern that Sirianni had asked some "funny questions" about the crime that gave her pause. Leavy wanted to force her to confirm that she'd told Sirianni she'd been with Santo and Perkins—and she did. But Barbara added the explanation that she only did so because she was afraid Sirianni would back out if she didn't—which she'd already explained many times before. Leavy didn't like that answer, so he continued to ask the question in the hope of getting the answer he wanted. It didn't work.

Leavy read from another letter—in the same line-by-line style—and leaned hard on the ending, which said, "You know him, don't you, Doll? He said he knew you. God, if I thought for one minute that there was one thing phony about this . . . Well, like I said, baby, it is a chance. We are all set to go to court Friday, and I am ready for it. My attorneys are great and will fight like hell for me. So now, doll, it is all up to fate. I am not worried, honey, for I see no reason to beat my head against a stone wall. Let the chips fall where they may. If we make it, doll there is much more in store for us, and I love you very sweet and there is much I want to do for you."

Barbara confirmed she'd written that and said, "I tried to be cheerful in my letters to her. I didn't want her to know how morbid and low I really felt about this."

Leavy: "And did you also write: 'Oh, another reason for my suspicions this afternoon was they let us visit for about 45 minutes, and you know that is very unusual, don't you think? Maybe the captain said it was all right because she knows my trial starts Friday.' Did you write that?"

Barbara: "Yes. What I meant by that was I figured everyone was running around feeling sorry for me, and so they thought, well, she is going to trial, and things look bad for her, so we will let her—just have a little this or that, I don't know."

Leavy: "Did you follow by saying, 'Well, doll, want to get this to K.' What is 'K'?"

Barbara explained *K* referred to kites, which meant notes.

Leavy: (Reading) "'Stay real sweet, baby. Love you much, and baby, I miss you terribly.' That completed the letter, did it not?"

Barbara: "Yes, it did."

It would later be confirmed by the jail deputies that although visitors were usually only allowed twenty minutes with the inmates, they were instructed to give Sirianni as much time as he wanted with Barbara. But to avoid drawing suspicion from prison officials who weren't in on the scheme, they were instructed to record the time spent for each visit as only twenty minutes. So no one was feeling sorry for Barbara. To the contrary, they were secretly maximizing their opportunity to wring as many incriminating statements out of her as they could.

The next letter was written around August 1, two weeks before the trial was supposed to start and a week before Barbara met with Sirianni.

Leavy: "And did you write as follows, after addressing Donna as 'Hi sweets,' or whatever that is. Is that what it is?"

Barbara: "Yes, it is."

Leavy: "Did you write as follows: 'I should have written last night, but I was a little tired. Hon. I got a letter from my attorney yesterday and the captain had me read it in her office and she thought I might get upset over it. In it he informed me that I was definitely facing the death penalty as we haven't been able to locate the two people that I had in mind. [Barbara clarified that the two people were her husband and Mr. Logan]. One I wasn't too sure of anyway. [Barbara clarified that was Mr. Logan.] He said that unless I would cooperate with the police there was no way out for me. [Barbara clarified that the "he" she was referring to was Hardy.] Well, as you know there is nothing I know about the case so if that is what is to be that will have to be it I guess. (The short happy life of B.G.).' You mean 'Barbara Graham,' is that correct?"

Barbara: "That's correct."

Leavy then clarified that this letter was written before Donna set up the meeting with Sirianni, yet again straining to prove that securing a witness to testify to a false alibi was Barbara's idea. I don't fault Leavy for wanting that to be true. It certainly looked better for him if Barbara had been the one begging Donna to get her a witness who was willing to lie. But as Leavy well knew, that simply wasn't the case. Not only did the evidence fail to back up the claim, but Donna herself had disproven it. He should've given up on this canard by now, but he apparently refused to let it go. Barbara's answer corrected his effort to skew the truth:

Barbara: "She had told me all along she could get someone for me if I wanted to. All I had to do was say the word."
Leavy: "That is the way it was, right?"
Barbara: "That's correct."
Leavy: "All you had to do was say the word, is that right?"

Here again, Leavy was trying to make it seem Barbara was the one who came up with the idea to put on a false alibi. But Barbara caught his drift.

Barbara: "Let me think. Sometimes you misconstrue the statements I make. I make them one way and you make them another."
Leavy: "You tell me."
Barbara asked for the question to be reread, and then answered:
Barbara: "She told me all along that if I needed help she would give it to me, and if I wanted to just say so to her, she would go ahead with the plans."
Leavy: "But you understood that all you had to do was say the word and Donna would provide somebody, is that right?"
Barbara: "If I would agree with her, yes."

Whether Leavy thought he'd made his point is unclear. To me, it sounded the same as it had all along: Donna had been offering to provide Barbara with an alibi—euphemistically referred to as "help" (because what other "help" could Donna provide?)—from the very start, and Barbara had held her off, thinking it wouldn't be necessary. Although they'd talked about it two weeks before the trial was to begin, it was only in the last few days that Barbara realized she had no choice and finally caved in.

Leavy continued to read from that letter: "So baby if you are able to do anything it will have to be right away as there is so little time left. Fourteen days to be exact, and the trial starts on the 14th day."

Barbara confirmed she'd written that but said, "I still hadn't made up my mind."

Leavy: "Then you wrote, 'Won't that be cute if I go up there without an alibi and just say I wasn't there.' Did you write that?"

Barbara's answer gives you some idea of the ugly twist Leavy gave that reading:

Barbara: "I did, but I didn't mean it to sound the way you made it sound."

Leavy disingenuously replies, "I am just reading what is here, am I not?"

Barbara: "I know, but look at the expressions you put into it, Mr. Leavy. How would you write?"

I can only imagine the tone of voice he used when he read the word *cute*. But I've got to hand it to Barbara. Leavy was in the driver's seat. He held all the power, and he was intentionally using it to distort her words so he could undermine her credibility. To her credit, she refused to be intimidated and called him out for it. That took some kind of mettle—and presence of mind. Especially knowing she was playing to a full house of spectators and reporters. I'm sure she was scared and anxious; her heart was probably pounding hard enough to break a rib. But she sure didn't show it.

Leavy moved on to ask whether she followed up that statement by writing, "'Think they will believe me?' Did you follow it up with that?"

Barbara: "I did. My attorney told me it was very unlikely they would."

They meaning the jury.

Leavy: "Did you follow then: 'Well anyway I am not worried about it as there is nothing I can do about it.' Did you say that?"

Barbara: "Yes, but I was worried."

Yes, she was. Barbara was very clearly telling Donna that she was concerned, because she knew there was very little chance the jury would believe she was at home on the night of the murder if she didn't have a witness to back her up. The balance of the letter confirms that she certainly was worried.

Leavy: "Then you said, 'Baby, I don't know why you should do all these things, but you will never be sorry, that much I can assure you and when I finally get out of this mess (one way or another)—' Did you write that?"

Barbara: "Yes, I did."

Leavy: "What's the 'one way' in parentheses, and what's the 'another'?"

Barbara: "Actually, I don't think I know."

Leavy continued to read from the letter: "I have some terrific plans and you are included in all of them (the kids too). Well sweetheart I want to finish this before your bath time. Be very careful and under no circumstances let anyone read this or know a word of it. And let's keep our fingers crossed. You can tell your friend that I will make it very much worth their while."

Again asked whether she'd written the letter, Barbara confirmed she had. Leavy then asked whether the reference to "your friend" was the person Donna was going to provide to testify to a false alibi.

Barbara answered: "I still don't think we had decided definitely on it, even though we had been writing back and forth like that . . . I just didn't want to do it and these were the plans we were making if I were to do it. Do you understand me?"

Leavy: "We will leave that to the jury."
Barbara: "Do you understand my answer?"

Leavy dismissed her, saying, "It doesn't make too much difference at the moment."

He then continued on to the remainder of the letter—which, as always—ended on a romantic note:

"Bye for now, Baby. You look so pretty today. Wish I was there with you. Above all, I would like to be outside with you so I could take care of you in the way you should be. There are so many things I want for you and that is the way it will be in the future, I am sure of it. Stay sweet and pretty for me baby."

Leavy: "Did you mean those affectionate terms that are contained in [the note] with respect to Donna?"
Barbara: "I think I did at the time."

Finally, Leavy produced the last letter. The date was never made clear.

"Hi Baby doll. You will have to excuse the writing tonight but I can barely see. [Barbara explained that she'd been writing in the dark.] The money finally got here this morning. You are so sweet for sending it. I wish I could do things for you, but my hands are tied in here. You know how I feel, though, or do you? Do you remember what I told you the other night? Well, honey, we will see what your friend has to say and take it from there. It's pretty risky, but I'll take the chance. I only hope he doesn't breathe a word. I could be caught in an awful trap, you know. No one is to know but you and me and the other party. Sometimes I get to wondering why you are doing this. Do you fully realize what it is?"

Leavy asked Barbara after every line whether she'd written those words and she confirmed she had. She explained that by getting caught in an "awful trap" she'd meant getting "caught here on the stand lying." She also explained what she meant in saying she wondered why Donna was doing this and whether she realized what it was:

Barbara: "She had written in those letters to me, telling me that she loved me and I thought maybe she was getting carried away with her love. I wanted her to understand what she was doing."

Leavy read the next lines of Barbara's letter: "Then I also wonder why I take the chance on trusting you like this. I want to and if we are given the chance to be together in the future there are many things I want to do for you. You would never have another worry, baby. But on the other hand if you are crossing me, do you know what I would have to do?"

Leavy: "Did you write that?"

Barbara: "Yes, I did. Break off our relationship."

Leavy: "Didn't you mean that if she was double-crossing you and sending you someone who might be an informer or someone working as an operator for the police—isn't that what you meant?"

Barbara: "No, I don't think I did, Mr. Leavy . . . Donna had written me these affectionate letters, and I had written the same. I reciprocated, and I liked her very much; and she professed to love me very much. In fact, she would cry over it. I just wanted her to know that I just didn't know what I meant about crossing, exactly, but I wanted her to know that I would have to break off the relationship with her."

Leavy telegraphed his disbelief: "That is what you meant when you said, 'Do you know what I would have to do?'"

Barbara: "That's right."

Obviously, that wasn't the answer he wanted. He was hoping she'd admit she was threatening to harm or even kill Donna if she turned out to be a snitch. But he was stuck with the answer that was most likely the truth. And I'm not just saying that because Barbara had never shown any violent tendencies or even because—in context, given the loving sentiments expressed throughout the letter—a breakup was logically the most likely "threat." I'm saying that because Coveney was reading all those letters as they came in. And probably so was Leavy. If either of them had thought Barbara posed a real threat, Donna would've been moved out of harm's way, or offered some kind of protection, in about ten seconds. There is no evidence whatsoever that any steps were taken to protect Donna after she got that letter.

Leavy then finished reading the letter:

"Forgive me for writing this way, baby, but I think a lot of you and I want you to know how I feel. I am sure you would feel the same way if the position were reversed. As it is now I have the utmost trust in you and I would hate to have it broken. I wouldn't care if I didn't think as much of you as I do. You are the sweetest girl I know and I wish we had met under different circumstances. Maybe things will work out all right anyway. Let's hope so. Honey I fell off this damn top bed today and landed right on my head, so I don't feel too well. Will end this for tonight and will write during the day and give it to K to give to you at dinnertime if I can. Be real good and stay sweet. I miss you and think of you always. I always love to see you looking so pretty when I go by. Nite for now, hon. XOX."

Leavy: "What are those three marks at the bottom, 'XOX'? Is that 'love and kisses'?"

Barbara: "It is."

That concluded Leavy's cross-examination, a fitting note to end on for questioning that'd focused far more heavily on the largely irrelevant romantic liaison between Barbara and Donna than proof of guilt, and the presentation of evidence that was deliberately orchestrated to mislead the jury.

From the time I began reading the trial transcripts, my opinion of Leavy had been shifting. At first, I'd been excited by the prospect of getting to see a celebrated icon in action. But as I saw the prosecution make one sleazy move after another over the course of the trial, the shine on his coat of armor had worn off. And my opinion of him hit rock bottom when I realized what he'd done with Donna Prow and then read his cross-examination of Barbara. Barbara's letters to Donna were the kind of bonanza few prosecutors ever get lucky enough to find. Her willingness to set up a false alibi was all there and in her own handwriting, no less. But instead of training his aim on those admissions, he spent hours dunning her with every *honey*, *baby*, and *love you* he could in an effort to pander to the jury's bias against homosexuality. It was shady, low-class lawyering that focused on ad hominem attacks to the point of detracting from the wealth of legally relevant evidence he had to draw on.

The slippery-as-an-eel lawyer who manipulates jurors through a verbal sleight of hand, putting a twist on the truth that turns up and down into upside down is a common trope. There may be some truth to it. After all, clichés are clichés because there's a kernel of truth to them. But it does not—and never was supposed to—apply to prosecutors. For all that I've pointed out changes in the law since Barbara's trial that would've prohibited the more grotesque Fifth and Sixth Amendment violations permitted in her case, the law requiring prosecutors to answer to a higher standard of ethics had been established long before 1953.

A prosecutor stands in a very different position than that of a defense attorney. A defense attorney's only allegiance is to the client. A prosecutor's duty is to see that justice is done. Not to see how many convictions he can rack up or how many bodies he can put on death row. The prosecutor's duty is to fight fairly, to present the evidence accurately and coherently to ensure that the jury is able to make a reliable determination of the facts.

In the landmark decision *Berger v. United States*, handed down in 1935, the United States Supreme Court explained how the prosecutor's unique obligations required fealty to a higher standard of ethics: "As such, [the prosecutor] is in a peculiar and very definite sense the servant of the law, the twofold aim of which is that guilt shall not escape or innocence suffer. He may prosecute with earnestness and vigor—indeed, he should do so. But, while he may strike hard blows, he is not at liberty to strike foul ones. It is as much his duty to refrain from improper methods calculated to produce a wrongful conviction as it is to use every legitimate means to bring about a just one."

What Leavy did violated that standard of ethics in myriad ways, some subtle—like refusing to read the letter Barbara wrote to her husband that would've directly contradicted the point he wanted to make—and some devastating, like hiding Donna Prow. The combined impact of those violations could not help but have a negative effect on the jury. Especially in a case that hinged on the testimony of an inherently untrustworthy accomplice.

The prosecution in this case—and in specific J. Miller Leavy—went after Barbara with an inexplicable zeal. No experienced prosecutor could see her history of petty nonviolent crimes and believe she was a likely candidate for the atrocious pistol-whipping of an elderly woman. But the two rough-looking men flanking her in court were the very epitome of the kind of violent career criminals who'd be likely to do exactly that—and more. And J. Miller Leavy was well aware that they were suspected of having committed other murders in Northern California. Yet he made no effort to put a cop in their jail cells or hire an inmate to lure them into a trap.

Instead, he took lethal aim at Barbara and stacked the deck against her with every cheap trick and underhanded tactic he could lay his hands on, choosing to champion the testimony of an accomplice he had every reason to know was not only a liar, but also the likely villain who'd brutally pistol-whipped Mabel Monahan.

CHAPTER SIXTEEN

How Barbara had fared in the eyes of the jury after Leavy's cross-examination is hard to say. She surely wasn't cowed by him. In today's world that'd probably earn her some points. It would have with me, anyway. But this was the era of *Leave It to Beaver* and *Father Knows Best*, where wives were expected to greet hubby at the end of the day with dinner on the table and a drink in hand—wearing heels and a welcoming smile. Barbara's defiance and peppery attitude might well have done her more harm than good. Women in Barbara's position were supposed to be penitent and cowed . . . whether they were guilty or not.

But at the eleventh hour a ray of hope appeared. Barbara had suggested that her neighbor's young daughter might be able to say she was at home on the night of the murder. As it turned out, Barbara was right. And she was the alibi witness of their dreams: Corrine Perez was a strikingly pretty, innocent-looking nineteen-year-old who had an unspecified disability that required her to wear leg braces and largely confined her to a wheelchair.

Corrine was certain Barbara had been at home on the night of March 9, 1953, because she'd been home all day and she'd heard Barbara and Hank fighting throughout the day and into the night. That was far from an unusual occasion, but Corrine could pinpoint the date because that was a Monday and her mother always worked late at her department store job on Mondays.

To top it off, she had a sweet, gentle demeanor that would soften the heart of the most skeptical juror—even the notorious Juror Number 5. And it seemed she did. Corrine was the very next witness called for the defense after Barbara testified, and according to the *Daily News*, the jury fell in love with her. The reporter wrote that Corrine had a "birdlike voice and her face, transfigured by a lifetime of suffering into an unearthly loveliness, fascinated the jurors and they bent forward to catch every word of her seemingly sincere testimony."

Corrine posed a unique problem for the prosecutor who had to cross-examine her. The goal was to shake her confidence, make her doubt her own memory so the jury would doubt it, too, but it had to be done delicately. The slightest hint of an aggressive posture with a little sweetheart like this and the jury would turn on the prosecutor in a split second. Leavy handed her off to Alexander.

Alexander got her to admit that she'd initially told the cops she didn't know where Barbara was on March 9—no real feat since it was written in the police report—but she explained, "I did not want to tell them about it." She was firm in her insistence that she'd heard Barbara and Hank arguing until late into the night on the ninth and that when she went to bed at 11:30 p.m., they were still fighting.

Her testimony panicked the prosecution. Barbara—the prized "get"—was about to "get" away. They flogged their investigators to find a way to rebut the testimony. The result was a string of witnesses who testified to hospital records that purportedly proved Corrine was at the hospital getting one of her treatments on March 9, and that she didn't get home until 8:00 p.m. at the earliest. But the defense fought back with their own parade of hospital employees whose testimony called into question the accuracy of those records. In the end, what emerged from the fracas was the reality that no one—not the ambulance drivers tasked with taking patients to and from the hospital, nor the clinic that adjusted Corrine's braces, nor the hospital itself—kept reliable records of the dates or times that patients were seen. And when the defense recalled Corrine to the stand in surrebuttal, she again firmly insisted that she'd been at home, that she kept a calendar of her hospital appointments, and that it did not show she had an appointment for treatment on March 9.

The next alibi witness was not someone the defense wanted to put on the stand. Hardy had spoken to Barbara's husband, Henry "Hank" Graham, in late August and was not impressed. Hardy had told Barbara his testimony would be "valueless," that he was "dreamy and incoherent," his memory shrouded in a fog of drugs.

But Leavy forced Hardy's hand. Near the end of Barbara's cross-examination, Leavy brought Hank into the courtroom and had her identify him. Leavy's little ploy of parading Henry Graham in front of the jury like an exhibit was meant to show that he wasn't out of state—he was right here in Los Angeles, ready and willing to testify. The prosecution couldn't make him testify. He was still married to Barbara, which meant spousal privilege applied. So either Barbara or Hank could invoke spousal privilege to prevent the prosecution from putting him on the witness stand. But the defense could call him. And by producing him in open court, the prosecution made sure they had to. If they didn't, it'd be a giant red flag to the jury that they knew Hank wouldn't back her story, and that Barbara's alibi—correction, her *second* alibi—was no more credible than her first. Which is why Leavy brought him into the courtroom and asked Barbara—with Hank standing there before her in the gallery—whether she still maintained she'd been with him the night of March 9, 1953. She said she still thought so—that she was either with him or with Mr. Logan.

Legally speaking, Leavy's little stunt of using Hank Graham like a human exhibit wouldn't fly today. First of all, this was—once again—a case of ambush. The defense had no notice he intended to bring Barbara's husband into court to make him part of her cross-examination. But second of all, in California, at least by 1965, the law of privilege has included the right not to even be called to the witness stand. Dragging Hank into court is tantamount to calling him as a witness. At least, that's what I would argue. In any case, legal or not, that move basically boxed in the defense. Once Leavy had produced Hank in court, the defense couldn't object without telegraphing to the jury that they knew he wouldn't support her alibi.

Was it clever? Certainly. Was it legal? Probably. But was it ethical? No. Even if hauling Hank into court was permissible, it violated the spirit of spousal privilege, which was intended to prevent exactly what Leavy had done: pit a husband against his wife.

But Leavy knew how to craft a dramatic moment, and of course, the press ate it up with a spoon. The story carried two-column photos of Barbara and Hank. Though they were clearly taken separately, the photos were positioned to show Barbara in profile seemingly fixing Hank with a tight-lipped stare, while Hank faced outward, with a soft, almost sad expression, the very picture of an average-looking, mild-mannered guy. No mystery who the heavy was in this match-up.

A reporter from the *Daily News* reminded the public that Barbara had "pitted her slim story that she was home with her husband against the crushing evidence" that showed she was in the house of Mabel Monahan. "But yesterday, as she neared the end of her long, arduous session on the witness stand, the doors of the courtroom of Superior Judge Charles W. Fricke banged opened and in strode the fateful figure of her husband. Barbara straightened in her seat as she saw Graham and her eyes constantly sought his face as he made his way to a seat in the spectator's section."

The next bit came straight out of a romance novel—a very badly written one: "At first she smiled tenderly and her eyes filled with tears as she seemed to beg for forgiveness for having spent a night away from home with Emmett Perkins, one of her co-defendants. But as the blank-faced Graham shunned her mute appeal, studiously avoiding her eyes, she mixed momentary glares of anger into her gaze, tightening her face into a mask of fleeting hatred."

A "mask of fleeting hatred"? How does a mask show a fleeting emotion? I don't care what they say: metaphors need to make sense. And mixing "glares of anger" into her "gaze" sounds like a baking recipe. Mix in three glares of anger with two glances of hatred, stir vigorously. What editor let that drivel go to print? Bear in mind, the *Daily News* was not a tabloid rag like *Globe* or the *National Enquirer*. This was supposedly a reputable news publication.

But it wasn't just the *Daily News*. The *Los Angeles Times* also got into the act, claiming that as Barbara stepped off the witness stand and walked back to the counsel table, she "glared malevolently" at Graham, who was seated in the second row of the gallery.

Remember all those sympathetic stories when Barbara first took the stand, about her downcast eyes and nervous hand-wringing as she clutched her handkerchief? Yeah, not so much now. The press had a new, much juicier story to tell. I think there was also something else in play at this point. When Barbara first took the stand, she was the frightened little doe the press—and the public—demanded. But now, she'd gone toe to toe with the prosecutor for almost two days, refusing to cower or show fear, giving almost as good as she got. That show of moxie ended the brief nod to any sympathy for Barbara.

After Leavy's little show-and-tell with Hank Graham, the press was on the alert, so when the defense called him to the witness stand, they were ready and waiting with fangs bared. They cast Hank as the poor, misbegotten man whose wildcat, she-devil of a wife had landed him in the hot seat with her cooked-up alibi. Reporters seemed to have forgotten that this man was a drug addict and a loser who'd spent all their money on heroin and downers, forcing Barbara to go back to work at the gambling house and write bad checks to put food on the table for him and their little baby, Tommy. And he still was a drug addict and loser. He'd recently been busted for drug possession yet again and only managed to come to court because he'd just bailed out. The news outlets buried that little tidbit in a terse few lines at the end of the article. It didn't fit the favored narrative of the soft-spoken little man who'd found himself hitched to the evil murderess Barbara Graham.

Unfortunately, the defense was forced to call him and take their chances. But good old Hank wasn't good for them. He said he'd moved out of the duplex on March 7 or 8 and moved in with his mother. He remembered those dates because he'd received his next-to-last unemployment check on March 6, 1953. But he confirmed that he'd gone back to the duplex to see the baby the following day—which *could've* been March 9—and Barbara had been there. During that visit, he and Barbara had again quarreled, and he'd stayed until 9:00 or 9:30 p.m. The murder occurred at roughly 8:00 p.m., so that actually gave some wishy-washy support for Barbara's alibi. But it was hardly the ringing endorsement the defense needed.

Hank's failure to fully corroborate Barbara's alibi sent the press into a frenzy of "she-had-it-coming" finger wagging. Here, at last, was the payback for infidelity and lawlessness she deserved. "Unfaithful wife Barbara Graham paid for her erring ways yesterday when her husband flatly refused to support the alibi that is believed to be her only hope of avoiding the gas chamber . . . as Barbara looked into the sad, accusing eyes of her husband and saw there was no forgiveness in them, she wept."

Far from Hank being at all moved by Barbara's tears, Hank Graham's brief testimony was heralded as having dealt the defense "a smashing blow," and the reporter rejected any possibility that it might be the vindictive retribution of a scorned spouse. "There was no ring of vengeful anger or outraged hurt as he stammered the words that may condemn Barbara to the gas chamber. There was instead something close to triumph."

"Triumph"? Doesn't that indicate he was taking some pleasure in trashing her alibi? But more to the point, Hank hadn't really nixed Barbara's alibi. That didn't make for a great story, though. The utter disdain for the truth was very clearly shown in what was purported to be the description of Hank Graham's actual testimony: "Yes, they had quarreled all right . . . but that was on the 7th or 8th of the month, and he had left. And although he may have dropped by the house on the 9th, it was only to see his 15 month old son, and the visit was brief."

No, the visit was not brief. Graham had actually said he'd stayed at the house—with Barbara—until 9:00 or 9:30 p.m.—well after the murder was committed, well after the gang had left the Monahan house. So if he had gone back to see the baby on the ninth, then he'd just backed up Barbara's alibi. Even the usually less reckless *Los Angeles Times* got it wrong, claiming that Graham said he may have gone back to the duplex on the ninth for a brief visit, but that he'd been alone—the implication being that Barbara had not been there, a direct misrepresentation of his testimony.

As for the letter Barbara had written to him on May 19, 1953, Hank admitted he'd received it but never answered it. At that time, although the press had written she was suspected of the Monahan burglary-murder, she'd only been charged with writing bad checks, and she'd told him she was confident the murder charges would be dropped. Hank knew all about the bad checks. Those checks had paid for dinner and put the roof over his head. So why didn't he write her back? No one asked, no one cared. And no reporter commented on it. But it was probably because he was high as a kite and couldn't be bothered. Later though, when he learned she'd been charged with conspiracy and murder, he made sure she wouldn't bother him again. He told his mother to lie and say he'd moved to Arizona. No reporter mentioned that either.

The newspapers' description of Barbara's reaction to all this once again resorted to the caricature of the icy-veined murderess: "While Graham was doing his best to convict her, Barbara showed plainly that she had no more tears to shed over him. She rested her determined chin on her clenched fist as he spoke and her pretty hazel eyes were two pools of gleaming hatred."

Apparently, Hank hadn't noticed those "pools of gleaming hatred," because he returned to the witness stand a few days later and recanted his earlier testimony. Graham said he'd found a memo showing his unemployment card had been stamped with the date March 11. He knew he'd been with Barbara until then, so he must've been home with her on March 9. He'd tried to reach the prosecutors to tell them, but he was told that they were out, so he called the defense attorneys.

Graham now remembered that he'd moved the last of his clothes out of the duplex on March 11, so he still had some belongings there as of March 9. He remembered that he'd gone to the duplex on the morning of the ninth at 9:30 or 10:00 a.m. to see the baby, and Barbara had been there. Graham took the baby out for a ride and found her still at home when he returned at 1:00 p.m. As they had many times before, they got into a fight about his lack of employment that continued until he left at 9:30 p.m. So Hank was certainly not "doing his best" to try and convict Barbara. But this testimony was virtually ignored by the press.

Hank's mother, Anne Webb, confirmed that Barbara had asked her where he was on more than one occasion during her visits to Barbara in jail and that she'd told her Hank moved to Arizona. That offered some support for the possibility that Barbara thought he might be able to corroborate her alibi. But that didn't necessarily mean her alibi was true. It could also just mean she was hoping he'd back her up, whether it was true or not. All in all, I'd say the mother's testimony was a wash. As was the testimony of William Croff, the friend who'd helped Hank move out of the duplex. He'd told Hardy privately that he knew he'd been at the duplex on the night of March 9 and that he'd seen Barbara there. But Croff went south on the witness stand, and said he wasn't sure what day it was when he went there. Hardy was infuriated but helpless to do anything about it. Croff was useless.

Incidentally, this was another example of how the defense was hobbled by the inability to hire an investigator. A lawyer is not allowed to testify in his own case, because it turns the lawyer into a witness. That's why, when a lawyer interviews a witness, they've got to have someone else present, ideally a cop or an investigator. If the witness forgets or denies what they'd said, the investigator can take the stand and testify to their earlier statement. In this case, because Hardy had been alone when he'd spoken to Croff, he had no one who could testify to Croff's initial statement that he'd been certain he helped Hank move out on March 9. So the jury never got to hear it.

That left the defense with Barbara's testimony—which was burdened by not only the damning weight of Sirianni's recordings but also her conviction for perjury—Hank Graham's vacillating testimony, and the testimony of Corrine Perez. Hank's belated turnaround was too little, too late. Somewhat wifty to begin with, his secondary claim of recovered memory just wasn't all that persuasive. The only real hope was that it might gain traction when viewed in conjunction with the far more credible testimony of Corrine Perez. Whether the combination of the winsome Perez and the "stammering" ex-husband would be persuasive enough to remove the stain of Sirianni's testimony was the big unknown.

CHAPTER SEVENTEEN

The press made no mention of Perkins's and Santo's reactions to Barbara's testimony, or the witnesses who testified in her defense. Since reporters were constantly on the lookout for even the slightest show of emotion by the three defendants, I'd guess that meant the men had maintained their habitually casual, disaffected attitude.

But now it was time for their defense. The ball was passed to attorney Ward Sullivan, who represented them both. Here again, was another example of something that would never happen today. Since an attorney is prohibited from representing a client whose interests conflict with another client, criminal defense lawyers nowadays almost uniformly opt to avoid even the whiff of a conflict by taking on only one defendant in a multidefendant case. Even when—as in this case—the defendants obviously have no conflict. Perkins and Santo were not at odds—neither one was pointing the finger at the other to say, "It was him, not me." Still, it's highly unlikely any lawyer would so much as think about taking on both of them. Especially in a death penalty case. Nor would a judge be inclined to allow it. If a lawyer did represent two defendants and a conflict were to arise—for example in this case, if Perkins suddenly decided to say he was at the gambling house that night and Santo did it all—it'd almost certainly cause a reversal on appeal if Santo got convicted.

Ward Sullivan had likely seen enough of his clients to be confident that neither of them would turn on the other. Besides, with the felony murder rule in play, the only viable defense for either Perkins or Santo was alibi; i.e., that neither one was at the scene. Since the felony murder rule meant all defendants were liable for murder if the killing occurred in the course of a felony—even if the killing was accidental—alibi was the *only* available defense. So, Ward Sullivan had no choice. He had to go for an alibi defense for both men.

Perkins's witnesses did a nice job of accounting for his whereabouts—until about 4:00 p.m. on March 9, hours *before* the burglary. And for some reason he thought it was helpful to call witnesses who could say he was at the dentist on the morning of March 10—the day *after* the burglary. But since the crime took place at approximately 8:30 p.m. on March 9, that didn't do him any good. And the only one who could say where he was for the critical period was his wife, Eleanor. She, of course, said he was at home with her. It's unclear why anyone thought this would persuade even one juror to doubt his guilt. But lawyers have to work with what they've got. At least his defense didn't blow up in his face.

Which is more than could be said for Santo. It wasn't the greatest idea to call his mistress, Harriet Henson, as his primary alibi witness to begin with, and Sullivan didn't seem to think so either. His entire direct examination took up less than five pages in the reporter's transcript. Probably no more than ten minutes of court time. Henson testified that Santo had driven to her home in Auburn, a rural town near Sacramento, on the afternoon of March 10, 1953. John True had arrived alone later that night. The inference they wanted the jury to draw was that Santo couldn't have made it all the way up to Auburn by the afternoon of the tenth if he'd been in Burbank murdering Mabel Monahan on the night of March 9. But John True—who'd arrived much later—could have.

An interesting aspect of Harriet Henson's testimony was that she saw John True palling around with both Perkins and Santo up in Auburn in late January, and that all three had taken a trip out of town together for a few days around that time. True had testified with certitude that he had only met Perkins in Los Angeles, a few days before the murder.

As zealously as the prosecution tried to protect True's credibility, they couldn't discredit that aspect of Henson's testimony.

Presenting Henson as Santo's only alibi witness wasn't much better than Perkins having his wife say he was at home with her that night. What else do you expect the girlfriend/wife to say? But that was far from the only problem with Henson's testimony. On cross-examination it was quickly revealed that Henson had tried to recruit a man named "Ike" to give Santo a false alibi, but he'd backed out. She then approached a mechanic named Jack Furneaux. Though she admitted to having met with him, she denied having tried to recruit him to provide a false alibi.

This time it was Alexander's turn to have some fun. He picked up a transcript and began to read. Within seconds it was revealed to be the transcript of a recording that'd been made of Henson's meetings with Furneaux. Alexander—following Leavy's style—went line by line, asking Henson again and again whether she'd asked that question and whether Furneaux had given that answer. Henson denied every word. When Alexander finished his cross-examination and turned the witness back over to the defense, Sullivan declined to ask any further questions. What *could* he ask? The defense had exploded in spectacular fashion. Surrounded by the shrapnel that'd been his case, Sullivan announced that the defense for Santo and Perkins had rested.

On rebuttal, Department of Justice special agent Harry Cooper explained how the bomb had been built. When Henson asked Furneaux to give Santo a false alibi, Furneaux had gone to the police, and they'd contacted the DOJ. With Furneaux's permission, Cooper and another agent wired him up, followed him to each meeting, and identified the woman he'd met with as Harriet Henson. Unlike the setup used by Sirianni, this one worked well, and it produced a recording that was crisp, clear, and utterly damning. With those recordings in hand, Cooper contacted the Los Angeles District Attorney's Office on August 21, 1953, and said he had a present for them. And in case anyone doubted the accuracy of the recordings, Jack Furneaux took the stand and verified every line.

With the testimony completed, Hardy and Sullivan each made their own Hail Mary passes. Hardy moved to strike all of Sam Sirianni's and Shirley Olson's testimony on the ground that their actions constituted a violation of due process. The judge denied the motion—to no one's surprise. But to be clear, in today's world, Sirianni's testimony would've resulted in a complete reversal for Barbara.

Sullivan moved for a mistrial on the ground that the defendants had been denied the right to a fair trial due to the negative publicity, and produced four portfolios of newspaper and magazine articles that blasted headlines during the trial, like "'Bloody Babs' Secret Record Tells Murder," "Link Monahan Girl in SF Vice Robbery," and "The Blond Iceberg Burns."

Sullivan argued, "I know that your Honor has cautioned them [the jury] that they were not to read the newspapers about this, but it is almost common knowledge that you can't walk down the street, can't walk out of this courtroom and go across on to Broadway and attempt to take a streetcar without observing some of the glaring headlines and these types of headlines are calculated to convey to their minds matters which have nothing to do with the evidence in this case. They are calculated to bias and prejudice the jury as well as the public in general."

Sullivan also argued in his written motion that the routine searching of courtroom spectators and the constant presence of uniformed guards contributed to the bias against the defendants, creating an atmosphere that depicted them to the jury as an ongoing danger. The judge conceded those security measures had been taken, but stated he'd been alerted to the possibility that someone with a gun might show up in court, so he'd considered it best to have everyone searched. The judge ruled that it couldn't be presumed the jury knew everyone was being searched since it wasn't done when they were present. As for the negative publicity, the judge noted for the record that he'd admonished the jurors not to read or listen to any news about the case and there was no affirmative evidence that the jury had violated that order. The motion for a mistrial was denied.

The thing is, I don't know how the jury could've missed the shrieking headlines no matter how hard they tried. Even if they managed to avoid television or radio news, back then, newspapers were kept in glass cases that purposely allowed passersby to see the front page, and those glass cases lined the downtown LA streets, especially the streets around the Hall of Justice courthouse. That was the whole idea of putting shocking headlines in bold type: to grab readers' attention and entice them into dropping a coin in the slot. And I wouldn't have expected anyone to tell the judge that they'd seen those headlines. No juror wants to suffer the embarrassment of admitting that they'd disobeyed a court order—even by accident.

Just as an aside, those glass cases were still ubiquitous in the '90s during the O. J. Simpson trial. I used to get an eyeful of the day's headlines about the case every time I stopped at a local drive-through for tacos or hamburgers.

I will give Judge Fricke this much, though: he'd refused permission for the press to take "motion pictures" or bring in "candid cameras" during the trial. I sure wouldn't have minded a ruling like that.

In any case, whatever the jury had or hadn't seen, it was now all over but the shouting. On to closing arguments.

CHAPTER EIGHTEEN

It was stifling in that courtroom. September in Los Angeles is always hot, and the sixteenth day of September in 1953 was no exception. It didn't help that the courtroom was packed, and it was standing room only. Spectators squeezed together on the benches in the gallery, filling every square inch of space. Men loosened their collars, and women dabbed sweat from their hairlines with handkerchiefs. But no one was about to give up a ringside seat for what promised to be the dramatic highlight of a trial that'd splashed headlines on an almost daily basis about the dizzying twists and turns in the case over the past month.

Speaking from my personal perspective as a trial lawyer, closing arguments can be daunting. It's no easy thing to weave together the testimony with the applicable law to form a cohesive and compelling story. Go too deep into the legal weeds and the jury gets bored, too complicated and the jury gets frustrated, too simplistic and the jury gets insulted. And the bigger the case, the more daunting the task, simply because there's so much evidence to discuss. I always wound up wishing I could just sit down and take questions, talk *with* the jury instead of just talking at them.

But closing arguments are also exciting. There's at least a bit of an actor in every trial lawyer, and taking center stage to address the jury always brings with it an adrenaline rush. It's a performance, yes. But it's also a chance to communicate with the silent watchers—the jury—who've taken this journey alongside you, a chance to tell them what you think about all that you've collectively seen and heard. And it's doubly exciting when you can feel that they're with you, on your side.

So I have no doubt that J. Miller Leavy savored every moment as he approached the jury. This was his last big moment. And he had a lot to say.

He started by admitting, "I supposed you might say we are relentless. Yes, relentless to our duty, because if we were otherwise in this case, on the evidence which you have heard, we would be derelict in our duty to the members of this community who prefer to live in it peaceably and law-abidingly."

Too bad he wasn't just as relentless about doing his job ethically. I'll give Leavy this much: he was consistent. His closing argument was true to form. From the moment he started to talk about the evidence, he pulled one cheap shot after another. He brought up Baxter Shorter's statement to the police, implying that it was similar to the testimony of William Upshaw and John True. But since Shorter's statement was never presented to the jury, no lawyer was allowed to use—or even refer to it—for any purpose. Leavy did it in a sly way. He said that the jury could "wipe out" True's testimony and just rely on either the testimony of William Upshaw or "in the original instance Baxter Shorter."

The implication is clear: Baxter Shorter's statement would be consistent with Upshaw's and True's testimony. But the jury had never heard Shorter's statement. So Leavy was flat-out testifying that Shorter's statement backed up John True. This was a double violation of law and ethics. Lawyers—and particularly prosecutors—aren't allowed to vouch for the credibility of witnesses. It implies that the prosecutor has secret knowledge that proves the witnesses' honesty.

But it's ten times worse for a prosecutor to vouch for the credibility of a party who never even appeared in court, indeed, whose statement wasn't even presented to the jury. There's no gray area here. Lawyers are not allowed to refer to matters outside the evidence. They can draw inferences from the evidence, but they can't claim—either explicitly or implicitly—that a statement the jury never heard is consistent with the testimony given in court. So Leavy's argument was a serious legal and ethical violation. A clear case of prosecutorial misconduct.

Hardy jumped to his feet, stammering in shock. "Pardon me just a minute . . . may the Court please—Baxter Shorter—there is no testimony concerning Baxter Shorter in this case. He is not a party—"

The judge inexplicably ruled, "He has been referred to in the testimony."

Hardy asked that Leavy's comment be read back and again objected: "May I submit there is no testimony of Baxter Shorter, no proper reference to testimony of Baxter Shorter in this record."

The judge repeated the comment: "I don't know. I sat here and heard his name mentioned a number of times."

But the judge was wrong. And the fact that he'd "heard [Shorter's] name" certainly didn't justify the conclusion that his statement had been presented to the jury. Hardy again pointed out that Shorter's statement had never been introduced into evidence in any way, but the judge again replied that he'd heard the name mentioned, then insisted Leavy hadn't said Shorter had testified. Hardy insisted, "That was the implication."

Hardy was right. That certainly was the implication of Leavy's remark, and the judge should've told the jury it was improper, that there was no evidence of what Baxter Shorter said to anyone, and admonished the jury to disregard it. Leavy sought to short-circuit the objection by telling the judge, "Perhaps my later argument in the case will clarify Mr. Hardy's present impression. May I proceed?"

The judge said, "Yes." And Leavy proceeded to make matters even worse, saying that although Upshaw's testimony alone proved the case, they still needed to present John True, and that "Baxter Shorter's testimony was available at one stage of the presentation of this case."

But that wasn't the point. Whether it was "available" or not—a legal question that'd never even been posed, let alone answered—the statement had never been presented to the jury. So any reference to the contents was simply illegal. Period.

Once again, Hardy objected: "I submit that is a misstatement and cite that as misconduct on the part of counsel. There is no evidence his testimony was available, it has never been available, it is not available. It is not admissible in this case."

Hardy may have been right. While Baxter Shorter's statement *might* have been admissible as a declaration against interest—an exception to the hearsay rule that prohibits statements made outside of court—it might not have qualified for that exception. The problem is, that legal question had never even been posed, let alone answered, since neither side had ever attempted to get Shorter's statement admitted. So Leavy had no business saying it was even "available" and certainly had no business claiming that the content of the statement was consistent with the testimony of either True or Upshaw.

Judge Fricke, who seemed to have suddenly forgotten not only the evidence but the law, replied, "I don't get the form of the objections. The statement was merely that the testimony was available."

Hardy: "That is—there is no such evidence that his testimony was ever available."

Finally—but only after Leavy had rung the bell twice, ensuring that the jury would hear and remember it—the judge agreed to try and unring it, half-heartedly: "Well, just to protect the record, I am going to instruct the jury to entirely disregard that portion of Mr. Leavy's statement."

Great. Thanks, Judge. Very helpful. As the Fifth Circuit once said, "if you throw a skunk into the jury box, you can't instruct the jury not to smell it." That lame, reluctantly given admonition was guaranteed to be utterly useless.

Leavy then turned back to the jury and said, "You folks keep in mind in my argument here I have a right to base it upon certain evidence, what are reasonable inferences that can be drawn, can be drawn from the evidence and when I do it, I will draw only those reasonable inferences which I feel can be drawn from certain facts and circumstances in this case; and I believe later in the case you will understand what I am referring to here in my argument."

No. The jury would not understand what he was referring to later, because he never went back to the subject of Shorter's statement. Because as he was well aware, he never should have raised it to begin with.

Now to be clear, Leavy went on to commit many transgressions that were far worse than that. But this one was particularly galling because Leavy knew very well that Shorter's statement actually contradicted John True's testimony on significant key points—especially his testimony that Barbara pistol-whipped Mabel Monahan—and showed True was certainly not Monahan's savior as he'd claimed.

So for Leavy to tell the jury that Shorter's statement would corroborate True's testimony was not only unethical and unlawful; it was an outright lie. But it was a lie he knew he could get away with, because the jury would never hear that statement.

Leavy then moved on to a description of the evidence that often veered into inflammatory hyperbole on the one hand, and a deification of John True on the other. For example, he dramatically described how when the defendants met up at the Smoke House that night, they were "planning [Mabel Monahan's] death," because "these people steal to live, and they kill to steal. That's one of their philosophies."

There was no such testimony nor even any basis to infer that anyone was "planning" to kill Mabel Monahan. Quite the opposite. If that'd been the plan, someone would've shot her as soon as they got inside. In fact, the unrefuted testimony was that they'd planned to settle Mabel Monahan on the couch and keep her out of the way while the others looted the place. And that also goes for the claim that it was their philosophy to "kill to steal." There was certainly no evidence of that.

Oddly, Leavy then contradicted what he'd just said, arguing that "John True thought no one would be harmed." How on earth could True think that if the plan had been to kill Mabel Monahan? He'd been at the Smoke House when they'd made the plan. So how come he didn't know that the philosophy of "these people" was to "kill to steal"? By all accounts, John True had known Santo for some time—they'd been buddies up in Auburn, taken trips together. How would it escape his notice that at least Santo—if not the others—believed in stealing to live and killing to steal?

Leavy also repeatedly—and I have no doubt deliberately—made a blurry mess of the legal requirement that an accomplice's testimony must be corroborated. In order to qualify as corroboration, the evidence has to connect the defendants to the crime. If the evidence only helps to prove that a crime was committed, then it doesn't count as corroboration. So the fact that the forensic pathologist confirmed Monahan had suffered blunt force trauma to the head—even though consistent with what True described—did not qualify as corroboration. It only went to the proof that a crime had been committed. Not who committed the crime.

Yet, time and time again—over counsel's objections, which the judge repeatedly overruled—Leavy pointed to such evidence not only as proof of True's credibility but as proof of corroboration.

Ironically—and fairly outrageously—Leavy even claimed True's testimony was corroborated by the fact that an ambulance had been called for Monahan. But he knew very well that although True claimed it was his idea, that was a lie. Shorter's detailed statement showed he was the one who'd said they had to get an ambulance and then tracked down a phone booth to call for help.

The truth is, the only reason the police managed to confirm that someone had actually called for an ambulance was because *Shorter* gave a detailed description of the route he took and the location of the phone booth where he'd made the call. But Leavy trumpeted that as proof of *True's* honesty, saying, "I tell you, that is no coincidence, that is a fact and circumstance which, in my judgment, confirms or strengthens the testimony of John True; makes you believe, and makes me believe, in my own heart and my own mind, from the evidence in this case, that he has spoken the truth. That is not coincidence, because it has been testified to here that True told Shorter to call an ambulance . . ."

And who gave that testimony "here" about calling an ambulance? John True. Leavy, knowing that True had lied and simply coopted Shorter's role to whitewash himself, touted that lie to claim that it was further proof of True's honesty.

But all of that paled in comparison to the personal attack he launched against Barbara. It was—bar none—the ugliest, most unethical argument I've ever seen a prosecutor make.

Leavy began with a reference to the letter in which Barbara said she had to "get out of this mess (one way or another)." He proclaimed that now they knew the "one way" was a false alibi—conveniently ignoring the fact that at the time she wrote that letter, Barbara herself didn't know she'd have an alibi witness—false or otherwise. He then pointed out that when he asked her what "another" way was, she never gave an answer. Actually, she said she didn't know. But Leavy had the answer: "I have an idea what it is . . . after we blasted her with Sam Sirianni— just some reason to get up here and flaunt herself before you, flaunt herself—because the Sirianni alibi was gone. Some reason, yes. You gentlemen, you're on the spot. She believes she can turn your heads from the performance of your duty in this case, and I don't believe so."

He was accusing her of trying to seduce the men on the jury. And not just that once. He returned to that theme again and again, saying that Barbara only took the stand to give a second alibi "so she could flaunt herself." And that "she's got to get onto the stand so as you gentlemen can see her, and she's got to say something, as she said in the letter, 'I don't have an alibi' and 'I'll just get up there and look pretty.'" And she said she was "at home with the husband . . . so as she could take the stand, so as you gentlemen could see her."

According to Leavy, then, Barbara wasn't forced to testify because her lawyers had been ambushed by the devastating testimony of Sam Sirianni that made a death sentence a demonstrable reality. No, she only took the witness stand so she could "flaunt" herself in front of the male jurors.

It was morally repugnant and outrageous that Leavy, the man responsible for engineering the very predicament that left Barbara with no choice but to testify, would now claim she'd only done so in order to bat her eyes at the men. And his interpretation of the lines in that letter was patently wrong. The line "I'll just get up there and look pretty" was clearly meant to be a joke, a form of gallows (quite literally) humor. There were many other remarks in her letters that showed Barbara was painfully aware that her chances of persuading the jury without a corroborating witness were very slim. No matter how "pretty" she looked.

But Leavy didn't stop there. He moved on to take a sideswipe at Barbara's lawyers, citing a little-known section of the Business and Professions Code as proof that even Barbara's lawyers didn't believe her alibi. Quoting from section 1268 in that code, Leavy argued that criminal lawyers were required to present a defense whether they believed it or not, and therefore: "Even though they might believe that wasn't the truth, it would be their duty to present it." (Actually, the correct code section is Business and Professions Code section 6068.)

That argument was yet another instance of prosecutorial misconduct. Even back in those days, prosecutors were not allowed to disparage defense attorneys' motives or speculate about what they do or don't believe. Not only is it highly unethical, it's irrelevant. What an attorney believes or doesn't believe matters not at all.

The defense should've objected to that shoddy insult, but they didn't. Very possibly because they had little reason to believe Judge Fricke, whose prosecutorial bias had been increasing on a daily basis, would sustain the objection.

To add insult to an injury, Leavy then accused Barbara of deliberately falling down the stairs at the beginning of the trial in order to buy time because Sirianni had not contacted her lawyers as he'd promised to do. "Now, she needs time. Something was happening, something had happened to Sam Sirianni . . . She needed time, folks, and according to her testimony the next day [after he failed to meet with lawyers] she falls down the back stairs. She needed time. She got it, she got three days."

It was yet another cheap shot, and one that failed to mention the fact that her supposedly fake fall was serious enough to land Barbara in the hospital with a concussion. In fact, Barbara had fallen a few times during her stint in the county jail, and she'd even told Donna about one of them in a letter—a letter Leavy had read to the jury when he cross-examined Barbara.

And he topped it off by reminding the jury that Barbara had invoked her right to remain silent when she was forced to appear before the grand jury. "She stood on her constitutional rights, refused to answer. That's good advice, if you're guilty. She says that's the advice of her attorney. That's good advice if you're guilty."

As the United States Supreme Court made abundantly clear, no prosecutor should be allowed to make such an argument, and no prosecutor could get away with making it today. In fact, more recently in 2014, a similar remark by a prosecutor—in part—caused the Tennessee Supreme Court to reverse the murder conviction against Noura Jackson.

Leavy made short work of Santo's and Perkins's defense. Not hard to do because they really didn't have one. Perkins's alibi stopped hours short of accounting for his whereabouts at the time of the murder, and Santo's exploded on contact when Alexander produced the recording of Santo's witness/mistress trying to suborn a false alibi.

Leavy then moved on to exhort the jury to vote for the death penalty for all three defendants. He made a point of reminding the jury that during voir dire they'd promised they could impose the ultimate penalty, and he expected them to keep their word—emphasizing the fact that Barbara was to be treated no differently than the other two defendants, that the instructions made no distinction as to gender. "You all gave us your word. That's why we settled on you folks. I said it was no formality. To use the expression, we mean business!"

Leavy then—in an effort to bludgeon the jury into returning a death verdict—hit the jackpot of prosecutorial misconduct:

I'm going to tell you folks something, so as you can exercise your sound discretion. This little bit of . . . argument with respect to the law, doesn't appear in the instructions of the Court in a murder case . . . and I tell it to you, because it is the law under our indeterminate sentence law in this State. Listen to this—because you are the ones who are going to be called upon . . . to exercise sound discretion. Sure, the law says for first degree murder the penalty shall be death or, as the words are, life imprisonment. Those are the words in the statute, or life imprisonment. But that is not the effect or application of those words under our indeterminate sentence law. No, sir. Listen to this!

Under our law, for life imprisonment for murder, a prisoner is entitled, after seven calendar years, to apply for parole. Sure, the state says death or life imprisonment, that's what the statute says, for punishment for murder. But we have other statutes, including the one I just mentioned, after seven calendar years a person under a life sentence for murder may apply for parole; and under our indeterminate sentence law our Adult Authority has the right to parole that person thereafter . . . I would say the average term for life imprisonment is about fifteen years for first degree murder. Some of them serve more; some of them serve less.

This argument was aimed straight at the layperson's fear that anything short of a death sentence means the defendant could get out of prison at any time. It's wrong and outrageously unethical. In any courtroom today, those remarks would've earned him a mistrial and a sanction by the state bar. No prosecutor is allowed to even hint that a defendant might get paroled, or that "life" doesn't really mean their whole life. Why? Because it invites the jury to speculate about something that neither they nor the prosecutor can possibly know. The prosecutor has no idea whether or when a prisoner will get parole—and neither did Leavy. A defendant might very well wind up in prison for the rest of his life. And Leavy's assertion that the "average term" was fifteen years is even worse. What's the source for that claim? There was no evidence to back it up. None. And what does the "average term" have to do with the evidence in this case? Nothing. While Leavy was allowed to talk about whether the death penalty was appropriate for this crime and these defendants, he had no business telling the jury how much time they'd serve if they got a life sentence.

And that argument might well have impacted the jury's decision on guilt as well. It wouldn't be the first time a reasonable doubt got pushed aside due to fear that a "likely"—but not beyond a reasonable doubt—guilty defendant would go free. Today, there's a standard jury instruction that prohibits the jury from considering what sentence a defendant might get in deciding whether they're guilty. But at the time of Barbara's trial, no such instruction was given. This meant Leavy's illegal argument had the potential to unfairly impact the guilt verdict as well as the penalty decision.

Now it was up to Hardy to show the jury why they should reject Leavy's claims and find Barbara not guilty. Being tasked with the responsibility of defending someone who's facing the death penalty is the kind of burden that keeps a lawyer up at night, second-guessing every move, trying to make sure they've thought of every possible argument and marshaled every fact that might persuade the jury to acquit.

Hardy began by telling the jury how that burden weighed on him. And he became emotional as he told the jury how much harder it was for the defense, because—as Leavy had pointed out—he was a court-appointed lawyer and there was no provision for funds to pay for an investigation. Every penny came out of his pocket. He vowed that no matter what happened with this case, he would "try to do something about it," because it wasn't fair to the defendant. As he pointed out, the prosecution not only had a staff of investigators who worked for the district attorney's office, they also had the Burbank Police Department, the Los Angeles Police Department, and the Department of Justice. Whereas "Barbara Graham has had Jack Hardy and Ben Wolfe and their cohorts . . . I feel this very deeply—it's been a rough road." The *Los Angeles Times* reported that Hardy's voice broke as he said, "The prosecution in this case has had every resource of money and manpower."

Hardy then took on the quagmire that was Barbara's alibi. He said that from the beginning she had no memory of where she'd been on the night of March 9. He recounted an exchange they'd had on July 10, when he'd first been appointed. He'd asked her, "Where were you on the ninth of March?" And she'd said, "Mr. Hardy, I don't know where I was. Where were you? Nothing unusual happened that night. I was probably at home or I may have been with Mr. Logan."

He then took the unusual step of distancing himself from his client. "Now I know more about Barbara Graham than most of you, and she told me a lot of things about her life—and I don't admire Barbara Graham at all. She wouldn't be my kind of a girl—but she isn't on trial for that. She's on trial for her life, for a murder, and I don't care what she has done in the past, she's not on trial for any of those things."

The press obviously hadn't agreed with him about that. They'd damned her for her life of petty crime before the first witness was sworn in. Hardy could only hope the jury would be a little less judgmental. But he also had to contend with the fact that the jury knew she'd lied to him, telling him she'd been with Sirianni in an effort to get him to present a false alibi. No question about it, he had his work cut out for him. So although his tactic of admitting he disapproved of his own client was unorthodox, under the circumstances, I'd say it was a necessary strategy to earn credibility with the jury.

Hardy then showed why he hadn't objected to Leavy's little stunt of citing the Business and Professions Code to claim criminal lawyers don't have to believe their clients' defense. Hardy told the jury that Leavy was no "moral God" to say why Barbara should be condemned, that they should make very sure of who had done it, "and not just because someone has been accused. For twenty years Mr. Leavy has been in this court and in these courts saying that every accused person, every defendant was invariably guilty. For twenty years."

Now the shoe was on the other foot, and Leavy didn't care for it one bit. He hotly objected: "That's a misstatement . . . there is no evidence of that; and to the contrary, I have gotten up and said otherwise and I won't stand for that statement."

The judge issued a mild rebuke: "I don't know as the statement should be made in that form, Mr. Hardy. You may proceed."

Hardy took some decent swings at John True as well: "A confessed murderer comes in here and asks you to give credence to save his own lousy life—and also he's not completely free because there's still a conspiracy charge on file here against him, which has not been dismissed, and if he hadn't delivered he could still be tried on that, don't ever forget that—talk about motives for testimony—True would say anything about anybody to save his own rotten skin, and he has."

That was an important point, and one the jury had likely forgotten. And Hardy made another important point: the fact that prior to his appearance at the trial, True had full access to the grand jury transcript, which allowed him to see what everyone else had said and make sure his testimony matched up with theirs. I suspect True was also allowed to study Baxter Shorter's statement.

Hardy didn't spend much time on all the logistical absurdities of True's claims about how Barbara had attacked Monahan. It would've been a tough tightrope to walk: to argue that Barbara wasn't there, but that even if she were, she couldn't have been the one who pistol-whipped Monahan.

Still, he did make some smart observations. He pointed to the crime scene photographs that showed Mabel Monahan's glasses were near her head where her body had been found, in the hallway next to the linen closet. But that's not where she'd initially been attacked. According to True, Barbara was standing near the front door when she struck Monahan. But if so, then Monahan's glasses would surely have fallen off right there, near the front door. Not down the hallway where she'd later been dragged by Perkins—probably assisted by True. As I've said, there were many reasons to doubt True's story, but this was yet another one.

And Hardy also made the more obvious point that with four big, strapping men on hand to do the job, "Why in the world would a girl that size be called upon to do the dirty work?" They wouldn't. Barbara, at five foot three and 121 pounds, is the last one they'd pick to get physical, but that's what made her the best choice to get Mabel Monahan to open the door.

Hardy then moved on to the subject of Donna Prow. Pointing out that Coveney used their "friendly" relationship to enlist her help, he said, "I think it is a part of our law enforcement and part of our American tradition not only to prosecute but to find out where the facts are, and also to protect the innocent . . . Now, Donna Prow was told to advance a friendship with Barbara Graham. She wasn't told to find out what the truth was . . . She was told to get Barbara Graham." And he pointed out that the jury never saw the notes Donna wrote to Barbara, or even all the notes Barbara wrote to her. Because, as Coveney testified, Donna had been too "embarrassed" to let him see the more amorous letters (cough, bullshit).

That—at a bare minimum—left a number of unanswered questions about exactly what Donna had really said and done. Chief among them, whose idea was it to seek out a false alibi? Although Barbara's letters show she was increasingly worried about her inability to find witnesses who could testify to her whereabouts, she never mentioned any desire to hire someone to lie for her until Donna talked about her underworld friend, "Vince"; i.e., Lieutenant Coveney. By that time, the trial was just two weeks away, and dear Donna was under the gun to produce. That

Coveney was pressuring her to get Barbara on board with a false alibi is more than just likely—it's highly probable.

Blumfeld, the head of the women's jail, testified she was under orders to make sure Donna's visits were conducted in private on the tenth floor and to keep no records of those visits. But even with that private access—which allowed Coveney to make an untold number of secret visits—the records showed that he also went to see her on the thirteenth floor *over seven times* just between August 4 and August 20 alone. This indicates two things: (1) that Donna was getting a lot of attention—read that as pressure to deliver—and more importantly (2) that persuading Barbara to go along with the program had taken a lot of doing.

And Hardy reminded the jury that although Barbara and Donna were writing at least once a day—and often more than that—from June until mid-August, of all those letters, only seventeen were produced in court. That means the vast majority of letters Barbara wrote were never produced, because she would've written Donna *over seventy letters* during the course of those months.

Granted, many were probably just chitchat and jail gossip. But certainly not all. Because Donna had a job to do, and her main source of contact with Barbara was via letters. So she had to do most of her work on Barbara in writing. And there's no way to know how many of Barbara's letters professed innocence or rejected Donna's offer of "help." Since Barbara's letters were picked over, first by Donna and then by Coveney and *then* Leavy, it's very likely only the most incriminating letters were preserved. Thus, Hardy concluded, "I would be awfully suspicious of that kind of a prosecution and that kind of a State's case." I couldn't agree more.

And obviously, it would've helped enormously if only they could've found Donna. During trial, Hardy had read the subpoena return to the jury in which the sheriff's deputy said he was unable to find her at any of the listed addresses. Now, he drove that point home again. "We tried to find her. We had no law enforcement agency. We tried to use the Sheriff's office and they . . . couldn't find her. Why didn't the State produce Donna Prow? No, that would have been a little too risky, the truth might have come out." He pointed out the very suspicious timing of Donna's disappearance, how Sirianni testified on August 27 and Donna got released the very next day.

As I read this part of Hardy's argument, I wondered whether the significance of what he was pointing out was registering with the jury. Even though neither Hardy nor the jury could know the lengths the prosecution went to in order to hide Donna Prow, they did know that not only had the prosecution declined to call her as a witness themselves, but the prosecution had also refused to help Hardy find her. Knowing that, the jury would have to conclude the prosecution didn't want Donna Prow to show up in court. But why? There was really only one reason: because she'd expose the fact that she was the one who'd suggested the fake alibi—not Barbara.

Next, Hardy tackled the thorny problem of Sirianni's testimony. Hardy did what he could, pointing out how hard Sirianni had pushed to get Barbara to admit that she'd been with Perkins and Santo, that she only did so after Sirianni had threatened to back out. And as for Barbara's damning statement that she knew Baxter Shorter wouldn't appear because he'd been "done away with," it was believable that—like everyone else who'd read about his kidnapping in the news—she'd only guessed he'd been killed and tried to make it seem like she had inside intel so Sirianni wouldn't back out of the fake alibi.

But Hardy was most passionate about his own role in driving Barbara to go along with this ill-advised scheme. As he urged the jury to understand the forces that drove her to go along with it, he confessed, "I want to say that I have said this privately and I'm going to say it publicly, I think that I was probably in a large measure responsible for Barbara Graham falling into Sirianni's police trap . . . Because I was convinced in my own mind, as I told her, that saying you are innocent and being innocent are fine, but in a case of this kind . . . you simply cannot say, 'I wasn't there, I don't know where I was.' And I said, 'It's a matter of desperation. You must remember where you were.' And she kept working on it, trying to figure out where she was . . . Finally, after it got to be a week before trial and Donna Prow kept egging her on—'Well, come on, I can help you. I can help you. I can help you—' And under the pressure that I exerted on her, of the utter necessity, as a matter of survival, that she had to remember where she was, she reached out like a drowning person for a straw and grasped at anything. And that was not an admission of guilt, ladies and gentlemen, that was consistent with innocence." Hardy quoted from Barbara's cross-examination, when she said, "Mr. Leavy, I was desperate!" and he added, "I wonder what some of us, including Mr. Leavy, might do under similar circumstances? I don't know."

It was the only viable way to counter Sirianni's testimony. But it was nevertheless legitimate. Between the pressure Hardy and Wolfe were putting on her and Donna's persistent efforts to make her accept "help" from the mysterious "Vince," not to mention the looming threat of the gas chamber, Barbara was under incredible pressure to make a choice: either stick with the non-alibi that she couldn't remember where she was—a surefire ticket to the gas chamber—or take Donna up on her offer.

If only she'd known that Corrine Perez—a witness so credible the prosecution tied themselves in knots trying to impeach her—would come through, she could've stuck to her original claim that she'd been at home. That would've given Hardy a good argument that there was a reasonable doubt about whether Barbara was involved. That argument might not have gotten Barbara an outright acquittal, but it very well might have left the jury deadlocked. At the very least, it likely would've spared her the death penalty.

Hardy—who by now had to be wrung out, emotionally and physically—ended his argument on an issue that haunted me throughout the many months I'd spent studying this case and continues to haunt me still. I could feel his anguish as he said, "The prosecution in this case . . . went to the lengths that I have never seen the like of to try to pin this atrocity on someone, and there wasn't too much difference who they pinned it on." He reminded the jury of Shirley Olson, the undercover cop planted in Barbara's cell to try and get her to confess, and described how Donna kept pushing until Barbara caved in and agreed to meet with Sirianni. "I never saw a case in my life where such utterly ruthless means with a person trapped up there in the County Jail—were taken to try to trap them and to get them to convict themselves."

Neither have I. And the way those efforts were focused almost exclusively on Barbara was as perplexing as it was repugnant. The way the prosecution systematically took aim at Barbara, the myriad ways they targeted her for character assassination—both behind the scenes in whispered asides to reporters, and in court, hammering home the romantic sign-offs in her letters to Donna—did not speak to a determination to see justice done. It spoke to a vendetta. I understand the desire to convict the guilty, particularly for a crime this heinous. But the way they went after Barbara, crashing through all ethical and legal guardrails in their zeal to take her down, was unprecedented in my experience—either as a prosecutor or a defense attorney. So I shared Hardy's utter incredulity at the way the prosecution had mistreated Barbara. I could actually picture him shaking his head as he walked back to his seat at the counsel table.

Sullivan's closing argument for Perkins and Santo rode on the back of Hardy's theme that the prosecution had employed underhanded tactics throughout this case. His point was that the prosecution wouldn't have gone to such lengths if they'd believed in their case, and the very fact that they'd done so cast doubt on the strength of the evidence. The problem with that argument was that his clients weren't the ones who'd been targeted. Barbara was.

The only reason the prosecution wound up with a recording of Santo's girlfriend trying to buy an alibi witness was because the person she tried to solicit went to the cops. The prosecutors hadn't set up anything; they just happened to get lucky. So, Sullivan really had no defense to work with. He did his best, but of necessity kept it short.

Now, the prosecution would present their rebuttal argument. This was their chance to answer the defense. And their last chance to persuade the jury.

CHAPTER NINETEEN

Alexander gave the rebuttal argument for the prosecution. He began by commenting on Hardy's emotional upset that the defense was given no resources to investigate their case, while the state had the assistance of multiple agencies. Hardy had only pointed out the truth. It was an undeniable—and huge—disadvantage. But Alexander saw it as an opportunity to take a shot at both Hardy and the defendants, stating,

> It's always a matter of regret that tears are shed by counsel. It's a difficult thing to see and watch a man shed tears, particularly counsel . . . I have been in this courtroom where people sat in the chairs where Santo, Perkins and Graham sit, people charged with the violation and mutilation of the bodies of babies, and their murder; and I have seen tears for those people, just as you have seen tears for the Grahams, Santos and Perkins. And you stop to analyze what are those tears for? Are they for the innocent victim that these people placed in that yawning chasm? Or are they for the miserable lives of those who destroy those innocent people?

Hardy's concern had obviously been the fact that the defendants could not get a fair trial given the disparity—a real "yawning chasm"— of resources. Alexander had no valid argument to counter that point, so instead he criticized Hardy's emotional response as tears shed for the mutilators of babies. It was a gratuitous, deliberately inflammatory remark that not only denigrated defense attorneys generally—and Hardy in particular—but also implied that the defendants in this case were no different than the mutilators and murderers of babies.

Not one word of that argument should've been allowed. But by the way, Hardy eventually got his wish: the system did change to ensure that attorneys who defend the indigent—whether they're court-appointed private counsel or public defenders—are compensated for their work and given the necessary funds to hire investigators and experts.

Alexander moved on to answer Hardy's criticisms about the way they'd treated Barbara by reading from the letters she'd written to Donna Prow. Leavy had already used them for cannon fodder during his argument, but determined to get his licks in, Alexander read them again, making sure to include every intimate or romantic word. His point was supposedly to show that their friendly tone proved Barbara wasn't really all that desperate—Hardy was.

But the excuse doesn't fly, because that was clearly untrue. Barbara repeatedly wrote about how worried she was, and more than once even said that she knew her lack of alibi might lead to a death sentence. I'd call that a pretty clear sign of desperation. It was a stupid argument that had no basis in the evidence or in logic. Of course she was desperate—who wouldn't be? And beyond that, it was largely irrelevant. Who cares if she was desperate? That didn't mean she was innocent. I'd have argued it meant just the opposite. So there was no valid reason to read Barbara's letters. It was just another excuse to highlight the fact, yet again, that Barbara was having an affair with a woman.

Alexander then tried to counter Hardy's criticism of the extreme manner in which they'd specifically targeted Barbara by using a line in one of her letters. She'd once written that if the police tried to question her, she wouldn't talk. This, Alexander insisted, meant the police had to pull out all the stops to deal with her: "Now, that's just another little insight into the lady we're dealing with, and why extra precautions and extra energy was expended in this case."

I admit, I'd been getting angrier and more disgusted by the minute as I read the prosecution's arguments, to the point where I'd had to get up and go walk it off several times. But when I read this one, I burst out laughing. Apparently in Alexander's world it's the rare, supremely dangerous, and wily defendant who prefers not to talk to the police. And when they come upon that uniquely nefarious creature, the police and prosecution have the right to go to any extreme to incriminate them. So of course, since Barbara said she'd refuse to answer questions, that meant they had carte blanche to do whatever it took to get her convicted and put to death—including planting an undercover cop in her cell, recruiting an inmate to lure her into a trap, and then using another undercover cop to force her to admit she was at the scene of the crime.

Alexander then turned to Hardy's accusation that the prosecution had willfully failed to help find Donna Prow. Aware of the serious implications of Hardy's charge, Alexander stooped to a new low. He had the unmitigated gall to claim Hardy never asked for their help in locating Donna, and that they'd had nothing to do with her release from custody. Both were blatant lies, disproven on the record. The following colloquy took place in full view of the jury:

Alexander: "I tell you now that at no time did Mr. Hardy ask the District Attorney's office to locate Donna Prow for him and I say that in his presence, at no time did he ask us to locate Donna Prow. And he knew he didn't have to ask us to locate Donna Prow. You heard him tell you that Donna Prow was on probation. If I were to locate Donna Prow I would go right across the street or make a phone call across the street and get Donna Prow's probation officer and he would know where Donna Prow is, if I wanted Donna Prow. There is no reason for me to bring Donna Prow in."

Hardy objected to this claim about the probation department as an improper reference to information that was not in evidence. Maddeningly, the judge disagreed, saying the subject of probation had been mentioned and that "one of the uniform conditions of all proba-tion is that the address of the person who is on probation shall be given to the probation officer and the probation officer continually informed of any change of address."

What Judge Fricke seemed to have forgotten was that not only had Hardy asked the prosecution—and the judge—for help in finding Donna in open court, *and* on the record, but he'd also read the sub-poena return for her that showed the sheriff's deputy had done exactly what Alexander had prescribed: he'd gone to the probation department and obtained the addresses Donna had given. But when the deputy went to those addresses, he was told she was not in either location. And he put all that on the subpoena return—which the judge signed.

In fact, Hardy had closed the defense case by again reading that subpoena return on the record: "I hereby certify that after diligent search and careful inquiry, I have been unable to find Donna Prow—unable to locate at either address given. No longer living at Longview address, not in at Marsh St. address. State they have no knowledge of her whereabouts; being the witness named in within subpoena, in the County of Los Angeles. Dated 31 August, 1953. Sheriff of the County of Los Angeles. By A.R. Cabanis, Deputy Sheriff."

So it was very, very clear that Alexander was wrong. Not just wrong, but lying. Because he knew very well that they'd refused to help find Donna Prow, just as he knew they'd made sure to spring her from jail before Hardy could get to her. But Alexander wasn't finished. He had the nerve to add, "Donna Prow became a rather prominent figure before August 28th, and had he [Hardy] wanted Donna Prow up until the 28th of August she was here." Meaning, she was in county jail.

That was wrong for two very obvious reasons, and Alexander knew it.

First of all, Donna was certainly not a "prominent figure" before August 28. The very first time the defense even heard her name was when Sirianni mentioned it during his first day of testimony on the afternoon of August 27.

The prosecution had to keep her existence a secret until then, because Sirianni was a surprise witness. If they'd released Donna Prow's name to the defense before he testified, it'd reveal the whole plot, because she was the connection between Sirianni and Barbara. That'd be the end of their big bombshell. So Donna Prow's existence had to stay under wraps until the very last possible minute.

And there's no question that the prosecution had ambushed the defense with Sirianni's testimony. Leavy, during his closing argument, very proudly took credit for the way he sprang Sirianni on the defense: "They do not discover until August 27th . . . when we marched him into this courtroom, and for the first time they learn, Barbara Graham learns, that Sam Sirianni whom she thought would testify falsely for her, was a Los Angeles rookie policeman, working as an agent of the Burbank Police."

Hardy also made it clear in his closing argument that he'd been ambushed. He described his shock when Sirianni took the stand: "When Sam Sirianni came in here and was sworn as a witness and I recognized that name from what Barbara told me, the roof fell in on me. I tell you, it took me two days to realize what had happened and why it had happened."

So Hardy had no way of knowing about some woman named Donna Prow. But he moved quickly once he did and sent out a subpoena for her the very next day, as shown in the trial transcript and the subpoenas for Donna Prow that'd been filed with the court, dated August 28—further proof that he'd had no idea she existed until Sirianni testified.

Second of all, Donna could not have been found in the county jail on August 28—thanks to the actions of the prosecutor sitting right next to Alexander, who surely was well aware of that. J. Miller Leavy had called for an emergency hearing before Judge Mildred Lillie requiring Donna to appear in court on August 28. His whole purpose for demanding that hearing was to make sure she got released from custody.

Compounding the lie, Alexander went on to insist they had nothing to do with Donna's release, that it was all Judge Lillie's fault: "Now, if you want to question [Donna Prow's] release you may question the conduct of a judge of the Superior Court, who sits in another department, but I don't think you can honestly question the conduct of that judge when you consider the fact that Barbara Graham in writing told her, 'But Honey, if you double-cross me you know what I'll have to do.' In other words, very sweetly, 'I'll have to slit your throat from ear to ear!'"

Hardy objected to the latter statement as misconduct, but—of course—the judge overruled it.

Apart from the inflammatory nature of the remark, Alexander's claim that Judge Lillie released Donna Prow because of Barbara's veiled threat was a load of garbage. At the time Judge Lillie released Donna, Barbara hadn't testified, so none of the letters had been produced in court, and Leavy never showed them to Judge Lillie or even tried to use that particular letter to justify Donna's release. I guess—unlike Alexander—Leavy didn't really think it meant Barbara was threatening to kill Donna. That's likely why Leavy instead cooked up an obviously fabricated threat by another inmate who'd supposedly threatened to poison Donna. By the way, neither the note nor the inmate who supposedly wrote it was ever produced.

But Alexander—who surely knew what Leavy had done to get Donna released—doubled down on the lie and claimed Judge Lillie's decision to release her was a sound one, arguing, "Now let me ask you—Donna Prow up in that County Jail with Barbara Graham there, along with many others who think like she does, what chance would Donna Prow have for her safety? And if a judge in her discretion decides to release Donna Prow—and I say 'her' and advisedly, it was a female judge and a good one—can we quarrel with that?"

Yes, we can quarrel with that. Even a "female judge" can get hoodwinked by a dishonest prosecutor. And even if Judge Lillie had been justified in releasing Donna, the prosecution never explained why they let her disappear at will and refused to help the defense find her after her release.

Finally, Alexander moved on to the centerpiece of the prosecution's case: John True. He argued that True chose to talk; he didn't have to: "Now if True wanted to save his own hide as you were told, all True had to do is look me in the eye and laugh and say, 'I don't know what you're talking about. I wasn't there.' He had done it once in April and done it successfully . . . So had he wanted just to save his own hide he could have maintained that attitude." But True instead "endeavored to make himself right with man and God, and take that stand and tell the truth as to what occurred."

The fact that Alexander could make that argument with a straight face shows he must've been a pretty decent poker player. But if he actually believed it, it only proves he was a fool. And I don't think he was. In reality, True *had* been arrested in April, and then released when he claimed he wasn't involved. But what he learned during the days of his time in custody as he was questioned for hours at a time was that the police already knew a great deal about who'd done what. So he knew it was just a matter of time before someone else got arrested and decided to spill their guts. He could either beat them to it and make a sweetheart deal that would get him off scot-free, or he could keep acting dumb and wind up sitting next to at least two of his former compatriots.

And don't forget: when True was being held in custody in San Francisco, Lieutenant Coveney said he had the indictment for murder in his pocket and told him in no uncertain terms that if he didn't talk, he'd be facing the death penalty. Coveney even enlisted True's friend Seth Terry to help pressure him into giving a statement. Between Coveney's threats and the likelihood that if he didn't take the deal, someone else would, it really wasn't a hard call. True opted to "save his own hide." Alexander tried to dismiss his obvious motive to lie by describing True as a none-too-bright but useful idiot, saying he was "a powerful brute with not much between the ears." But it didn't take a genius to figure out which way the wind was blowing—and that was straight into prison if he didn't cooperate. True chose freedom.

In this way, Alexander largely ignored True's motive to lie, choosing instead to laud him as a brave truth teller, too dim witted to fabricate. To that end, he made a point of reminding the jury that neither Santo nor Perkins testified, saying their failure to take the stand was further proof of their guilt. But he took it even further and argued their failure to testify even qualified as corroboration for True's testimony.

Alexander's finale ended with an exhortation to vote for the death penalty that was yet another prime example of what—in any court-room today—would not only cause a mistrial but would also land him in hot water with the state bar: "We don't ask for the death penalty in every case . . . We try to find some redeeming virtue, something in the evidence which may be considered mitigating, something which by any stretch of the imagination we can say, while it is not an excuse, it is understandable . . . but where in this case can you find a single redeeming virtue for any one of these defendants? Where can you find a single mitigating circumstance? Where can you say under the facts of this case the extreme penalty is not warranted?"

This pronouncement that "we" only ask for the death penalty where "we" can't find any mitigating factors invokes the opinion of the district attorney's office and the personal opinions of the prosecutors in this case. This is absolutely forbidden. The reason is, it implicitly asserts a superior knowledge of what kind of case and what kind of defendant is deserving of the death penalty. "We don't ask for the death penalty in every case" sends the message that the prosecutors have insider information that led them to decide death was the appropriate verdict. It says, "Trust us, we're the experts" and "We know better than you."

That is exactly what the prosecution should never say and what the jurors should never do. The jury is there to impose the moral perspective of the community based on the evidence that has been presented to them in a court of law. Not to take a prosecutor's word for it based on some secret information supposedly known only to them.

Alexander wrapped up his presentation with an emotional plea: "Can you leave unheeded the cry of Mrs. Monahan from her grave? She cries for justice! The entire State cries for justice! Can you leave that cry go unheeded? I don't think you are the kind that will." He then exhorted the jury to sentence the three defendants to death, thanked them, and sat down.

What made Alexander's numerous misrepresentations and outright lies even worse was the fact that the defense had no opportunity to counteract them. No further arguments are allowed after the prosecution presents their rebuttal. That means it's up to the jury to catch those falsehoods. But in a trial that went on for weeks, it's unrealistic to expect that even the most diligent juror can remember everything that'd happened—let alone understand the legal significance of it all.

I can only imagine how Hardy felt as he watched the jury file out of the courtroom to begin deliberations, knowing how their ears were ringing with the many untruths and distortions he'd never get to counter. From personal experience, I can tell you that the moment when the jury leaves the courtroom is one of the worst. There's nothing more you can do. You can't call another witness, make another argument, or show another exhibit. You're helpless. Now, it's all up to those twelve. And they may see through the smoke to get to the truth . . . or not.

The jury would not only have to decide whether the defendants were guilty but also whether they should live or die.[7] If they found a defendant guilty, they would then have to decide on the penalty. But

---

7   In 1953, a capital case was handled in one single phase, and the jury decided both whether a defendant was guilty and what sentence should be imposed at the same time. Today, at least in California, a capital case is tried in two separate phases: the guilt phase is conducted first, and the penalty phase is conducted second. The jury must first render a verdict finding the defendant guilty of capital murder before even proceeding to the second phase. Only at that point does the trial proceed to the penalty phase, where evidence pertinent to the sentence is presented. The jury then votes only on whether the death penalty is appropriate.

the jury only filled out a verdict form for the penalty if they chose to show leniency and impose a life sentence. If they decided on death, they didn't have to fill out any verdict form. So if they sent out a verdict of guilty with no further statement, that meant the jury had voted for death.

Just two hours after they'd begun deliberations, the jury came back to the court with a question: "Does the penalty we select require the unanimous vote of all, or does a split vote give the death penalty?" The question spelled doom, but the answer was easy. The judge said, "Your verdict must be unanimous; in other words, as to both issues, the jury must be unanimous. Does that cover the question?"

The foreman: "That covers the question."

It also provided a very clear answer: if the jury was debating the penalty, that meant they had already decided to convict the defendants. Now, the only question was whether they would allow them to live.

After the judge answered their question, the jurors, who were now being sequestered until they reached a verdict, were escorted to dinner and then to the lodgings that'd been provided for them by the county: the Rosslyn Hotel on Fifth Street in downtown Los Angeles. Built in 1914, with an annex added in 1923, it was once the largest hotel on the Pacific coast, with 1,100 rooms. Though it was considered luxurious at that time, today, it's the site of "market-rate lofts and low-income housing." In other words, not so luxurious now.

Reporters focused almost exclusively on Barbara's reaction to the jury's question. According to the *Los Angeles Times*, she was the only one of the three who seemed to be "visibly upset" by it. The reporter said her eyes were "red-rimmed and watery" and her "pale, set face" showed signs of worry. But even in this most dire moment, they felt the need to again describe her hair—this time saying her "reddish blonde tresses" were "curled" in a "mass of tiny ringlets."

The *Daily News* reported a rumor that some jurors were "holding out against sending blonde Barbara Graham to the gas chamber." That article also said Barbara was the only one to show the "strain of the long trial" as Alexander gave his rebuttal argument, and that "deep shadows circled her eyes and her face was drained of color." It was also reported that she had spent a sleepless night despite being given a sedative. By way of contrast, Santo and Perkins—whose chances of escaping the gas chamber were deemed "slim"—reportedly had the same "noncommittal" expressions they'd worn throughout the trial.

But the *Valley Times* must've had a source inside the women's jail, because it led with a description of what'd happened when Barbara went back to her cell after the nine-man, three-woman jury posed their question. "A flood of pent-up emotion broke loose" and she "wept and sobbed in her jail cell" while a friendly matron "combed her now-darkening hair." She allegedly wailed, "My stomach feels all knotted up. Now it begins, waiting, waiting, always waiting. Why did this have to happen to me? Life is so short. Is mine to be shorter?" Santo and Perkins, on the other hand, were described as "calm" and "icy cool." This article, too, reported the rumor that the jury was hung on the issue of penalty.

At noon the following day, Hardy told a reporter that Barbara was "praying and reading her Bible." By 2:00 p.m. the jury announced it had reached its verdict. The judge took the bench at 2:45 p.m. Silence blanketed the courtroom as he examined the verdict forms, then handed them to the clerk. I envision Barbara staring at him, barely breathing as she waited to hear the words that would decide the rest of her life. The clerk read the first verdict. It was for Barbara. "We, the jury in the above entitled action find the defendant, Barbara Graham . . . guilty of murder in the first degree."

Barbara blew her nose into a small handkerchief, but remained calm. Now was the time for the clerk to read the penalty verdict—that is, if the jury had recommended leniency and voted to spare her life. But instead, the clerk continued to read the verdicts for Santo and then for Perkins: "Guilty of murder in the first degree."

It took a moment for Barbara to register what that meant. As the reporter for the *Los Angeles Times* put it, "The realization that she had been condemned to death in the gas chamber seemed to take root slowly as Mrs. Graham listened to the clerk intone the verdicts. Then tears welled in her eyes and she wiped them away with her handkerchief."

A reporter ran out of the courtroom when the last verdict was read. Outside in the hallway, a shout rose up from the waiting crowd as he told them the jury's decision. The jury was then polled individually to confirm that this was their verdict. Barbara, along with Santo and Perkins, watched as each juror confirmed that it was. The judge thanked the jury and dismissed them.

Barbara whispered to Hardy, "As long as they found me guilty of something I didn't do, I'd rather take the gas chamber than life imprisonment." But although "her face was chalky-white" and "her eyes red-rimmed," there were "no hysterics from this well-tailored murderess." The reporter seemed almost disappointed as he wrote, "Barbara doesn't kick over the traces. She doesn't leap to her feet to scream vile abuse at the jury. She doesn't swoon. She sits there and takes it with unexpected calm."

The *Los Angeles Mirror* drew a very different picture of Barbara's reaction to the verdict. While that reporter, too, quoted Barbara's words to Hardy, he claimed Barbara's "face was deathly white under her knotted reddish-blonde hair" and that "the 30-year-old Barbara broke into hot, blinding almost silent tears."

Perkins, as usual, appeared "unperturbed," and "his bony face with its waxlike skin is Sphinx-like. He glances over the jury seemingly unconcerned." But Santo's "eyes dart," they "seem red" and he "leans over and almost apologetically blows his nose vigorously." A strange description for Santo, who'd never come close to looking apologetic at any point. I wonder whether it was just wishful thinking on the part of the reporter, who was looking for any trace of vulnerability from the man who'd shown so little emotion throughout the trial. According to the *Los Angeles Mirror*, both Perkins and Santo "accepted the sentences with the same demeanor that has characterized their appearances in court for five weeks. Their faces remained pallid, expressionless, stoic."

The moment the judge left the bench, reporters and cameramen crowded around the three defendants at the counsel table like vultures landing on the dead carcasses of their prey, until guards hustled the defendants out of the courtroom. The spectators that'd filled the gallery gathered in the hallway outside, ostensibly to talk about the verdict. But the jurors had no intention of joining them. The foreman, on his way out of the jury room, told a reporter, "Our deliberations were our own and we voted as we saw fit. The job is done and we want to forget it."

One juror however—not the foreman—was more than happy to talk to the press. He admitted that "several jurors," both men and women, had hesitated over whether to vote for death for Barbara. But he "strongly denied" having any sympathy for Barbara: "That show she put on in court certainly had no effect on me."

But Leavy's argument sure did. That juror's remark showed Leavy had scored a direct hit with his warning to the male jurors not to be swayed by her effort to "flaunt" herself before the jury. That juror heard him loud and clear—and refused to be the dupe who fell for "that show she put on." Anyone who thinks a prosecutor's closing argument doesn't matter should let that juror's declaration sink in. As stated by the Ninth Circuit federal court of appeal: "Closing argument matters; statements from the prosecutor matter a great deal."

Back in the courtroom, District Attorney Ernie Roll and his two prosecutors were basking in their victory. The *Los Angeles Times* reported that Roll posed for photos as he congratulated "his two assistants who so vigorously and successfully prosecuted this case of stark, brutal murder—Adolph Alexander and Miller Leavy, saying, 'They did a terrific job.'"

Meanwhile, Barbara nearly had to be carried out of court. Reportedly, "two husky female deputies" took her to her jail cell on the thirteenth floor of the Hall of Justice. There, she tearfully refused the sedative that was offered, and asked for her little son, Tommy, saying, "I want my baby! Please bring me my baby!" Then, "she put her head down on the desk and bawled like a baby." Barbara cried throughout the night and "kneeled by her steel bunk . . . clasping a paper-bound Gideon's Bible in her trembling fingers."

By all accounts, her mother-in-law, Hank's mother, had been bringing Tommy to see Barbara in jail throughout the trial. As for Barbara's two older sons, she apparently lost contact with them after her mother ruined her effort to reestablish ties in the years before the trial.

I take no position on whether the death penalty should be allowed, other than to point out that the advances in forensic science have increasingly revealed that wrongful convictions—while still rare—happen more than anyone had suspected. And there have also been changes in the law that reflect a more nuanced approach to the felony murder rule. Back in 1953—or even 1977—a defendant who drove the getaway car in a liquor store robbery where someone accidentally got killed was not only guilty of murder, but they'd be eligible for the death penalty or life without the possibility of parole, even if they'd never planned to kill anyone or even knew someone had a gun. Today—at least in California—that defendant would likely only be liable for robbery. As the United States Supreme Court has held since at least 1982, a getaway driver in a bank robbery shouldn't necessarily be sentenced to death because his cohort spontaneously panics and kills someone. The fact that our sensibilities have changed so dramatically in a relatively short period of time gives reason to consider whether a sentence as irreversible as death should be available.

But I do take a position in condemning the procedure that allowed a jury to choose a death sentence merely by saying nothing. At the very least, a jury's vote for the penalty that will end someone's life at the hands of the state should require that they memorialize that decision with a written declaration signed by the foreperson. And require that the jury be polled individually and answer out loud when asked if they'd chosen the sentence of death—as they routinely do for a verdict of guilt. To allow an absence of any declaration to serve as an affirmative vote for such a momentous, irrevocable decision encourages cowardice and irresponsibility. A jury that believes beyond a reasonable doubt that a defendant deserves to be put to death should be willing—and obligated—to actively and publicly say so. Today, at least in California, that is the procedure.[8]

The day the jury handed down Barbara's verdict was the last day of Hardy's involvement in the case. He'd worked tirelessly—and exclusively for her—over the past several months, with no pay. He had to revive his flagging practice and make a living again.

But because she'd been given a death sentence, Barbara was entitled to an automatic appeal to the California Supreme Court. That meant she'd get a new lawyer to represent her on appeal.

On October 6, 1953, Al Matthews agreed to take on the mantle. He would be Barbara's lawyer and protector to the very end.

---

8 As of this writing, however, the governor of California has declared a moratorium on capital punishment and ordered the dismantling of death row in San Quentin State Prison.

CHAPTER TWENTY

Both Matthews and Sullivan made motions for a new trial on behalf of their clients. Predictably, those motions were denied. On October 6, 1953, Judge Fricke pronounced the sentence of death as to Santo and Perkins. One week later, on October 13, 1953, he pronounced death for Barbara as well.

Now, the case would go up to the California Supreme Court on an automatic direct appeal, as was—and still is—required for death penalty cases. Direct appeals in criminal cases involve written briefs that present arguments based on any legal errors reflected in the transcripts. No new evidence is allowed. And in order to win a reversal, the errors have to be serious enough to show that the defendant would have fared better if those errors had not occurred. It's no easy thing to do, which is why appeals in any criminal conviction seldom result in reversal. And unless there's a request for oral argument, there are no more personal court appearances.

The only other avenue to overturn the conviction lay in a petition for a writ of habeas corpus. But back then that was an even tougher burden to carry. Al Matthews would have to show one of two things: (1) that there was newly discovered evidence that couldn't have been found by the time of trial and that would have justified an acquittal, or (2) that her trial lawyers had rendered such ineffective assistance that their unprofessional mistakes and failures caused her to be convicted when she ordinarily wouldn't have been if she'd had a competent attorney.

The bar for proof of ineffective assistance of counsel is very high. Courts have rejected a claim of ineffective assistance even when a lawyer was proven to have fallen asleep during trial. Given the prodigious efforts put in by Hardy and Wolfe, that claim would never fly.

So Matthews's only real hope for overturning the conviction was the discovery of new evidence—and not just any new evidence would do. The law at that time required that the newly discovered evidence had to point "unerringly to innocence."[9] That's an incredibly high bar.

If all those options failed, Matthews was left with a bid for a grant of clemency from the governor. That wouldn't set Barbara free, but it would spare her life. The search for new evidence might help here too. Because even if Matthews's investigation didn't turn up the kind of evidence that'd justify a reversal, it might be enough to persuade the governor to reject the death penalty. However, the governor at that time was Goodwin Knight, a Republican, so that, too, was an uphill battle. The one small ray of light was that the attorney general, Pat Brown, was a Democrat and an opponent of capital punishment. If they could win him over, he might be able to persuade Knight to let Barbara live.

All of these options were long shots. Still, Matthews set about trying to find the evidence that three law enforcement agencies and all the lawyers had missed. I would've thought he'd hire a private investigator, which usually means a retired cop. But he decided to go in a different direction. Carl Palmberg had a degree in criminology, and some of the comments in his reports offered insights that indicated he might've also studied psychology. He was certainly an unorthodox choice. But it turned out to be a great one. Carl was smart, resourceful, and tenacious, and his diligent investigation would turn up all the information on Donna Prow's history, and her connection to Lieutenant Coveney.

Carl met with Barbara frequently, and he became convinced she couldn't have killed or even assaulted Mabel Monahan. It seems he may have conducted psychological testing on her as well, because he found

---

9   In re Branch (1969) 70 Cal.2d 200, 214.

that Barbara had a positive aversion to violence. So at least now—finally—she had a team working for her that included an investigator.

And as her letters reveal, Barbara grew close with both Al Matthews and Carl. They became as much friends and confidants as a legal team. In a letter to Matthews dated October 12, 1954, she wrote about her memory of a funny personal story he'd told her: "Dearest Al, I was very happy to see you yesterday. And honestly, Al, I'll never recover from what you said about that party, it is just too much, I was lying here this morning listening to Verdi's Rigoletto, and as you know, there is not one on [sic] thing funny in that opera, when all of a sudden the vision of your knocking on your desk, saying 'here here' [sic] and the eyes looking reverently up at the wall, passed thru my mind, and it was too much for me. I burst out laughing, right out loud. Couldn't help myself . . . I owe Carl a letter, but it is such a task to pick up the pen these days, in fact I owe everyone. I thought I would write him today, but I will try again tomorrow."

She bared her soul to Matthews on multiple occasions in letters like this short note written on December 29, 1954: "I am in a deplorable frame of mind. At my lowest ebb, I might say. Nothing seems to have any meaning. Do you have any suggestions as to how to fill these empty days and nights."

And Barbara's little team soon gained an unexpected—but dedicated and valued—member: Ed Montgomery, a Pulitzer Prize–winning investigative reporter for the *San Francisco Examiner*. He'd been solidly on the side of the prosecution and contributed to many of the scathing commentaries about Barbara throughout the trial. But toward the end, as he sat in the courtroom, he began to have doubts. He eventually realized that he'd been taken in by the relentless drumbeat of overheated rhetoric by the prosecution, the police, and the press who—right from the start—had condemned Barbara as a depraved, heartless villainess whose life of crime had left an untold number of victims in its wake. And in that revelatory moment, Montgomery was forced to admit his own role in that demonizing chorus, bent on the destruction of a woman who might very well be innocent. Rather than summarize the moment he made that turn, I'm going to let him speak for himself. This is an excerpt from the book he began to write—but never finished—about the trial:

From the Burbank and Los Angeles police and from the district attorney's staff diatribes flowed like water—small tributaries of adverse information, fact and fancy alike, which helped swell the mounting current of public indignation—an insurmountable tide of lasting prejudice. A dope fiend gun moll. The mistress of Jack Santo, that ruthless killer of men and children. A hop head sadist who told the police to go to hell. This was but the beginning of the printed abuse heaped upon Barbara Graham by eagerly competing newsmen as each succeeding edition went to press. Here were the sparks, once kindled, that mushroomed into the all encompassing flames of public prejudice and bias. Accepted as gospel truth on the mere say so of some quote hungry official and broadcast at large on the traditional surmise that you can not libel a loser.

As though hypnotized by our words, nearly all of us bought outright the prosecution's premise there could be no good in Barbara Graham. Newsmen covering the trial from day to day in the heavily guarded courtroom and those of us in distant city rooms doing rewrite from the extensive wire coverage were of a common mind—Barbara Graham was guilty as hell and it was up to me to let the world know it. The public was given no respite from the constant doctrination that here was a girl that was every bit as rotten and as vicious as the two men seated to the right of her at the counsel table. Three of a kind—three of the worst.

Montgomery went on to describe the hulking Santo, forty-one years old, who'd called the shots on a "series of brutal robbery murders," and Perkins, his shrewd, conscience-free, homicidal lieutenant who'd aided and abetted Santo in the beating death of a young father and three young children, leaving the fourth—a three-year-old—near dead.

As Montgomery described it, his turnabout came when he sat in the courtroom during the last phase of the trial, giving him a chance to observe the three defendants at close quarters. But now, without the remove of his "distant city room," he was struck by the contrast in both looks and demeanor between those two men and Barbara Graham.

"While Perkins and Santo looked the part, Barbara resembled anything but the brazen hophead she had been depicted as being. The sadism the prosecution claimed constituted her very being was not reflected in her hazel eyes and almost delicate features. She looked more the part of an attractive young matron—the charming housewife—than she did the murderess."

As I read those passages, I imagined Montgomery processing the initial shock of the stark contrast between the Barbara he saw in person and the woman he'd heard, read, and written about. Then, how that shock kicked his journalistic instincts into gear, propelling him into an investigation of his own to find out whether the doubt that'd sprung up in his gut would find roots in evidence yet uncovered.

It did surprise me that he was shocked. Montgomery was an experienced reporter who'd covered criminal cases for years. He surely knew that murderers come in all shapes and sizes. There's no such thing as a "look" that invariably brands someone as a murderer. It'd been my job as a prosecutor to remind jurors of that fact for years, in one trial after another. And I made a point of saying that was true from either perspective: that a defendant who looked like someone who'd commit murder might very well be innocent, just as a defendant who looked like a choirboy might be a killer. The old adage that you can't judge a book by its cover happens to be true. If you want to know what that book is about, you have to read the thing—i.e., see the evidence.

So I have to believe there was something more to Montgomery's revelation in the courtroom that day. That he was picking up on the kind of inchoate, intangible signals that form connections on a subconscious level.

We aren't usually aware of it, but we make connections like those every day. I have a vivid memory of one such experience. I was in an elevator with a male friend—not a boyfriend—and another man stepped inside. As he pushed the button for the third floor, I was hit with a wave of violent energy radiating from him. I fought the instinct to back away, afraid to draw his attention—and doubting my own intuition. When he got off the elevator, my friend turned to me and rolled his eyes as he exhaled. "Wow, that dude had some kind of evil intention going on there. Did you feel it?"

That was certainly not the only time I'd had a visceral reaction to someone just based on a feeling. But I remember that particular experience because someone else had felt it too. That time, I couldn't dismiss it, thinking, "It's probably just me." Thus do we gaslight ourselves far too often. Women in particular.

In Montgomery's case, that feeling must've been very strong because it inspired him to go to great lengths to explore Barbara's case. He collaborated with Barbara's attorney, Al Matthews, in her bid for clemency, searching for information that might show there was reason to doubt her involvement in the crime. After the trial, he met with Barbara several times—and with Perkins and Santo as well. He'd hoped the two men, and especially Perkins, might break down and admit she was innocent. Carl Palmberg predicted that particular effort would fail. He'd interviewed them, and they'd made it clear they'd never take the fall and exonerate her. They were convinced the state would never put her to death, and if she—the pistol-whipping savage—were spared, then the state would have to spare them too. Not the most brilliant strategy. But they weren't brilliant—and they didn't have a lot of options.

And yet, one of Montgomery's last visits with Perkins had given him hope. Referring to the pistol-whipping of Monahan, Perkins had said, "You'll never convince me that she [Barbara] did it." On hearing that, Montgomery told Perkins that if he had information that would exonerate Barbara, he owed it to her to tell him. When Perkins subsequently did ask to see Montgomery, it seemed he'd decided to do the right thing. But when Montgomery went back to take his statement, Perkins was angry and in no mood to help anyone. The guards hadn't kept his request to see Montgomery confidential, so everyone knew about it, including Santo—and he'd told Perkins to keep his mouth shut, that they had to keep "the girl out in front." Santo was still hopeful they could ride Barbara's coattails to a commutation, if not a reversal.

Still, for what it's worth, the fact that Perkins had asked to meet with Montgomery after having said in the past that he'd never believed Barbara killed Monahan is some evidence that he knew Barbara hadn't been the one who'd attacked her. Perkins's word never would've been enough to get her conviction reversed. The only way it could've helped was in Barbara's bid for clemency. The governor is allowed to take information like that into account in deciding whether to spare someone from a death sentence. Whether it would've made a difference to Governor Knight, we'll never know.

Although Montgomery's efforts with Perkins hadn't panned out, he did have some luck in other areas. He'd pitched the idea of making a movie and writing a book to drum up support for Barbara's cause, and film producer Walter Wanger saw a good story in it. With his help, Montgomery unearthed John True's original statement to Alexander on June 4, 1953, that had never been given to the defense. He pointed out the inconsistencies between that statement and True's testimony, which would've helped to cast doubt on his reliability, and he later successfully spearheaded the demand for an inquiry into the need for better discovery rules based on the prosecution's failure to turn it over.

Montgomery wrote and spoke often about his change of heart and the guilt he felt for the part he played in blackening Barbara's image with the public. His announced belief in Barbara's innocence made some other reporters take another look at the woman they'd so universally condemned. Now, they revealed that "Bloody Babs," the hard-hearted blond murderess, had been neglected and abused from birth, rejected by a cold, unfeeling mother who'd never wanted her. Barbara's two-part article in the *American Weekly* in April 1954, as told to Stuart Palmer, which described her impoverished, desolate childhood and thwarted efforts to find a normal, law-abiding life as an adult, was republished in the *San Francisco Examiner*.

And Bernice Freeman, a reporter for the *San Francisco Chronicle*, who often did columns about death row inmates in San Quentin, and—like Montgomery—had initially been convinced of Barbara's guilt, also found reason to doubt that belief after digging a little deeper.

Freeman interviewed Barbara at length when she was on death row. In those meetings, Barbara steadfastly maintained her complete innocence. She insisted she hadn't been with Santo and Perkins that night. But Freeman knew Barbara had never been able to come up with a solid alibi, and she also knew Barbara had been arrested in the company of Santo and Perkins. So at first, she was fairly certain Barbara was guilty. But over time, she began to waver. Barbara had no violence in her past. And as Freeman came to know her, she found that Barbara had neither the inclination—nor the stomach—for an act as savage as the pistol-whipping of anyone, let alone an elderly woman.

In Freeman's book *The Desperate and the Damned*, the description of Barbara presented a sharp contrast with the image of the vicious murderess that'd continually been depicted in the news: "A small brunette of about thirty years, she had huge brown eyes fringed with long, dark lashes, and soft olive skin. She wore her floor-length, navy-blue housecoat like an evening gown, and around her slender neck was a narrow band of black velvet ribbon. As she talked, she waved a long, black cigarette holder, which she held in one tiny, well-manicured hand. The girl was a little beauty."

Freeman's description of Barbara's "tiny, well-manicured hand" in particular intrigued me. It was totally at odds with the way reporters had highlighted Barbara's "strong" hands and fingers—a very unsubtle effort to show she was entirely capable of violently clubbing the victim with the butt of a pistol. It was yet another example of the gross sensationalism that had infected the press so completely it was difficult to believe anything beyond the most basic dates, times, and places.

Their talks ultimately compelled Freeman to track down John True. He was living in a trailer in Sausalito at the time, a beautiful little seaside town outside San Francisco—though not so beautiful in the low-rent neighborhood where True lived. Freeman described him as small, "quick-moving and quick-thinking," and handsome, with iron-gray hair and "sea-blue eyes." Over the course of their conversations, he gave brief accounts of the murder that varied with each telling, but during their last meeting he went into greater detail. He said that after someone put the pillowcase over Monahan's head, she was still moaning, and that Santo told Barbara to shut her up. Barbara "belted" Monahan with the pistol, and then "lost her head." She "took one of her shoes off and whacked the old lady with the heel of it. She kept on smashing away with the pistol in one hand and the shoe in the other until Santo and Perkins got disgusted." He claimed he'd had to "haul her off that poor old lady," and that even then, he "couldn't stop Barbara from dragging her all over the house." The lurid, hyperbolic tale bore little resemblance to even his own testimony.

Small wonder that Freeman concluded John True was "careless with the truth" and that "his word, even under oath, should have been subject to more careful scrutiny than the jury had given it."

Barbara, who knew Freeman had met with John True, asked during her last meeting with the journalist, "Did you ever notice his hands?" At an earlier visit, Barbara had told her to look closely at True's hands, saying, "They're supple and strong. A man with hands like that can do anything." Now, Freeman said she had looked at them and thought they were "firm and powerful." Barbara then remarked, "Such hands! They're square and strong and quick, like the rest of him." When Freeman wondered why Barbara had asked her to look at his hands, Barbara replied, "Remember how that old lady was beaten and mauled? Put two and two together and you might make John True and Mrs. Monahan instead of four—or instead of me doing it."

It was the closest Barbara had ever come to admitting she'd been present. But when Freeman pointed out that was the only way she could know that it was John True who'd pistol-whipped Monahan, she again denied having been there. Freeman asked if Perkins and Santo knew it'd been True who "mauled" Monahan. Barbara said, "Of course." When Freeman suggested Perkins and Santo might make a "last-minute attempt" to save her, Barbara gave a dry laugh. "Do you think they're that kind? You know them. They don't care about anyone."

No question about that. Those two monsters clearly didn't care about anyone.

Still, for Barbara, it seemed the tide was beginning to turn.

CHAPTER
TWENTY-ONE

But on the legal front, things were not looking up. At Carl Palmberg's suggestion, Barbara offered to take a lie detector test to prove she hadn't committed the murder of Mabel Monahan. Al Matthews made the pitch to the district attorney's office and the state director of corrections, Richard McGee. Barbara was quoted as saying, "The only reason I want a new trial is because I'm not guilty of the Monahan thing. I don't want a commutation, I wouldn't want that because I couldn't stand to spend the rest of my life in prison."

Barbara had been offered a lie detector test when she was first arrested, but she said she'd refused because "there were about 60,000 cops around calling me all sorts of names." I can believe that. The police probably weren't all that polite to anyone they'd arrested. And they'd asked everyone—not just Barbara—to take a lie detector test, including John True, who'd stopped the test the minute the cops started to ask about the burglary and murder.

But District Attorney Ernie Roll wasn't taking any chances. His deputies had relied on John True's claim that Barbara had beaten Monahan nearly to death. If she passed the polygraph, it'd call the entire prosecution into question. He refused to allow Barbara to take it, stating that since she'd refused the first time it was offered, "nothing useful" would be served by letting her take the test now.

At that time Barbara was being housed in San Quentin, the high-security men's prison in San Francisco—a very unusual arrangement. Since she was the only female, they had to block off a section of the hospital wing and put a blanket over the bars so the male inmates couldn't get to her or even see her. That also meant Barbara—unlike the men—was alone for twenty-two and a half hours a day.

She'd originally been sent to the women's prison in Corona, but after learning in November 1953 that death threats had been made against her, the authorities decided to move her to San Quentin. The source of those threats wasn't specified, but it was believed that certain criminal elements thought she knew enough to be dangerous if she decided to talk.

My money is on Santo and Perkins. During the Monahan murder trial, it'd been reported that they were being investigated for other murders up north. By the time they got convicted for the murder of Mabel Monahan, two of those cases—the quadruple murders of a father and three small children up in Chester and the robbery-murder of a miner in Auburn—had been filed. If they got convicted, they were likely to get another death sentence in at least the Chester murder case, so they'd probably do whatever it took to keep Barbara quiet. But whatever the source, those threats must've been credible because making it safe for Barbara as the lone female in a men's prison was no easy thing. The extra security measures cost a bundle. So, unsurprisingly, when in 1954 it seemed the threat had passed, the legislature refused to authorize any more additional funds, and Barbara was transferred back to Corona.

I'm guessing Barbara found out about those threats. That'd explain why she wound up testifying for Santo and Perkins in the Chester murders in April 1954. She had nothing to do with those murders, and in fact didn't even know Santo at the time they were committed in 1952. But supposedly, an agent who was assigned to the Chester case had come to see Barbara in May 1953, while she was in jail, awaiting trial in the Monahan murder case, and offered to set her free if she'd testify that Santo and Perkins had committed the quadruple murders.

Barbara claimed she'd told the agent she couldn't help him, that when she'd asked them whether they'd committed the crimes, they told her they hadn't.

Calling on Barbara to tell that story was surely a sign of the defense attorney's desperation. I very much doubt anyone bought a word of it. I know I sure don't. I think it's highly unlikely anyone would've offered Barbara a complete pass for the Monahan murder, no matter what kind of information they thought she might have. And even if the jury believed her, I can't imagine why they'd give a damn that Santo and Perkins had denied their guilt. In a shock to no one, they got convicted in both cases and were again sentenced to death.

And things were not going well for Barbara either. Her legal prospects dimmed further when, on August 11, 1954, the California Supreme Court turned down her direct appeal and affirmed her conviction and sentence. Matthews now had to prepare the federal petition for habeas corpus that would take her case into the federal district court.

Barbara was distraught by the denial of her appeal, and it seemed that life in the women's prison in Corona was miserable. In a letter to Matthews dated September 23, 1954, she begged, "Please, please, if we cannot get a commutation, do not get me any more stays, I cannot stay here under this sentence any longer than Dec. 3. I have taken all the indignities they have heaped on me that I can. The insult that was handed to me today was really the crowning glory. Oh Al, you just don't know. I can't write more now, but please Al, no more stays, at least I *know* I can leave here in December. Sincerely, Barbara."

What those indignities were or what the insult that'd been the "crowning glory" was, she didn't say. Her next two letters to Matthews, written on October 12 and 15, 1954, didn't mention either subject. But the reason she knew she'd be leaving Corona in December was because Judge Fricke had set her execution date—and that of Santo and Perkins—for December 3, 1954, after the California Supreme Court affirmed the conviction and sentence. Since executions were performed only in San Quentin, Barbara knew they'd have to send her back by then.

Although Barbara seemingly blamed the conditions in Corona for her unhappiness, her letters reveal an inner turmoil and angst that likely had little to do with where she was housed. In her October 15 letter to Matthews, her emotional state seemed to swing from one end of the spectrum to another. After mentioning that Stuart Palmer—a columnist who'd collaborated with her on the two-part article for the *American Weekly*—had tried to visit her, she said, "Al, sometimes I get to thinking of people as I sit alone in here. And know something? I find myself pitying them, their scope of life is so limited, that they really don't know what it is to live. Do you understand what I mean? I don't know what made me write that, but it is true. My music must be affecting me. (smile)."

She frequently listened to classical music. In her previous letter, in addition to Verdi, she said that she'd also been listening to *Carmen* and particularly enjoyed the part where she did the Gypsy song and dance, but said that "for the most part it is the music that moves me."

But for all that she'd said she pitied people for their "limited scope of life," she then sank into an abyss of despair, writing, "The other day I was feeling so badly, and I had no shoulder on which to weep, so I sat down and wrote poor Sherry the longest, saddest, most morbid letter I have ever written. She said it took her hours to read it, because she had to cry every few lines. You're lucky you have never seen me when I am depressed."

So it seems her mood swings were fairly extreme. Given her circumstances, that was more than understandable. And Barbara herself remarked on it. She closed that letter to Matthews saying it was time for bed and that she was always "so happy" when she could "chalk off another day. Believe me, I have them down to a T. Bet you never had another client who thought the way I think. That's a woman for you. 'Nite for now, take good care of yourself, am thinking of you and praying for us. My regards to Mike and Polly if you see her. Most sincerely, Barbara."

In November, a Beverly Hills attorney joined Al Matthews on behalf of all three defendants. William Strong filed an application for a stay of execution with the California Supreme Court. In addition, he sent a telegram to the court via Western Union stating his request to add three federal grounds to the application based on the violation of the right to due process: "1) denial of effective representation of counsel by State's surreptitious use of Prow and Sirianni to obtain recorded statements, 2) involuntary nature of such admissions obtained by trickery and fraud, 3) use at trial of Graham's grand jury refusals to answer on grounds of incrimination."

Until this application and telegram, none of these issues had been raised. Al Matthews had focused his appeal on the argument that the evidence offered to corroborate John True's testimony was insufficient as a matter of law. As a practical matter, arguments that the evidence is insufficient as a matter of law are very hard to win on appeal. The court—whether it's a court of appeal or the California Supreme Court—would have to find that no rational jury would believe the evidence was strong enough to prove the charge—or in this case, that it was sufficient to corroborate John True's testimony. But the quantum of evidence legally required to corroborate an accomplice's testimony is minimal. Barbara's statements to Sirianni alone were more than enough to corroborate True. As long as those statements were admissible, Matthews's claims were doomed.

But the federal constitutional issues William Strong raised were right on the money. The scheme that put Sirianni in the visitor's room with Barbara after she'd been indicted for murder and was represented by Hardy deprived her of the effective assistance of counsel by maneuvering behind her lawyers' backs—a clear violation of the Sixth Amendment right to the effective representation of counsel. In addition, Sirianni's questioning was violative of the Fifth Amendment because it was coercive, forcing Barbara to confess or face the loss of an alibi. And Leavy's cross-examination and comment on Barbara's invocation of the right to refuse to incriminate herself was also a violation of the Fifth Amendment.

The only problem with these arguments was that they were ahead of their time. It'd be years before the courts acknowledged that these practices were gross constitutional violations. Still, the United States Supreme Court had the power to take the lead on these issues and set the bar higher if it chose to. And the court had long ago recognized that it was a violation of the Fifth Amendment for prosecutors to argue—as these prosecutors did—that a defendant's invocation of the right to remain silent was proof of guilt. It would only take one more step for the court to apply that federal constitutional holding to the states. So, Strong's move of taking the case to the United States Supreme Court was the only realistic possibility of getting Barbara's conviction reversed, though it too was a real long shot.

And that was clearly Strong's plan all along. He was required to file his claims in state court first to "exhaust state remedies"; i.e., give the state courts a chance to rule on them. But there was no way a state court was going to break with precedent and reverse on those issues. When the state courts predictably rejected his arguments, Strong immediately put them before the United States Supreme Court in a request for a stay of execution. And finally, there was a glimmer of hope: Justice William O. Douglas agreed to issue the stay to allow him to file a petition for a writ of certiorari. That writ asks a higher court to review the ruling of a lower court, and it's the typical way a case reaches the United States Supreme Court.

That was good news, but it was followed by a crushing blow. In her letter to Matthews on December 12, 1954, Barbara wrote that she'd just heard Carl Palmberg was in the hospital. "I feel simply terrible about him being ill. I wrote to him last night, but when I think of the letter now, I don't believe I was very cheerful. Will see if I can do better tomorrow . . . is his illness very serious?"

While Barbara was worried about Carl, she at least was having an easier time at Corona. Things had apparently improved. She wrote to Matthews, "Don't faint now. But I do not want to go back to San Quentin. Personal reasons. Will explain at a later date." She asked after Matthews and his family and guessed he was preparing for Christmas and New Year's, then asked him to give her regards to William Strong. Showing she was in a better frame of mind at this point, she closed by saying, "G'nite now, hope my letter finds you happy and in the best of health. You know don't you, how much I appreciate everything? I do. Sincerely, Barbara."

But just two months later, she got devastating news. Carl Palmberg had died of leukemia. His investigation—so close to being completed—now would never be finished. His notes remained unorganized, his final report forever unwritten. The *San Francisco Examiner* mentioned his passing in a brief note, stating, "With the greatest secrecy—and financed by several lawyers and newspapermen—he had been working to establish that blonde Barbara Graham, under sentence of death for the murder of an elderly woman in Burbank, is innocent . . . With his death died Barbara's last chance for survival. Small wonder she almost collapsed when she heard the news in prison."

Barbara wrote of her grief over the loss to Matthews. "Carl's death is a terrible shock to me. It seems impossible that I will never see him again. We have lost a very loyal friend. I wish I could attend his funeral, but of course I know I cannot. I wrote Sherry and told her to send flowers, but just received a letter from her this A.M. and she is in San Francisco. Two friends gone, for now I will not see her . . . Gosh, Al, I have had two horrible days and nights since Carl died. There is a saying the good die young, it was certainly true in this case."

One month later, Barbara wrote a letter of condolence to Carl's wife: "I have been intending to write for some time now, but words seem so inadequate at a time like this. I do know what a terrible loss Carl's death is to you, you have my deepest sympathy . . . Your husband was a fine man, Mrs. Palmberg, and I feel his loss deeply. I am sure that all who knew him, loved him. Will close for now, with the hopes that we can meet soon and that you always have the best from life. Most sincerely, Barbara."

Just a few days after writing that letter, on March 7, 1955, Barbara got still more bad news. The United States Supreme Court rejected attorney William Strong's petition for a writ of certiorari. In addition to the grounds he'd set forth in the Western Union telegram, he'd also argued that all three defendants had been "convicted by the newspapers, radio and press long before they were tried in the trial court." Justice Douglas, who'd issued the stay that vacated the December 3, 1954, execution date, dissented from the denial of Strong's petition without a statement.

It was the final, crushing blow. Any hope that her conviction might be reversed was now gone. Barbara wrote,

> I feel as though the bottom of everything has given way in me. What a horrible feeling, Al . . . Oh, Al I do feel terrible, out of it all tho, I want you to know how very much all you have done for me means to me and aside from the legal end of things, I value your friendship. I received your last two letters, and always I am pleased when I hear from you or see you. Funny, this morning when I heard the news, I was shocked to numbness, now the enormity of it has fallen full force on me and I cannot hold back the tears, yet they bring no relief. Life is such an odd game. To a degree Al, God has answered my prayers, for I did plead with Him to bring this to an end soon, and so He has. The suspense is almost over. I have never been one to show much emotion, but I am sure that if people could see into my heart, they would know that I am incapable of murder. Knowing that myself, I find a certain amount of peace in my heart, but even with that, the blow is hard.

Guess I should bring this to an end, I see I am becoming maudlin, forgive me, it was not my intention.

Do you believe there is any hope at all on the commutation, Al? I would appreciate your honest opinion, bad or good, remember how I felt about one at the beginning? I have changed now. Life does seem very dear to me. I do want to live . . . What a deplorable situation Al, at times it is still hard to realize that I am the main figure in all this. Insignificant Barbara Graham. If it wasn't all so serious, it would be funny, but my sense of humor has failed me at this point. I do hope all is well with you and yours. Please give my regards to Mike and Sig. Most sincerely, Barbara.

But by the end of May, just a week before the date set for her execution on June 3, she struck a surprisingly brave note that signaled resignation to her grim fate. The reporter who wrote the piece was remarkably sympathetic. For a change, there was no mention of her hair as the reporter described how Barbara spoke "casually" of her impending execution. "If I have to go to the gas chamber, I'll go with my head held high." Barbara said she knew her lawyer had exhausted all appeals but still hoped for a commutation. "You always hope, but if it is the will of God that I die, then I'll die. I'm at peace with God and with myself. I have no animosity toward people who have hurt me." Barbara said she'd been held in isolation for the last twenty-two months and that "even death would be relief from this hell." Asked what she thought of prison officials' fears that she'd try to commit suicide, she replied with a smile, "In a place like this it is easy to wish that you were dead, but I've never thought of such a thing. I'm a Catholic, and it is against my religion."

Straightening her shoulders, she said, "If people don't believe me and I must go, I'm not going to do anything dramatic about it. The date is close, but everything is in the hands of God now."

Or in the hands of Al Matthews, who at that very moment, was filing yet another habeas petition in the Los Angeles and San Francisco federal district courts, alleging that Sirianni's recording of his conversations with Barbara violated her right to privacy and amounted to coercion, fraud, and trickery. Both petitions were denied on June 1, 1955. Refusing to give up, Matthews went to work on the final push: a petition in the Ninth Circuit, the federal court of appeals.

But the very next day, on June 2, 1955, Barbara was moved to San Quentin, and into a cell that was right next door to the gas chamber.

CHAPTER
TWENTY-TWO

Warden Harley Teets was a kindly man by all accounts. He'd gotten to know Barbara during her last stay in San Quentin, and he'd grown fond of her. When she came back for her last visit, he did what he could to make it as palatable as possible. They put Barbara on the third floor at the end of the psychiatric ward. Her "suite" consisted of three rooms: a cell with a standard steel cot (Barbara got the royal treatment of getting sheets and pillowcases—something the men were never allowed) and a toilet, next to which was a small enclosed area with a portable shower fixture. Across from her cell was a matron's office and a corridor where they'd put an easy chair for the matron's rest breaks. Since the matron was there to ensure Barbara didn't try to harm herself, she had to maintain watch throughout the night. It struck me as more than a little strange that they wouldn't let a condemned prisoner die by her own hand. My only—admittedly cynical—explanation is that they just didn't want to deal with the consequences of an unsuccessful attempt at suicide.

As before, since Barbara was the only woman in a male prison, special care had to be taken to shield her from view. Warden Teets had the window of her cell covered in green plastic and draped blankets across the bars in every area that might allow the male inmates to see inside. Also, because her "suite" was right next to the gas chamber, Teets had the guards put a tarp over the door to spare her the sight of it. Still, in spite of all those efforts, her arrival had an inauspicious beginning.

Barbara hated the matron from Corona who'd accompanied her to San Quentin, and she was in a foul mood when she arrived. So when she greeted the registered nurse, Barbara Cates, who'd been assigned to spend the next twenty-four hours at her side, she was a little less than cordial. Cates tried to lighten Barbara's mood as she introduced herself, saying, "My name's Barbara, too." But Barbara wasn't having it: "Who cares? And I'm Mrs. Graham to you!"

Not lovely. But given what she was facing, understandable. Fortunately, Nurse Cates didn't let it rattle her. She took it all in stride. Warden Teets had known she would; that's why he picked her. He had a feeling she and Barbara would get along. Cates was Barbara's age, thirty years old, and she had two little boys, who were three and five. She'd be able to talk motherhood with Barbara, who was very devoted to her youngest son, Tommy. Throughout the trial, Barbara's mother-in-law had brought him to the county jail to visit her. Cates was also fairly hip; she spoke Barbara's language (Teets referred to it as "jazz" lingo), and she had a great sense of humor. But their introduction got even rockier when Cates told Barbara she'd have to do a full rectal and vaginal exam. They had to make sure she didn't have anything she might be able to use to harm herself.

Barbara flamed out. "Oh no you're not! You're not going to touch me! If I was going to I would've killed myself a year ago!" Luckily, before matters could spin out of control, Warden Teets, accompanied by the associate warden and the doctor, showed up for the customary night-before-execution visit. Cates met him outside the suite and told him about Barbara's reaction. Teets wisely said, "Then forget it. Just examine her belongings." Barbara had brought a small plastic suitcase with a few clothes, toiletries, and makeup.

Teets and company then went to see Barbara. When he asked if she needed anything, she requested only the chance to see her lawyer that night, and Teets was happy to oblige. He offered to give her anything she wanted for dinner. Barbara wasn't interested in food. But they nevertheless sent up heaping trays that included baskets of fried chicken and whole pies. Cates thought it was sickening. They ate none of it.

When Cates told Barbara she didn't have to worry about the internal body exam, Barbara relaxed and calmed considerably. From that moment on, they got along famously. But Barbara didn't like the matron they'd assigned her any better than the previous ones, and she told Cates about it. Cates might've advised the matron to make herself scarce, or maybe the matron got the message on her own, but whatever the reason, she stayed out of the way and spent the night napping in the nearby kitchen. Barbara and Cates sat in companionable silence for most of the evening, Cates sitting on a pillow on the floor next to the cell, Barbara inside the cell on her cot. Cates noticed that even now, Barbara was fastidious. After Teets left, she scrubbed her face, applied a liberal dose of bath powder, changed into a pair of red and black pajamas, then rinsed her stockings, folded her slip neatly, and hung up her skirt and blouse on the bars of the cell.

Matthews came to see her, and Cates moved to a position where she could see them but not overhear what they were saying. But Cates did hear one thing Barbara said to him: "If they ever realize the injustices they have done to me—if they ever write up my life or make a movie of it, I want Tommy to benefit from it. Someday they'll discover the wrong they've done." She gave Matthews a letter to give to Ed Montgomery in which she thanked him for all his efforts on her behalf.

The simple yet moving note would later be published in the book that accompanied the film about the case.

> Dear Mr. Montgomery,
> There isn't much I can say with words, they always fail me when most needed but please know that with all my heart I have appreciated everything you have done for me.
> Sincerely,
> Barbara Graham

Barbara didn't sleep; she chain-smoked and drank coffee all night, though she tried to lie down for periods of time. She and Cates shared stories about their children, and Barbara spoke of how much Tommy meant to her. They also talked about men. Predictably, since Barbara'd had her share of losers and Cates was trying to serve her deserting husband with divorce papers, the men did not fare well. A record player was in the room, but Barbara—who'd always loved jazz and classical music—never played any music that night. The radio was on in the background as they talked through the wee hours, and on occasion, the announcer would mention Barbara. Every time it happened, Barbara asked Cates to change the station.

At some point during the night, a sergeant who'd just been with Santo and Perkins came in. He was fuming, saying, "They could save that little girl if they would!" The sergeant had apparently suggested this was their last chance to exonerate Barbara. But her codefendants, who were in a separate wing, had instead just asked him for the baseball scores, then belched, rolled over, and gone to sleep, like the animals they were. Sometime later, a guard who'd been friendly with Barbara joined them to share a cigarette, and they all enjoyed their last visit together.

Early the next morning, the Barbaras got to talking about the crazy things they did in their high school days. They laughed about the weird food they ate, and one of them happened to mention hot fudge sundaes. Barbara said she didn't think she'd had one since she was in school, then said excitedly, "I'll eat one if you will!" Cates placed the order, and when the men in the kitchen heard who it was for, they made the biggest, fanciest sundae they'd ever seen. Cates offered to pay for it, but the sergeant insisted on picking up the tab.

After they'd finished, Barbara freshened her lipstick and combed out her soft, shoulder-length hair. She wryly remarked, "This is one time I wish it wasn't ladies first," commenting on the fact that she was scheduled to go to the gas chamber at 10:00 a.m. while the men were scheduled for later that afternoon. Barbara asked Warden Teets if she could wear a blindfold, and he gave her permission. The sergeant found a black sleeping mask and gave it to Cates. She put it in the kitchen where Barbara wouldn't have to look at it.

Cates later recalled that Barbara never once spoke of the case. Nor did she ever rail against her fate or indulge in self-pity. I have to believe that was fairly unusual.

Barbara must've known Matthews was papering the courts with petitions, feverishly searching for some way to stop the wheels that would crush the life out of Barbara from grinding forward. So when the call came in at 9:20 a.m., she couldn't have been completely surprised. The warden had been told to "delay everything for an hour." Barbara hadn't yet started to get ready, and Cates was convinced she was about to be saved. "You won't go, Barbara! You won't!" But Barbara was less sanguine. Nodding toward the room that had a tarp stretched over the door, she said, "That's the chamber out there, isn't it? I know it is. I know it." The guards had never said what was behind that door and they gave no answer now, still trying to protect her from the horror that awaited her.

But it wasn't Matthews who'd provoked that delay. It was William Strong. He'd placed a call to the governor at 2:00 a.m., saying he'd found a case that showed Sirianni's act of taping his interrogation of Barbara was illegal, which meant her statements to him should never have been admitted into evidence. Governor Knight had someone check out Strong and determined he really was a lawyer and that no one had previously mentioned the case he'd cited. After studying the case, the governor immediately woke up the chief justice of the California Supreme Court to tell him. He was apologetic, but the chief justice said no apology was necessary. That's what he was on hand for. He would convene the entire panel of justices at nine o'clock that morning to consider the new case Strong had cited. The execution was scheduled for 10:00 a.m. The governor's office called the warden to tell him to hold off for an hour.

The justices moved swiftly. By 10:24 a.m., they'd rendered their decision: the case Strong had cited did not justify reversal. Governor

Knight called Warden Teets. "I have talked with the Chief Justice of the state supreme court and with the Chief Justice of the circuit court of appeals. All of the applications have been denied. There is nothing further in my office or before me to prevent the carrying out of the sentence of the court."

Warden Teets made the sorrowful trek to Barbara's cell to give her the news. She changed out of her pajamas and put on her skirt suit, but her hands were shaking too badly to put on her earrings. Cates put them on for her. The doctor fitted the webbed harness over her chest with the hose that would attach to a stethoscope he would listen to outside the chamber so he'd know when to pronounce her death. Teets handed her the blindfold. The guards laid down carpeting between her cell and the door of the gas chamber, because the floor was cold and she'd have to go barefoot. But Barbara wanted to wear her high-heeled patent leather shoes. Warden Teets could hardly refuse her this one last wish. He gave the okay, and she headed toward the last door she would ever pass through. It was almost over. All the months of waiting, of imagining, of dreading would finally end. There might've been some measure of peace in that.

But just as she reached the doorway to the gas chamber, the phone rang again. Another emergency writ requesting a stay of execution had been filed with the California Supreme Court—this time by Matthews. Barbara had managed to maintain some semblance of composure up to now. But the unexpected delay at the very brink of the doorway finally broke her. It was too much to bear. As the guards escorted her back to her cell, she cried, "Why do they torture me? I was ready to go at 10!"

Finally, at 11:10 a.m., Teets got the last phone call. He entered the suite slowly. "Barbara, I'm very sorry, but this is it." He gave her the mask. Now weakened by the prolonged trauma, she needed the support of the priests on either side of her to manage this last walk. She leaned on them as she moved, head down, to the gas chamber.

J. Miller Leavy, in attendance to savor his triumph once again, witnessed the execution in the company of over a dozen journalists.

Points given to those reporters for consistency. As they had throughout the case, they once again focused on her physical appearance. The *Los Angeles Times* reporter adopted a heedlessly callous tone, writing, "The brashly attractive 32-year-old convicted murderess, her bleached blond hair turned to its natural brown . . . walked to her death as if dressed for a shopping trip." Following up on that theme, the *San Francisco Examiner* described her as though she were attending a fashion show: "She wore a beige wool suit with covered buttons, pumps, gold pendant earrings and wedding band." The *San Francisco Examiner* even treated her blindfold as though it was a fashion accessory: "Her face was an ivory cameo accented by the mask [blindfold] and her rouged crimson lips"; "the mask hid her tired eyes and she looked pretty in her beige suit"; her hands trembled, and "her small pendant earrings quivered nervously," but she retained her composure.

Barbara entered the gas chamber at 11:31 a.m., and because she was blindfolded, the guards talked her through the step up to the chair. As the guards seated her, "she was trembling in hand and body . . . and her lips moved constantly, apparently in prayer as the guards adjusted the straps across each arm, her chest and legs. One of the guards asked her whether the straps were all right and she briefly nodded and seemed to speak. He patted her on the shoulder as he stepped out of the chamber. The other told her to breathe normally, then left."

The pellets dropped at 11:34 a.m. The air began to fill with the noxious gas.

The reporter wrote, "She sat quietly, wetting her lips once or twice for almost a full minute. Then she breathed deeply and her head fell forward—either in a faint or from the first whiff of the hydrocyanic acid fumes."

Gene Blake of the *Los Angeles Times* described her final moments in graphic detail. He reported that "it seemed an interminable time before death came . . . She gasped and drew her head up twice. Then came another gasp. Then her head tipped far back, her mouth agape. Again and again she gasped until her head pitched forward for the last time at 11:37. Her gasps came slowly and fainter. And finally stopped." Journalist Al Martinez wrote that Graham "gasped and strained against the straps that bound her . . . foam bubbled at her mouth."

She died at 11:42 a.m.

The medical record of her execution bears the following notes: "Openly bitter over repeated delays in execution. Grateful to Chaplains and said she was resigned to go at 10:30 AM. Very brave and declares she will hold up to the end. No grimaces, dies very quietly."

By way of contrast, it went rather differently with Perkins and Santo. They slept soundly the night before, ate heartily, and joked with the guards as they got strapped into their chairs, telling the guards not to do anything they wouldn't do. The merry jokesters, a.k.a. mass murderers, were seated side by side in the gas chamber, and the pellets dropped for both of them at 2:34 p.m.

Attorney General Pat Brown, who would later become governor, commented on the horror of Barbara's execution, saying, "The way the death penalty has been administered in California in the last two years is a disgrace to the administration of justice. The way the Graham woman was executed was a sad commentary on legal killing in California."

It was indeed that. And so was the travesty of a trial that allowed it to happen.

CHAPTER
TWENTY-THREE

That should've been the end of the matter. But it wasn't.

In 1958, a film about the case was released, starring Susan Hayward as Barbara Graham, titled *I Want to Live!* It was a huge commercial hit and critical darling, earning six Academy Award nominations and Oscar and Golden Globe awards for best actress for Susan Hayward. The prosecution and police did not come off well in the film. Depicted as callous bullies who unfairly condemned Barbara based on snap judgments and little evidence, they were the villains of the story. Barbara, on the other hand, was the star of the show, the beautiful, sympathetic victim—flawed, a little rough around the edges, yet fundamentally sensitive and warmhearted—and sorely mistreated from birth by her mother, society, and especially the criminal justice system.

Though touted as a true story, the screenplay was in many ways a work of fiction. Barbara's criminal past was minimized and white-washed, her sharp edges sanded down to depict a vulnerability she'd never have allowed to show in real life. Overall, the film created an impression of Barbara that was at odds with both logic and reality given her life of abuse and neglect. A life that left her with deep emotional and psychological scars that foreclosed any real possibility of finding a place in the "straight" world. But the film's depiction of her excruciating death was widely acknowledged to be truthful and accurate—by both death penalty opponents and law enforcement.

Hollywood film producer Walter Wanger was a staunch death penalty abolitionist. So, when Ed Montgomery pitched the idea of making a film about the case, Wanger snapped it up on the spot. He'd immediately seen how the film would be a powerful vehicle to promote his agenda. To a certain extent, it was. The film inspired a state senator to draft a bill to abolish the death penalty in California. But it also shined a light on the trial itself, and that light was not flattering to the prosecution.

Incensed by the way the film had turned public opinion against him, Leavy waged a war to set the record straight. He hired a writer—William Walker, who'd covered the case as a reporter for the *Los Angeles Herald-Express*—to collaborate with him in writing a book, a screenplay, and a lengthy article in the magazine *Cavalier*, a poor man's version of *Playboy*. Though that magazine article had been shopped around to a number of outlets, *Cavalier* was the only magazine willing to publish it. It came out in April 1959, with a splashy headline on the cover, "Exposing Hollywood's 'I Want to Live!' Hoax." Since the case was still a fairly hot topic—thanks to the film, I wondered why the piece found no other takers. Then I read it and saw why.

It was total trash, filled with gross misrepresentations and outright lies. For example, a caption under Baxter Shorter's photo claimed that according to testimony, Barbara "jumped down in the grave and smashed Baxter in the face with a shovel." No such "testimony" was ever given by anyone in any forum, and in fact there is no evidence Barbara had anything to do with the kidnapping or likely—but unproven—murder of Baxter Shorter.

In a separate section of that article, Leavy discredited the film and singled out Ed Montgomery personally. Montgomery's eloquent and very vocal denunciation of the prosecution had only added fuel to the fire of Leavy's umbrage. Leavy retaliated by saying Montgomery's claim to have "covered" the trial was "false," and that "to [Leavy's] knowledge, he never covered a single session of the actual court proceedings." He challenged Montgomery to disprove that statement. Montgomery vehemently denied the claim and in fact was so upset by the allegation that he wanted to sue Leavy for defamation. He wrote to Walter Wanger about filing a lawsuit, and Wanger—eager to get more publicity for the film—enthusiastically supported the idea. But whether Montgomery ever filed a lawsuit is unclear.

Still, to issue such a personal attack on a reporter—not to mention an open challenge like that—was very odd. Leavy didn't even know who Montgomery was until *after* the trial, when he launched his crusade to prove Barbara's innocence. The likelihood that Leavy—years after the trial—could remember the faces of every reporter who'd ever been in the gallery, and remember that Montgomery was not among them, is virtually nil. And there's every reason to believe Montgomery did attend the trial at some point, even if he hadn't been there every day. He covered it as a reporter for the *San Francisco Examiner*, a reputable outfit that'd followed the trial closely.

As for the book Leavy collaborated on with Walker, *The Case of Barbara Graham*, although it had the advantage of Leavy's full access to all the police reports, I found it to be unreliable in many respects—especially about the trial. And its pro-prosecution and law enforcement bias was readily apparent. Since Leavy was the driving force behind the book, the bias wasn't surprising. But he'd also found a dedicated compatriot in Walker. The news outlet where he'd been a reporter during the trial, the *Herald-Express*, was responsible for some of the most inaccurate, sensationalized coverage of the trial, and the most noxious commentary on Barbara.

If Leavy hoped that book would sway public opinion in his favor, he was sorely disappointed. *The Case of Barbara Graham*, published in January 1961, didn't grace any bestseller lists. And the screenplay Leavy collaborated on with Walker, *Weep No More for Barbara*, went nowhere.

But fans of the film weren't Leavy's only detractors. In 1960, a subcommittee had been convened under the auspices of the Assembly

Interim Committee on Criminal Procedure to look into whether the prosecution had violated the defendants' right to due process in failing to provide the defense with the statement John True made to police and Adolph Alexander on June 4, 1953. Somehow, it'd finally been revealed that the defense had never been given this official, transcribed statement, and the possibility had been raised that if True's prior inconsistent statements had been presented to the jury, it might've altered the outcome of the trial. The ostensible goal was to determine whether the prosecution's failure to turn over the statement was willful and whether new, more stringent laws of discovery should be drafted.

But a question was raised as to whether such an inquiry was moot. Someone had recently claimed Barbara had confessed her guilt to the warden just before her execution. If so, the chairman of the committee observed, the question of whether her due process rights were violated by the suppression of John True's statement might be deemed "academic" to those "not familiar with the constitutional guarantees afforded every accused." In other words, even if that June 4 statement might've persuaded the jury to acquit Barbara, so what? If she confessed, she was guilty. So, what does it matter?

Actually, it did still matter, because if her rights were violated in a manner serious enough to believe she might've been acquitted had it not been for that violation, then guilty or not, regardless of that confession, she didn't get a fair trial. And neither would future defendants—some of whom might not be guilty—if the prosecution were allowed to get away with hiding exculpatory evidence. It wasn't just about Barbara et al. The chairman of the committee knew that, but he also knew the public wouldn't understand the importance of the principle involved. So, to forestall taxpayer complaints about wasting resources on a guilty dead woman, the subcommittee decided to find out whether it was true that Barbara had confessed to Warden Teets.

And who brought the possibility of a confession to the attention of the subcommittee? None other than J. Miller Leavy. Of course.

Leavy insisted on appearing before the state legislature during the debates on the bill to abolish the death penalty. There, on March 9, 1960, he publicly claimed that he'd been told Barbara had confessed to Warden Teets. It was a shocking revelation given Barbara's persistent assertion of innocence from the very beginning to the very end as far as anyone had known . . . until now.

Leavy said he'd heard about it almost a year earlier, in June 1959, from Marin County district attorney Bill Weissich. This raised an obvious question, and state senator Richard Richards of Los Angeles immediately asked it: "Why the secrecy of this confession? Was it not news of interest to the public at the time? Why the cloak of secrecy?" Good question. Barbara had been dead for five years by that time. Why was no mention made of it until now? And why, if Leavy heard about it almost a year ago from Bill Weissich, had he waited so long to reveal it?

Leavy's only answer was that the warden hadn't made a record of the confession. Warden Harley Teets had died in 1957, and Weissich claimed the warden told him about the confession two days before his death.

But that didn't explain why Weissich hadn't told anyone about it back in 1957, when Teets supposedly told him. More to the point, why hadn't Warden Teets made a record of such a momentous event in this highly publicized case? Why didn't he make it known publicly? And why tell Weissich—of all people—who had nothing to do with the case or the operations in San Quentin?

These obvious questions immediately raised doubts about the supposed confession. And more cold water was thrown on the claim by director of corrections Richard McGee, who said an event as significant as a confession was required to be officially recorded and reported to him. "Why he [Warden Teets] didn't bring this to me is difficult to understand," McGee said. McGee, who knew Warden Teets well, said Teets was not someone who played fast and loose with the rules, and that it'd be totally out of character for him not to report something as important as a confession to McGee. While such an event might not be important to the prison officials, it would certainly be important to the governor (who considers clemency applications), and Teets knew very well that McGee reported to the governor. Yet he never told McGee or made a record of this important event.

Leavy claimed Warden Teets "took the position that it should not be documented; it was a great burden to him." How Leavy—in whom Teets had never confided—would know that is a mystery. And tellingly, McGee didn't buy that explanation. He found the undocumented hearsay statement of a man who'd since died to be of little value and questioned Leavy's motive in making the claim publicly now. Reportedly, "[McGee] presumed Leavy was bringing up this story because of all the criticism implying that Mrs. Graham was innocent."

McGee was right. And Leavy's announcement at that senate hearing is a classic example of unintended consequences. Because—far from putting to rest the roiling doubts about Barbara's guilt—his claim that she'd confessed reinvigorated the whole debate and led to its own senate subcommittee inquiry. That inquiry would reveal Leavy's willingness to sacrifice the truth to satisfy his obsession with personal vindication.

It turned out that a rumor had circulated around the prison after Barbara's death that she'd confessed to Warden Teets. As any current or past prison inmate will tell you (and as many have told me), one of the biggest complaints about life behind bars is boredom. Every day is Groundhog Day, a gray, grinding routine of endless repeats. And the guards who work in that monotonous twilight zone suffer from it too. Rumormongering is a major source of entertainment, and it's rampant.

That rumor mill was likely responsible for starting the ball rolling, but it picked up considerable speed when it somehow made its way to the ears of the district attorney of Marin County, William Weissich. In his testimony before the subcommittee, Weissich explained how the story of Barbara's confession was brought to light. Leavy had somehow caught wind of the rumored confession, and at a meeting of district attorneys in February 1959, he sought out Weissich to ask him about Barbara's confession. Weissich had not previously known Leavy and was surprised to be approached by him. He was even more surprised when Leavy asked him to tell his writer, Bill Walker, about the confession—and Leavy's request that Weissich find out if anyone else knew about it. So basically, Leavy buttonholed a complete stranger and drafted him to contribute to a book and, while he was at it, go dig up some other sources for him. If I'd been Weissich, I'd have asked this guy if he also wanted me to do his laundry.

Weissich wasn't the most efficient investigator. He admittedly didn't act on Leavy's orders for months—until Leavy cornered him again in June 1959 at another prosecutor's conference and repeated his marching orders. Weissich at this point might've wanted to tell Leavy to go hire a cop and leave him alone. But since Weissich had opened the can of worms himself by telling Leavy about the confession, he might've felt he was obligated to follow through. Or, maybe he liked playing detective for Leavy—a famous prosecutor.

In any case, Weissich finally took action on August 20, 1959, when he attended the execution of Stephen Nash at San Quentin. While he was there, he paid a visit to the new warden and asked him about the confession. The warden searched all the files and found no record of any confession by Barbara.

The following month, Leavy dispatched his writing partner, Bill Walker, to Marin County to persuade Weissich to make a statement on the record about the confession. But Weissich was reluctant. Warden Teets had told him about the confession in confidence. Teets hadn't wanted it to be made public. In addition, Weissich didn't want to be the "only one" who claimed that Warden Teets told him about Barbara's confession. He didn't want to go on the record unless someone else backed him up. Weissich, describing what he'd said to Walker, testified, "I said, very frankly, to use my words, people will say, 'that's just bloody Bill Weissich again making up a story,' and I just didn't want to get involved in it unless there was corroboration." Weissich said he'd "made it quite clear" to Walker that he didn't want his statement to be used "unless corroboration could be obtained."

As I read that testimony, red flags popped up all over the place. Let me tell you right now, if my primary source said he was afraid to go public without corroboration because he'd been accused of "making up a story" before—implicitly *many* times before—I'd close my notepad and say, "Thanks, never mind." Someone who's been accused of "making up a story" so many times he himself admits it is not someone I'd rely on . . . for anything. But not Walker. And certainly not Leavy.

Issuing the caveat that Walker couldn't use it until someone else came forward, Weissich then gave a statement in which he explained that the only reason he hadn't told anyone about the confession before then was that Warden Teets had wanted him to keep it a secret. Weissich, still acting on Leavy's orders to find another source, then went back to San Quentin in October 1959 and again asked the warden about the confession. The warden again said he knew nothing about any confession but suggested Weissich talk to associate warden Louis Nelson, who'd been working at San Quentin during Barbara's stay.

Nelson initially refused to talk about it, saying he needed director of corrections Richard McGee's permission. When McGee grudgingly gave it, Nelson—who declined to appear in person before the subcommittee—wrote a letter in which he stated Teets had told him about Barbara's confession but that he was "hazy" about the details: "The details relative to the crime I do not remember," he said. With one exception. He claimed Teets said Barbara admitted to having "pistol-whipped Monahan until she was dead." This so-called detail had been so well publicized that one of the inmates could've recited it. Nelson also said that he was only willing to reveal the confession because Weissich had already done so.

Weissich's statement about the confession—both in writing and before the subcommittee—was even less detailed than Nelson's. He said his "mind is blank" on the subject of what Teets had said when he told him about the confession. He could only say generally that Teets had said Barbara admitted her guilt in connection with the Monahan case. Weissich did not remember Teets making any such "graphic" statement about the confession as the one Nelson had recounted. He reiterated his claim that he hadn't mentioned the confession publicly until now because he felt Warden Teets had told him about it "in confidence," but now that director of corrections Richard McGee gave associate warden Louis Nelson permission to make it public, he felt he could speak of the matter as well.

So basically, in a classic game of "telephone," one claim begat and built on another, and neither—coming years after the supposed initial revelation by Teets—provided any compelling details to ensure its authenticity. And the fact that Teets had made no record of the confession completely undermines the credibility of these stories.

But Weissich and Nelson weren't the only witnesses to testify before the subcommittee. And when the others showed up, the story sprang even more leaks. One particular question about the supposed confession had already emerged: Exactly when could Barbara have made it? The implication so far was that it'd happened when she went back to San Quentin for the last time, the day before her execution.

That made sense. With all hope of a reprieve now gone, Barbara would have nothing to lose. But Barbara Cates, the nurse who'd spent every moment with Barbara from the time she arrived at San Quentin on June 2, 1953, until her death the following day, made it abundantly clear that at no time did she ever confess—to Teets or anyone else. Ed Montgomery also testified that there was no possibility Barbara had confessed to the warden. He'd discussed the case with Warden Teets more than once during his visits to San Quentin, and Teets said that although he thought Barbara was present at the scene of the crime, he never believed she'd committed the murder. Montgomery had known Teets a long time, and if Barbara had confessed to him, he would've found a way to discourage Montgomery from continuing to look for proof of her innocence.

It was agreed by all parties that Cates's testimony ruled out the possibility that Barbara might've confessed when she went back to San Quentin for her execution. Even Weissich eventually conceded as much and claimed he never "contended the confession was made just prior to the execution." And McGee agreed that if Barbara had confessed, it could only have been during her first visit to San Quentin between November 1953 and June 1954.

Weissich, who'd previously admitted he had no idea when the confession had happened, jumped on that opening and insisted that Barbara might've confessed to Teets during her earlier stay in San Quentin in 1954.

But as the chairman of the subcommittee pointed out, at the time of Barbara's first incarceration at San Quentin, she "publicly maintained her innocence" and was still actively pursuing her postconviction appeals and petitions, which were all based on "the assumption of her innocence." And director of corrections Richard McGee agreed that would've made it even more critical for Teets to advise him of a confession so he could relay it to the governor, who had to rule on any request for clemency.

That was exactly right. Barbara had appeals and writ petitions pending in both the state and federal courts. Indeed, even in her interview just one week before her execution, when she believed all appeals were exhausted, the article ended by saying that Barbara continued to maintain her innocence of the murder.

Lastly, although he never testified before the subcommittee, even one of the chaplains who spent considerable time with Barbara during her first stay in San Quentin in 1954 and was again by her side on the morning of her execution adamantly denied that Barbara had ever confessed. In his book *Death Row Chaplain*, Chaplain Byron Eshelman stated, "I do not believe Barbara ever admitted the murder that brought her to the gas chamber."

Ultimately the subcommittee never resolved the question, nor did it ever come to a final decision about whether Alexander had deliberately withheld John True's statement. But in my opinion, the claims by Weissich and Nelson that Barbara had confessed to Warden Teets simply don't hold up. I don't think they're necessarily knowing lies, so much as the projection of a desired truth, influenced by the power of suggestion.

The possibility of a confession was welcomed by those who thought the film falsely exonerated a murderer. A confession would force the doubters to agree she was guilty. And Weissich admitted he was one of those who strongly disapproved of the film and the book based on the screenplay. As he testified before the subcommittee, "I have always felt that it was unfortunate that the administration of justice in the State of California should be subjected to the false impression conveyed by the book and the motion picture." It was likely this sentiment motivated Weissich to tell Leavy about the supposed confession.

But the story about Barbara's supposed confession very plainly doesn't hold up to the most superficial scrutiny. And Leavy surely knew it. That he nevertheless persisted in publicizing the claimed confession in the face of overwhelming evidence that it was utterly false speaks to a vainglorious obsession with winning, and a willingness to abandon all truth and justice in its service.

It's of a piece with the way Barbara's right to a fair trial was trampled from start to finish by a press who, instead of seeing a human being, saw only a juicy story that would generate splashy headlines, and a prosecution who, instead of standing above that fray to ensure justice was done, dived into the depths of that muck and mire along with them in order to score a high-profile win.

Thus was Barbara left to the mercy of forces beyond her control—just as she had been from birth. But while her bleak history of neglect and abuse may have doomed her to a life on the fringes, it didn't have to mean that life would end in the gas chamber.

EPILOGUE

I spent the better part of two years immersed in the case—the investigation, the trial, and Barbara's life—gathering, poring over, and analyzing thousands of pages of transcripts, books, magazine articles, and newspapers. The process of writing about it was at times harrowing, the emotional toll exhausting. When at last, I came to the end, I closed my laptop and stared out the window, overcome by the outrage, frustration, and utter sadness that washed over me. As both a prosecutor and defense attorney, the one principle I'd held most dear was the right to a fair trial. There can be no justice without it. And a fair trial means the jury gets to know the unaltered truth, not the abridged version created by a prosecutor's kaleidoscope twist that eliminates any evidence inconsistent with guilt.

At base, the jury had only the word of an accomplice—John True—to prove what each of the defendants did inside that house. There was no physical evidence to back it up. That made it all the more critical that every single piece of evidence bearing on his credibility be revealed. Instead, the prosecution willfully hid the evidence that would've exposed the myriad problems with his credibility—even going so far as to lie to the jury that Baxter Shorter's statement would back up True's testimony. This profound breach of ethics unquestionably impacted the jury's view of this key witness.

Although the senate subcommittee addressed the question of whether legislation was needed to ensure that this never happened again, they never came to a decision. Three years later, the United States Supreme Court took the matter out of their hands with the landmark decision *Brady v. Maryland* (1963) 373 US 83, holding that the prosecution's suppression of evidence favorable to the defense that is material to the issue of guilt or punishment violates due process: "Society wins not only when the guilty are convicted but when criminal trials are fair; our system of the administration of justice suffers when any accused is treated unfairly."

That holding came too late for Barbara. As did the holding in *Massiah v. United States*, which would've prohibited the prosecution from using an undercover cop like Sirianni to pressure an indicted defendant to confess.

But there is such a thing as basic fairness and decency that should matter to a prosecutor—especially when he intends to ask a jury to put a defendant to death. Leavy and Alexander not only showed very little concern for those ethical considerations, but also, when it came to Barbara in particular, they discarded all notions of fairness, going to grotesque extremes to chase her into the gas chamber. No doubt those excesses were motivated in part by their awareness that the entire case hinged on an accomplice of dubious credibility who had a hands-on role in the murder.

But there was a particularly personal angle to the way Leavy went after Barbara. Throughout the trial—and even after her death—he relentlessly pushed the obviously flawed theory that she'd pistol-whipped Mabel Monahan. Reading Leavy's pugilistic cross-examination and misogynistic closing argument remarks—in particular the odious accusation that this woman whose life was on the line took the stand only to "flaunt" herself to the male jurors—revealed a personal animus that was both shocking and baffling. I've seen serial killers and mass murderers get more humane treatment than Leavy gave Barbara Graham.

It seemed, in part, to be a matter of ego, a need to prove his prowess by taking down the defendant who posed the biggest challenge. And maybe it was also a gendered '50s attitude that particularly deplored and punished a woman who refused to conform to societal norms. Because I can't imagine a prosecutor today would load up their closing arguments with the kind of overtly misogynistic jabs Leavy threw at Barbara.

I had always planned to end this book by sharing my own opinion about what I thought had happened on the night of March 9, 1953. But I wanted to do it fairly, in as neutral and objective a frame of mind as possible. And as I finished reading the subcommittee hearing, I realized I was in no shape to do that. I was too angry. So I made myself take a break from the case and step away for a while. By that time, I'd written almost a full draft of the book.

Finally, I was ready. There is no question in my mind that Barbara was there. She'd agreed to be the decoy, a role that wasn't supposed to involve anything more than getting Mabel to open the door—maybe, at most, keep her out of the way while the others searched for the fabled safe. When Barbara got out of the car, she left her purse behind—the purse that, according to Baxter Shorter, contained a gun. There were only two guns. Perkins gave Barbara's gun to True, who admitted he was armed when he followed her inside. Santo gave the other gun to Perkins just before he went into the house. That meant Barbara was unarmed. It's possible she was trying to hold on to Mabel when True came in. But it's also possible Mabel hadn't even realized she was about to be robbed until True arrived. He said that when he approached the house, he found the door still ajar. So, at that point, Barbara had just stepped inside. But when True came in behind her, Mabel knew she was in danger and either started to scream or tried to run. That jibes with Baxter's statement that he heard a short scream and then a door slam. True grabbed Mabel, kicked the door closed, then grabbed her and pistol-whipped her, sending her to the floor. He went to the floor with her—not to save her but to keep her down. As Shorter said, he was holding her down, not "cradling" her head.

Perkins then entered with Santo, and while True held on to Mabel, they searched the house. When they realized there was no safe, no $100,000 stash, Santo went outside and waved Shorter in to prove there was no "take." He wouldn't be getting his promised 10 percent. When Shorter entered, he saw that Mabel was lying on the floor, her face and head bloody. The others continued to search the house, and at one point, someone complained that Mabel was making too much noise. Barbara suggested they "knock her out" to keep her quiet. Perkins then pistol-whipped her, prompting Shorter to protest and demand that they untie her and let her go. It was likely Perkins—as True initially said—who put the pillowcase over her head, after which Santo tied the gag around her neck.

True, by his own admission, left Mabel on the floor and joined in the fruitless search for a while. When he returned, she was no longer making any noise. Shorter begged him to take off the gag, but True was in no hurry. He asked Santo what he thought about it, remarking that it was probably safe since she wasn't going to cause them any more "trouble." When Santo gave the okay, True either loosened or pulled down the gag, though by then it was way too late. They left not long after that, and when Baxter Shorter got into his own car, he drove to a pay phone and called for an ambulance. It was symbolic of the whole tragic, ill-fated episode that he gave the wrong address. But I don't think it made any difference. By the time Shorter made the call, Mabel Monahan had already passed.

That's how I think it all went down. But my opinion takes into account a lot of evidence the jury never got to hear, such as Shorter's statement and John True's earlier statement on June 4.

One major question remains: Even without Shorter's statement, would it have made a difference to the jury if the prosecution had produced John True's prior statement and the defense had been able to put Donna Prow on the witness stand?

True's slippery memory of the facts, his initial statement that Perkins—not Barbara—had put the pillowcase over the victim's head, and his inconsistent description of how he'd pulled Barbara away from Mabel and told her to "just tell them what they want to know!" showed him to be—at the very least—an unreliable narrator.

And if the defense had been able to put Donna Prow on the witness stand, the jury would've seen more clearly how the prosecution had targeted Barbara by promising an inmate—who'd been convicted of manslaughter—freedom in exchange for her services. That meant two key witnesses—John True and Donna Prow—had been bought and paid for.

In addition, the defense would've been able to confront Donna with the statements she'd made to the press, which would've shown the jury how she'd been the one who initiated the relationship with Barbara, plying her with gifts, money, and promises of love and that she was the one—not Barbara—who'd suggested the use of a false alibi. That would've given the jury a clearer picture of the way Barbara, in an extremely vulnerable state, had been unfairly lured into a trap and then pressured to confess.

Would that have led to Barbara's acquittal? Maybe not. But I can certainly believe that a few jurors—and it only takes one—might decide they were suspicious of a prosecution that relied so heavily on the testimony of snitches. A suspicion like that translates easily into reasonable doubt. That means the trial would've ended in a hung jury.

And even if the jury did convict Barbara, I think it's far more likely that they would have voted for leniency instead of death. My belief is based in part on the fact that the jury reached a guilty verdict in just two hours, but spent almost a full day on the issue of penalty. But it's also based on what the foreman later said about the penalty deliberations.

Interviewed decades after the verdict, the jury foreman, Robert Dodson, still had a vivid memory of how, during the sentencing deliberations, a female juror fell to her knees and prayed aloud, agonizing over the decision of whether to sentence Barbara to death. According to Dodson, she wasn't the only one. Several jurors were troubled by the prospect of sending Barbara to the gas chamber—as was Dodson. But he felt that the evidence—in particular the taped statements Barbara had made to Sirianni—left him no choice.

Had the jury known of the reasons to doubt True's testimony that Barbara had wielded a gun, and known more about how relentlessly she'd been pushed into the false-alibi scheme, I think it's entirely possible they would've voted for leniency. If you're wondering why Leavy hid Donna Prow and why Alexander buried John True's statement, there's your answer.

Barbara never wavered in her denial of guilt for the murder of Mabel Monahan. Even when confiding in her lawyer after her last viable petition was denied by the United States Supreme Court, she said, "I am sure that if people could see into my heart, they would know that I am incapable of murder. Knowing that myself, I find a certain amount of peace in my heart."

According to the book *I Want to Live!* in her last conversation with one of the priests on the day of her execution, Barbara echoed that same sentiment. "I think it's going to be rather nice to come face to face with the one person in the world who knows I'm innocent."

The priest answered, "None of us is wholly innocent or guilty in the eyes of God."

Barbara explained, "I meant Mrs. Monahan."

BIBLIOGRAPHY

"Alibi Plot Baring Rocks Defense in Monahan Case." *Los Angeles Mirror*, August 28, 1953.

"Alibi Plot Told in Monahan Case." *Los Angeles Times*, August 28, 1953.

"Authorities Hide Indicted Suspect in Monahan Death." *Sacramento Bee*, June 10, 1953.

"Babs Graham, Santo, Perkins to Die Dec. 3." *Valley Times* (Burbank, CA), September 17, 1954.

"Barbara Graham Flares Up at Trial." *Los Angeles Times*, September 3, 1953.

"Believe 'Canary' Shorter Slain on 'Ride.'" *Valley Times* (Burbank, CA), April 16, 1953.

"Blonde Denies Ever Seeing Slain Widow." *Los Angeles Evening Herald-Express*, September 1, 1953.

"'Bloody Babs' Falls; Delay in Monohan Murder Trial." *Los Angeles Mirror*, August 19, 1953.

"Burbank Sleuth Trips Murder Trial Suspect." *Daily News* (Los Angeles), August 28, 1953.

Caen, Herb. "Sunday in Shorts." Baghdad-by-the-Bay. *San Francisco Examiner*, Feb. 13, 1955.

Cairns, Kathleen A. *Proof of Guilt: Barbara Graham and the Politics of Executing Women in America*. Lincoln, NE: University of Nebraska Press, 2013.

California State Legislature. *Reporters' Transcript of Testimony Before the Assembly Interim Committee on Criminal Procedure, Sub-Committee Hearing re: Alleged Discrepancies and Suppression of Evidence re: Barbara Graham Confession*, March 21, 1960.

Cates, Barbara. Walter Wanger Collection. Wisconsin Historical Society. Madison, WI.

"Cohen Henchman Tells Rob Plot in Monahan Trial." *Los Angeles Mirror*, August 26, 1953.

"Confession in Monahan Case Blasted." *Los Angeles Times*, September 17, 1953.

Cook, Gale. "Santo Murder Trio Executed; Delays Torture Barbara." *San Francisco Examiner*, June 4, 1955.

Crawford, Canoy. "Murder Defense Gets Delay." *Valley Times* (Burbank, CA), August 28, 1953.

"Court Denies Appeal of Monahan Murder Trio." *Los Angeles Times*, March 7, 1955.

Daily News (Los Angeles), August 28, 1953.

Daily News (Los Angeles), September 4, 1953.

Davis, Bernice Freeman. *The Desperate and the Damned*. Crowell, 1961.

"Defense Claims 'Babs' Trapped by Alibi Plot." *Los Angeles Mirror*, August 28, 1953.

"11 Guards Watch True on Stand." *Valley Times* (Burbank, CA), August 25, 1953.

Eshelman, Byron. *Death Row Chaplain*. New York: Signet, 1972.

"Evidence against Suspects in Monahan Murder Held Insufficient." *San Bernardino (CA) Daily Sun*, April 15, 1953.

"Figure in Shorter Case Bans Lie Detector Test." *Los Angeles Times*, May 15, 1953.

"File Away Monahan Murder." *Valley Times* (Burbank, CA), April 17, 1953.

"Find Burbank Widow Bludgeoned to Death." *Valley Times* (Burbank, CA), March 12, 1953.

First installment of *The Barbara Graham Story*. Walter Wanger Collection, Wisconsin Historical Society. Madison, WI.

"For Wayward Girls." *Los Angeles Times*, March 13, 1914.

"Former Actress Found Murdered." *Hackensack (NJ) Record*, March 12, 1953.

"Former Actress Found Murdered." *Meriden (CT) Journal*, March 12, 1953.

"Gambling Link Is Sought in Widow Strangulation." *Deseret News and Telegram* (Salt Lake City, UT), March 13, 1953.

"Girl Who Set Jail Trap Freed." *Valley Times* (Burbank, CA), August 29, 1953.

Graham, Barbara, as told to Stuart Palmer. "Pathway to Murder." Part One. *American Weekly*. Reprinted in *The Sunday Oregonian*, April 11, 1954.

Graham, Barbara. Letters, 1954–55. Walter Wanger Collection, Wisconsin Historical Society. Madison, WI.

"I'll Go with My Head Held High." *San Francisco Examiner*, May 27, 1955.

"Informant Provides Identity: Version of Slaying Outlined by Officers." *Evening Vanguard* (Venice, CA), April 14, 1953.

"'Informer' Kidnapped in 'Ride.'" *Valley Times* (Burbank, CA), April 15, 1953.

"Jail Mate Reveals Plot to Frame Murder Alibi." *Los Angeles Times*, August 28, 1953.

"Jury Believed Split on Babs' Death Verdict." *Daily News* (Los Angeles), September 22, 1953.

"Knight Sleepless Studying Santo Pleas." *San Francisco Examiner*, June 4, 1953.

"L.A. Fugitive Linked to Killing of 4." *Los Angeles Evening Citizen-News*, April 15, 1953.

"Last Minute Confession by Barbara Graham Is Revealed." *Sacramento Bee*, March 10, 1960.

"Last Minute Santo Case Please Rapped." *San Francisco Examiner*, June 5, 1955.

Letters, 1954–55. Walter Wanger Collection, Wisconsin Historical Society. Madison, WI.

Lexington (KY) Herald, March 12, 1953.

"Lie Test Denied Barbara Graham." *Citizen-News* (Hollywood, CA), March 16, 1954.

Los Angeles Conservancy. 2014. laconservancy.org.

Los Angeles Examiner, May 5, 1953.

Los Angeles Herald-Express, August 19, 1953.

Los Angeles Herald-Express, August 20, 1953.

Los Angeles Herald-Express, August 28, 1953.

Los Angeles Herald-Express, August 29, 1953.

Los Angeles Herald-Express, September 1, 1953.

Los Angeles Herald-Express, September 2, 1953.

Los Angeles Magazine, June 4, 2013.

Los Angeles Times, August 28, 1953.

Los Angeles Times, September 17, 1953.

Los Angeles Times, September 22, 1953.

Los Angeles Times, September 23, 1953.

"Mabel Monahan Found Slain in Her Residence." *Streator (IL) Daily Times-Press*, March 12, 1953.

"Mabel Monahan, Once Actress, Found Killed." *Concord (NH) Daily Monitor*, March 12, 1953.

Martinez, Al. "When the People Cry for Blood." *Los Angeles Times*, March 31, 1990.

"Monahan Case Figure Freed After Threats." *Los Angeles Times*, August 29, 1953.

"Monahan Jury Still Undecided." *Valley Times* (Burbank, CA), September 22, 1953.

"Monahan Murder 'Cracked.'" *Valley Times* (Burbank, CA), June 10, 1953

"Monahan Murder Suspect Linked to Mass Slaying." *Valley Times* (Burbank, CA), April 15, 1953.

"Monahan Murder Trio Convicted." *Daily News* (Los Angeles), September 23, 1953.

"Monahan Suspect's Own Voice Blasts Phony Alibi." *Daily News* (Los Angeles), August 28, 1953.

Montgomery, Ed. "Death Stay for Perkins." *San Francisco Examiner*, November 30, 1954.

"Mrs. Graham Hurt, Death Case Delayed." *Los Angeles Times*, August 20, 1953.

"Mrs. Graham's Alibi Blasted by Mate." *Los Angeles Times*, September 4, 1953.

Muir, Florabel. Florabel Muir Reporting. *Los Angeles Mirror*, June 10, 1953.

"Murder Case Suspect Held." *San Francisco Examiner*, April 14, 1953.

"Murder Suspect Kidnapped: Fear Underworld Vengeance for Reported Squealer." *San Pedro (CA) News-Pilot*, April 15, 1953.

"Murder Suspect on Stand." *Valley Times* (Burbank, CA), September 1, 1953.

"Nevada City Man Will Be Grilled in Murder Case." *Sacramento Bee*, April 14, 1953.

"New Appeal for Barbara." *San Francisco Examiner*, May 27, 1955.

Nichols, Ralph C. "Los Angeles Newspaper Coverage and Dramatization of the Barbara Graham Case." Master's thesis, California State University–Northridge, 1990.

"Nurse Says Mrs. Graham Did Not Confess Murder." *Fresno Bee: The Republican* (Fresno, CA), March 22, 1960.

O'Hara, Pat. "Barbara Graham's Husband Refuses to Back her Alibi." *Daily News* (Los Angeles), September 4, 1953.

Oliver, Myrna, and Ted Rohrlich. "J. Miller Leavy; Legendary Prosecutor." Obituary. *Los Angeles Times*, Jan. 5, 1995.

Palmberg, Carl. Report on Donna Prow. Walter Wanger Collection, Wisconsin Historical Society. Madison, WI.

"Perkins, Santo, Girl Arrested." *Valley Times* (Burbank, CA), May 5, 1953.

Peters, Bill. "Mystery Suspect Tells 'Kidnaping.'" *Valley Times* (Burbank, CA), April 15, 1953.

"Pathway to Murder." Parts One and Two. *American Weekly*. Reprinted in *San Francisco Examiner*, April 4 and 11, 1954.

"Police Kidnap Charges Seen: Chief Andrews and 3 Aides Accused." *Los Angeles Evening Citizen-News*, April 14, 1953 (Valley edition).

Pomona Progress Bulletin, August 26, 1953.

"Probe Figure Kidnap Victim." *Spokane (WA) Daily Chronicle*, April 15, 1953.

"Prosecutor Flies North in Monohan [*sic*] Inquiry." *Los Angeles Times*, June 5, 1955.

Rawson, Tabor. *I Want to Live! The Analysis of a Murder*. New York: Signet, 1958.

"Redhead Accused in Monahan Case: Sits Unmoved at Description of Alleged Beating in Murder Trial." *Los Angeles Times*, August 19, 1953.

"Roll Refuses Lie Test for Barbara Graham." *Los Angeles Times*, March 16, 1954.

"Rush Whittier Guards to Quell Girl Mutiny." *Los Angeles Times*, February 28, 1921.

San Francisco Examiner, June 4, 1955.

San Quentin Execution File for Barbara Graham, California Department of Corrections. California State Archives, Sacramento.

"Santo Gang Loses Death Stay Pleas." *San Francisco Examiner*, June 1, 1955.

"Santo Gang Moll Says Lie Test Welcomed." *San Francisco Examiner*, February 13, 1954.

"Santo, Jailed, Faces Chester Killing Quiz." *Sacramento Bee*, May 5, 1953.

"Shorter's Wife Identifies Trio." *Napa Register*, May 6, 1953.

"Slayers' Identity Known, Claim." *Redwood City (CA) Tribune*, April 14, 1953.

"Slaying Denied by Mrs. Graham." *Los Angeles Times*, September 2, 1953.

"Slaying Figure Victim of 'Last Ride' Kidnaping: Possible Informer in Burbank Killing of Woman Abducted." *Los Angeles Times*, April 15, 1953.

"Slaying Linked to Clark Gaming." *Reno Gazette*, March 12, 1953.

"Sordid Life Told at Monahan Trial." *Daily News* (Los Angeles), September 2, 1953.

Stanford, Sally. *The Lady of the House: The Autobiography of Sally Stanford*. New York: G. P. Putnam, 1966.

"State School Girls Riot, Twenty-Five in Jail." *Ventura (CA) Daily Free Press*, February 28, 1921.

Strong, William. Application for stay of execution and Western Union telegram. November 23, 1954.

"Suspect Gives Grand Jury Monahan Murder Details." *Valley Times* (Burbank, CA), June 10, 1953.

"Testimony in Murder Revealed." *Valley Times* (Burbank, CA), June 16, 1953.

"3 Cohen Hoods Held, Grilled on Burbank Murder." *Los Angeles Mirror*, March 26, 1953

"Three Men, Woman Indicted in Burbank Widow's Slaying." *Los Angeles Times*, June 4, 1953.

"3 Suspects in Burbank Killing Seized." *Los Angeles Times*, May 5, 1953.

"$3,000 Property Damage and Several Hurt in Riot." *Ventura (CA) Weekly Post and Weekly Democrat*, March 4, 1921.

"Tipster Marries Forbidden Lover, Leaves Country." *Long Beach Press-Telegram*, April 29, 1954.

"Upshaw Free After Quiz on Shorter." *Los Angeles Evening Citizen-News*, May 18, 1953.

"Upshaw Freed in Shorter Case Inquiry." *Los Angeles Times*, May 17, 1953

Valley Times (Burbank, CA), August 19, 1953.

Valley Times (Burbank, CA), August 19, 1953.

Walker, Bill. *The Case of Barbara Graham: The Ruthless Deals Between Informers and Cops in a Famous Trial for Murder*. New York: Ballantine Books, 1961.

"Wealthy Widow Beaten to Death in Calif." *Lebanon (PA) Daily News*, March 12, 1953.

"Witness Describes Monahan Slaying." *Los Angeles Times*, August 26, 1953.

"Woman Tells of 'Deal' in Santo Case." *San Francisco Examiner*, April 28, 1954.

ACKNOWLEDGMENTS

First and foremost, boundless thanks to John Valeri, a fantastic writer, who agreed to be my researcher on this book. Finding information on a case that happened so long ago is no easy thing, but John came through every time. I don't know what I would've done without him. A dear friend for many years whose wit and wisdom make my day—every day. It was an incredible gift to get to work with him on this book.

Dan Conaway, agent extraordinaire . . . What can I say? He's the best. This book would never even have been conceived, let alone published, without him. If I thank him for the next hundred years for all his sage advice, support, and genius, it won't even come close to expressing the breadth of my gratitude. Not many people get to honestly say they love their agent. I do.

Many thanks to my developmental editor, Celia Johnson, for her great suggestions and hard work. And thank you to my wonderful copyeditor, Stephanie C., for making one great catch after another!

My profound thanks to Gracie Doyle and Liz Pearsons at Thomas & Mercer for believing in this project. Their vision, support, and enthusiasm were critical and a constant source of inspiration. What a pleasure it's been to work with them!

I also want to thank the wonderful person at the Los Angeles Archives and Records Center who managed to dig out the clerk's transcripts on this over-seventy-five-year-old case. What a gem! And I also want to thank the court reporter who told me the reporter's transcripts were still available. I'll never forget the thrill of hearing her say that.

I also want to thank Kathleen A. Cairns, who so graciously shared some of her research and helped point me to sources for this book. I highly recommend her excellent book *Proof of Guilt*, which also discusses Barbara Graham's case but is more widely devoted to an examination of the death penalty and specifically the women who faced that ultimate sentence.

And as always, my undying gratitude goes to the brilliant—and brilliantly funny—Catherine LePard, who gave me the courage to write (and ignore the naysaying voices in my head) and helps to shape my vision in all that I do.

ABOUT THE AUTHOR

California native Marcia Clark is the author of *Final Judgment*, *Snap Judgment*, *Moral Defense*, and *Blood Defense*, all part of the Samantha Brinkman series. A practicing criminal lawyer since 1979, Clark joined the Los Angeles County District Attorney's office in 1981, where she served as prosecutor for the trials of Robert John Bardo, convicted of killing actress Rebecca Schaeffer, and, most notably, O. J. Simpson. The bestselling *Without a Doubt*, which she cowrote, chronicles her work on the Simpson trial. Clark has been a frequent commentator on a variety of shows and networks, including *Today*, *Good Morning America*, *The Oprah Winfrey Show*, CNN, and MSNBC, as well as a legal correspondent for *Entertainment Tonight*.

Follow Marcia on X at @thatmarciaclark.